critical thinking in the field of family law & human rights.

Alice

THE CONSTRUCTION OF FATHERHOOD

This book tackles one of the most topical socio-legal issues of today: how the law – in particular, the European Court of Human Rights – is responding to shifting practices and ideas of fatherhood in a world that offers radical possibilities for the fragmentation of the conventional father figure and therefore urges decisions upon what kind of characteristics makes someone a legal father.

It explores the Court's reaction to changing family and, more specifically, fatherhood realities. In so doing, it engages in timely conversations about the rights and responsibilities of men as fathers. By tracing values and assumptions underpinning the Court's views on fatherhood, this book contributes to highlight the expressive powers of the ECtHR: more specifically, the latter's role in producing and legitimising ideas about parenting and, more generally, in influencing how family life is regulated and organised.

Alice Margaria is a Research Fellow in the Law and Anthropology Department of the Max Planck Institute for Social Anthropology. She holds a PhD in Law from the European University Institute. Her previous book *Nuove forme di filiazione e genitorialità: leggi e giudici di fronte alle nuove realtà* (2018) explores the role of national judges in bridging the gap between the social and the legal realities of families created via assisted reproduction, from a comparative perspective. She was invited as a visiting scholar at various institutions, such as Emory University and Lund University. She also worked with international organisations, including the UNICEF Office of Research.

The Construction of Fatherhood

THE JURISPRUDENCE OF THE EUROPEAN COURT OF HUMAN RIGHTS

ALICE MARGARIA

Max Planck Institute for Social Anthropology
Department of Law and Anthropology

CAMBRIDGE
UNIVERSITY PRESS

University Printing House, Cambridge CB2 8BS, United Kingdom

One Liberty Plaza, 20th Floor, New York, NY 10006, USA

477 Williamstown Road, Port Melbourne, VIC 3207, Australia

314–321, 3rd Floor, Plot 3, Splendor Forum, Jasola District Centre, New Delhi – 110025, India

79 Anson Road, #06–04/06, Singapore 079906

Cambridge University Press is part of the University of Cambridge.

It furthers the University's mission by disseminating knowledge in the pursuit of education, learning, and research at the highest international levels of excellence.

www.cambridge.org
Information on this title: www.cambridge.org/9781108475099
DOI: 10.1017/9781108566193

© Alice Margaria 2019

This publication is in copyright. Subject to statutory exception and to the provisions of relevant collective licensing agreements, no reproduction of any part may take place without the written permission of Cambridge University Press.

First published 2019

Printed in the United Kingdom by TJ International Ltd. Padstow Cornwall

A catalogue record for this publication is available from the British Library.

ISBN 978-1-108-47509-9 Hardback

Cambridge University Press has no responsibility for the persistence or accuracy of URLs for external or third-party internet websites referred to in this publication and does not guarantee that any content on such websites is, or will remain, accurate or appropriate.

To my children

Contents

Foreword		*page* xi
Acknowledgements		xiii
	Introduction	1
1	**Fatherhood and the Law in Europe**	4
	1 Ideology versus Reality: Changing Families and Changing Fatherhood	4
	2 The Law's Reaction: New and Old Ways of Connecting Fathers to Children	9
	3 Introducing the Key Concepts	13
	'Conventional Fatherhood'	13
	'Fragmenting Fatherhood'	14
	'New Fatherhood'	15
	4 The Aim and Structure of the Analysis	17
2	**The ECtHR and Fatherhood: Limits and Potential**	19
	Introduction	19
	1 Family Relationships: Between Restraint and Innovation	20
	2 Core Provisions	24
	2.1 Article 8 and Fatherhood	25
	Two Stages of Review	25
	Positive Obligations	29
	2.2 Article 14 and Fatherhood	32
	3 Doctrines and Decision Making	35
	3.1 The Doctrine of the Margin and Strictness of Review	36
	3.2 The Variable Use of Doctrines and the Court's Moral Views	40
	4 Case-Law Selection	45

3	**Fatherhood and Assisted Reproduction**	48
	1 The Impact of ARTs on Conventional Fatherhood	48
	2 The ECtHR and ARTs: An Ambivalent Reaction	52
	2.1 Transsexuality and Fatherhood	54
	2.2 Not-Yet Conceived Children and the Ideal Father	58
	2.3 Surrogacy and Intended Fatherhood	63
	3 Conclusions	68
4	**Post-Separation and Unmarried Fatherhood**	72
	1 Fatherhood and the 'Crisis' of Marriage	72
	2 The ECtHR, the 'Crisis' of Marriage and Fatherhood	75
	2.1 Parental Rights after Family Breakdown	78
	2.2 Non-Consensual Adoption	85
	2.3 Paternity Proceedings	91
	Fathers Contesting Paternity	93
	Fathers Claiming Paternity	98
	3 Conclusions	106
5	**Fatherhood and Family–Work Reconciliation**	109
	1 Women in the Workplace and Conventional Fatherhood	109
	2 Childcare-Related Entitlements for Fathers and the ECtHR: One Step at a Time	114
	2.1 Restating Conventional Fatherhood	116
	2.2 Contemplating 'New Fatherhood'	119
	2.3 Pushing for 'New Fatherhood'	121
	3 Conclusions	125
6	**Fatherhood and Homosexuality**	128
	1 Homosexual Families and Conventional Parenthood: Points of Disjuncture	128
	2 The ECtHR and Homosexual Relationships: A Two-Stage Development	131
	2.1 Homosexual Fathers and Their Biological Children	135
	2.2 Single-Parent Adoption: Gays versus Lesbians	139
	2.3 Second-Parent Adoption and the 'Special Status' of Marriage	144
	3 Conclusions	151

7	**Fatherhood at the ECtHR**	155
	Introduction	155
	1 The Construction of Fatherhood in the ECtHR Jurisprudence	156
	Towards 'New Fatherhood'	156
	The Relationship between Change and Continuity	159
	2 The Role(s) of Doctrines	161
	European Consensus	162
	Positive Obligations	164
	3 Final Thoughts	166
Bibliography		169
Index		186

Foreword

It is an honour and a great pleasure to write the preface for this important, timely and fascinating book, a study that redraws the terrain of contemporary studies of fatherhood and law by turning the critical gaze to the construction of fatherhood in the context of the jurisprudence of the European Court of Human Rights (ECtHR). Alice Margaria has written a meticulously researched book, theoretically sophisticated in its approach yet written throughout in an engaging and accessible style. It is a work that I have no doubt will appeal to a wide readership across disciplines, making not only an important contribution to legal scholarship, and socio-legal studies in particular, but to interdisciplinary work on fatherhood generally and the growing body of international scholarship exploring the interconnections between gender, parenting and social change.

The scope and command of a diverse literature base in the work is formidable. The book encompasses, amongs other things, consideration of the complex relationship between law and the changing nature of families and fatherhood in a transnational frame; the core provisions, doctrines and decision-making of the ECtHR, blending detailed analysis of case-law with insights drawn from across diverse disciplinary perspectives. In her assessment of the limits and potential of the Court, the author carefully takes the reader through key areas of law that have, in the context of the ECtHR as well as other legal arenas, raised challenging and significant questions about social and legal understandings of fathering and fatherhood. These include the relationship between fatherhood and assisted reproduction (Chapter 3), the place of fatherhood in debates around family–work reconciliation (Chapter 5) and men's parenting in laws relating to same-sex relationships, in particular with regard to adoption laws and the privilege of heterosexuality in the jurisprudence of the Court (Chapter 6). Central to the book is consideration of another issue that has prompted extensive debate and dialogue across jurisdictions in Europe and beyond. In a discussion of the legal regulation of post-separation and unmarried fatherhood, the author charts how what is taking place in the law in these areas, on closer examination, reveals much about shifting understandings of marriage, divorce and, indeed, the politics of law and families.

What is truly original, and makes this work quite distinct from other studies of fatherhood, law and society, is the core focus on the jurisprudence of the ECtHR. It explores how, in this context, a closer examination of legal regulation can reveal much about the fragmentation of a traditional father figure and the nature of legal determinations of who, and by virtue of what kind of link, should be regarded as the legal father of a child. Exploring cases pertaining to family life and father–child relationships that have crossed national borders and reached Strasbourg, the book reveals a deep uncertainty across countries about social understandings of fatherhood and fathering; and how these constructions of fatherhood, as the book frames it, are enmeshed with an array of beliefs about social bonds, intentions, responsibilities and rights. Crucially, what emerges is not just the key role of the ECtHR in the production, reproduction and legitimation, through its binding decisions, of an array of (by no means consistent) ideas of what it means to be a 'father' and, in particular, a 'good father'. The book also considers the place of fatherhood at a conceptual level in a study of the power of law. More precisely, as the author puts it, it unpacks how the effects of the Court's jurisprudence do not stop at telling parties how they must behave but also involve messages about what values, and ideas – about, for example, care, family, responsibility and rights – are more important than others within specific legal contexts. What emerges is a picture of both shifts and continuity in the extent to which the Court can be seen as either resistant or receptive to changing notions and practices of fatherhood in society.

As the author notes, whilst several scholars have sought to explore the contribution of the Strasbourg Court in relation to wider notions of parenthood, fatherhood has remained a relatively unexplored subject. This book is unique in the way it places the law's 'fatherhood question' firmly on the agenda in the context of European jurisprudence. It is, in short, socio-legal scholarship at its best, most fascinating and most thought provoking – a book that deserves to be widely read far beyond the discipline of law and which will take its rightful place in the canon of work on fatherhood, law and gender and in socio-legal scholarship generally.

Richard Collier, Newcastle Upon Tyne, UK. March 2019

Acknowledgements

I owe a debt of gratitude to many people. I would like to start by thanking Ruth Rubio-Marin for bringing me to this interesting topic of research and for providing precious guidance during my PhD at the EUI. My thoughts on fatherhood have been greatly influenced by Richard Collier and Sally Sheldon, who – apart from producing wonderful scholarship – have been extremely generous and devoted time and efforts to read and discuss parts of my work. I am also grateful to Prof. Nancy Dowd, who has been a great source of inspiration and support especially during the initial phase of my PhD and to Prof. Martha Fineman for making my stay at Emory particularly fruitful. I am also thankful to Prof. Marie-Claire Foblets for encouraging me to bring this project to fruition whilst benefiting of the extraordinary resources provided by the Law and Anthropology Department of the Max Planck Institute for Social Anthropology (Halle). Special thanks go also to the library staff at the MPI, who always managed to satisfy my hunger for more and more sources and to retrieve copies of books and articles from different nooks and crannies all over the world. Many more colleagues have taken the time to read and offer comments on earlier versions of this work; I wish to thank all of them.

Each of my family members has played a crucial role in this journey. I wish to thank my father for making 'nurturing fatherhood' a reality in my daily life; my mother, for being an essential ally in my mission to juggle work and family obligations; my children, Aida and Ismail, for being patient and accompanying me throughout long and tiring working days; Skander, for being their engaged father and my supportive partner; and, my 'social' siblings, Noemi and Stefano, for their omnipresence despite our physical distance. I wish to thank also those who – by way of contrast – made some steps of my journey particularly arduous: they have helped me to realise the power of dreams and commitment.

Introduction

As of the 1970s, fatherhood has become a central feature of a range of legal and social policy debates in Europe. Social changes as diverse as the decline of marriage, rapidly developing reproductive techniques and women's greater participation in paid employment have all, in different ways, posed questions about the legal rights and responsibilities of fathers. In a world that offers radical possibilities for the fragmentation of the traditional father figure, who and by virtue of what kind of links should be regarded as the legal father of a child? Is the biological connection the most decisive factor? Do marital ties existing between the biological parents preserve a mediating role in defining the father–child relationship? Should fatherhood be understood in the sense of actually doing the fathering and, therefore, require the existence of social bonds? Or, should mere parenting intentions – although not yet substantiated by social fatherhood – be considered sufficient?

In all these discussions, the European Court of Human Rights ('ECtHR') has retained a central role, engaging – more or less directly – in the production, reproduction and legitimation of ideas of what it means to be a 'father'. Over the past few decades, indeed, several widely disputed – often morally and ethically charged – cases pertaining to family life and, in particular, father–child relationships have crossed national borders and reached Strasbourg. In addition to its more concrete and immediate influence through binding decisions that provide a floor on which Contracting States must stand,[1] the Court has contributed to delineating the contours of fatherhood through what theorists call 'the

---

[1] N. J. Wikeley, 'Same Sex Couples, Family Life and Child Support', *Law Quarterly Review*, 122 (2006), 544.

law's expressive powers':[2] the effects of its jurisprudence do not stop at telling parties how they must behave in certain circumstances, but go as far as to make statements on what values are more important than others. The Court's judgments, therefore, not only express how the applicant father is expected to behave or the features he is expected to possess in order to be granted the sought status or rights, but also they ultimately have an impact on how family life is organised by conveying wider messages on how (legal) fatherhood ought to be understood and regulated in today's society.

While a number of scholars have been intrigued by the contribution of the Strasbourg Court in shaping and reshaping the wider notion of parenthood[3] – and sometimes, motherhood – fatherhood remains a rather unexplored subject. A number of books and articles have indeed sought to document various aspects of the legal regulation of fatherhood, but focusing on national legal contexts or EU law.[4] This book, in contrast, offers the first sustained, socio-legal engagement with the way fatherhood has been constructed and redefined in the jurisprudence of the ECtHR. In thematically linked chapters, cutting across substantive areas of law in which the rights and responsibilities of fathers have been particularly controversial, it traces values and assumptions underpinning the Court's views regarding fathers and their role within the family. In particular, it examines to what extent the Court is either resistant to or receptive of changing notions and practices of fatherhood in society.

Apart from exploring the legal approach to fatherhood in a new terrain, the chapters to follow investigate the complex interactions between the Court's

---

[2] K. Lõhmus, *Caring Autonomy: European Human Rights Law and the Challenge of Individualism* (Cambridge University Press, 2015), p. 2.

[3] The closest works, in this sense, are S. Choudhry and J. Herring, *European Human Rights and Family Law* (Hart, 2010); A. Büchler and H. Keller (eds.), *Family Forms and Parenthood: Theory and Practice of Article 8 ECHR in Europe* (Intersentia, 2016); C. Draghici, *Legitimacy of Family Rights in Strasbourg Case Law: Living Instrument or Extinguished Sovereignty?* (Hart, 2017).

[4] To cite the most prominent authors, the extensive work by R. Collier and S. Sheldon (inter alia, their book *Fragmenting Fatherhood: A Socio-Legal Study* (Hart, 2008)) explores how fatherhood has been understood and regulated across different areas of English law and social policy. Outside Europe, N. E. Dowd (inter alia, *Redefining Fatherhood* (New York University Press, 2000) and 'From Genes, Marriage and Money to Nurture: Redefining Fatherhood', *Cardozo Women's Law Journal*, 10 (2003–2004), 132–145) has produced insightful scholarship on fatherhood taking US law as the object of analysis. Definitely less often, the legal regulation of fatherhood has been investigated in relation to supra-national legal orders. One of the few examples is E. Caracciolo di Torella's article 'Brave New Fathers for a Brave New World? Fathers as Caregivers in an Evolving European Union', *European Law Journal*, 20(1) (2014), 88–106, which brings to the fore the European Union's approach to fatherhood, particularly by looking at EU legislation and the jurisprudence of the Court of Justice of the European Union.

understanding of fatherhood, on the one hand, and the interpretative repertoire at its disposal, on the other hand. As such, this study contributes to clarifying the genesis of the construction of fatherhood emerging from the ECtHR case-law. In particular, it examines whether it is the result of a consistent application of its doctrines of interpretation and/or, rather, the outcome of a predetermined moral position of the Court.

1

Fatherhood and the Law in Europe

1 IDEOLOGY VERSUS REALITY: CHANGING FAMILIES AND CHANGING FATHERHOOD

Despite 'family' being a fluid concept, in Europe, the 'dominant ideology of the family' continues to identify the heterosexual nuclear family as the 'ideal', the 'norm' against which other family forms and practices are measured.[1] This ideology prescribes a set of formal as well as functional features. First of all, it refers to a 'white, heterosexual, married couple, with children, all living under the same roof'[2] and, as such, resonates with the image of the 'sexual family',[3] to use Martha Fineman's terminology. The 'dominant ideology of the family' rests, in fact, on the assumption that 'the family' originates from and revolves around a formally celebrated adult sexual affiliation.[4] Apart from being based on a particular family form, this ideology ascribes specific family roles in accordance with a gendered division of labour: while the wife is the primary caregiver, the husband is the main breadwinner.[5] A crucial dimension of the 'dominant ideology of the family', therefore, is a 'dominant ideology of motherhood', which glorifies the mother–child bond as sacrosanct to the child's wellbeing and, as a corollary, reduces the paternal role to economic provision.[6]

---

[1] C. McGlynn, *Families and the European Union: Law, Policy and Pluralism* (Cambridge University Press, 2006), p. 23. See also, K. O'Donovan, *Family Law Matters* (Pluto Press, 2003), pp. 39–41.
[2] McGlynn, *Families and the EU*, p. 23.
[3] M. A. Fineman, *The Neutered Mother, the Sexual Family and Other Twentieth Century Tragedies* (Routledge, 1995).
[4] M. Fineman, 'The Sexual Family' in M. Fineman, J. Jackson and A. Romero (eds.), *Feminist and Queer Legal Theory: Intimate Encounters, Uncomfortable Conversations* (Ashgate, 2009), p. 48.
[5] McGlynn, *Families and the EU*, pp. 24–25.
[6] Ibid., p. 25; C. McGlynn, 'Ideologies of Motherhood in European Community Sex Equality Law', *European Law Journal*, 6(1) (2000), 31.

In addition to reflecting the prominent sociocultural understanding of what a family is and should be, the heterosexual nuclear family has long since pervaded debates on law and families and shaped the ways in which family laws are formulated and implemented.[7] As an example, until fairly recently, the only form of adult relationship that enjoyed legal recognition was the marriage between a man and a woman. The marital family was also perceived as the only locus for ensuring adequate child's development and welfare and, as a result, children born out of wedlock were considered 'illegitimate' and denied equal protection. The 'dominant ideology of the family', therefore, sends out clear messages, produces and sustains stereotypes about the 'normal' family type and the 'proper' role of mothers and fathers within families.[8] These norms, even if not mirroring reality, ultimately serve as parameters against which the legitimacy of other family forms and practices as well as of individual claims is judged, with variable sanctioning effects.[9] The 'legal significance'[10] of this ideology, therefore, might go as far as to marginalise, to exclude and to deny equal protection to relationships and families who do not come close to the normative ideal.

Moving from ideal to real, the 'dominant ideology of the family' bears little comparison to the diversity and complexity of present-day family life in Europe. Despite remaining more or less prevalent depending on the country considered and an aspiration for many, over the last fifty years, the primacy of the heterosexual nuclear family has been profoundly challenged as a consequence of major demographic evolutions. Apart from providing new paths to partnership and parenthood, social change has made non-traditional family forms – that used to be largely invisible in society due to social stigma or lack of official recognition – increasingly visible. The changing landscape of European families can be linked to four main 'enlightenments':[11] (1) the advent of assisted reproductive technologies (ARTs); (2) the weakening of marriage, the ascent of unmarried cohabitation and extra-marital childbearing and, at the same time, an increasingly widespread resort to DNA testing; (3) the rise in female labour force participation and women's continuing engagement in paid employment

---

[7] D. Gittins, *The Family in Question – Changing Households and Familiar Ideologies*, 2nd edn (Macmillan, 1993), pp. 2–3.
[8] McGlynn, *Families and the EU*, p. 23.
[9] S. Boyd, 'Some Postmodernist Challenges to Feminist Analyses of Law, Family and State: Ideology and Discourse in Child Custody Law', *Canadian Journal of Family Law*, 10 (1991), 94.
[10] A. Diduck and F. Kaganas, *Family Law, Gender and the State* (Hart, 1999), p. 10.
[11] H. Krause, 'Comparative Family Law: Past Traditions Battle Future Trends – and Vice Versa' in M. Reimann and R. Zimmermann (eds.), *The Oxford Handbook of Comparative Law* (Oxford University Press, 2006), p. 1110.

after childbirth; and (4) the growing social acceptance and legal recognition of same-sex partnerships and, although at a slower pace, the expanding possibilities for them to become parents and to be legally recognised as such.

A central feature of all these transformations has been the heightened dissolution of the previously coextensive practices of sex, marriage and parenthood. Each through its own path, these demographic shifts have therefore led to an increasing split of biological families into different households, marriages and cohabitations.[12] Apart from resulting in 'fragmented' families, this process of disintegration has had a particularly strong impact on men's role as fathers, thus signifying to a great extent a fragmentation of fatherhood.[13] As a consequence of this changing social context, therefore, what was previously conceptualised as a unitary status and undertaken as a unitary practice tends now to be understood as displaying multiple shades and to be concretely shared between two or more individuals.

Starting from ARTs, these techniques hold the potential to disintegrate parenthood into different constituent parts, thus urging reflections and decisions upon who should enjoy the legal status, rights and responsibilities of parents. Advances in reproductive technologies have indeed given rise to new social and biological situations that, in turn, call old assumptions into question and create new dilemmas for the law. Donor insemination, for instance, challenges not only the importance that society attaches to biology but also the very traditional notion according to which there is a biological link between the father and his child. Thanks to the participation of third parties, the biological contribution can be split from the social context of interpersonal relationships[14] and, therefore, there might be two individuals who – by virtue of different types of input – could be regarded as fathers or, at least, as undertaking paternal functions: the sperm donor, as gamete provider, and the intentional/social father, on the grounds of his parental intentions and, after the child's birth, participation in the child's life.

As a further consequence of social change, the long-standing link between marriage and parenthood has also loosened up. While in the 1950s and 1960s, marriage in Europe was almost universal (almost 8 per 1,000 inhabitants), in the 1970s the crude marriage rate (number of marriages per 1,000 inhabitants) began to decline and, in 2010, it reached the low level of 4.4 per 1,000, thus

---

[12] C. Smart and B. Neale, *Family Fragments?* (Polity Press, 1999), p. 181.
[13] R. Collier and S. Sheldon, *Fragmenting Fatherhood: A Socio-Legal Study* (Hart, 2008), p. 87; S. Sheldon, 'Fragmenting Fatherhood: The Regulation of Reproductive Technologies', *Modern Law Review*, 68(4) (2005), 527.
[14] M. M. Shultz, 'Reproductive Technology and Intent-Based Parenthood: An Opportunity for Gender Neutrality', *Wisconsin Law Review*, (1990), 300.

halving over the period of forty years.[15] At the same time, unmarried cohabitation has emerged as a long-term alternative to marriage and, as a consequence, childbearing outside marriage has also become more frequent. In 2016, around 42 percent of children were born outside marriage in EU countries.[16] Overall, however, the number of people living as a couple is decreasing in most European countries and this decline is attributable to, inter alia, an increased frequency of union disruptions.[17] If the crude divorce rate doubled from 1 (1970) to 2 (2010) per 1,000, and, in 2010, around 50 percent of marriage ended in divorce, unmarried cohabitations have proved even more unstable than marriages.[18]

Apart from graphically illustrating the idea of the 'fragmented family', the decline of marriage and, more generally, the increased fragility of families are responsible for another dimension of the fragmentation of fatherhood. The institution of marriage has traditionally served as a vehicle to connect men with children.[19] Within the 'dominant ideology of the family', fatherhood is constructed not as an autonomous relationship between the father and the child, but rather as mediated by the father's marital union with the child's mother. In present times, however, DNA testing can demonstrate a divergent biological reality and, therefore, bring to light situations where children have a connection with two father figures: the biological father and the husband or new partner of the mother who acts as a social father towards the child. Moreover, after separation or divorce, although sole maternal custody is no longer the only option and joint parental responsibilities on the part of the parents tend to continue after their break-up, it remains the case that children are more likely to live with their mothers.[20] Men who retain parental roles and

---

[15] L. Toulemon, 'Fifty Years of Family Change in Europe: Diversifying Partnerships', in D. Mortelmans, K. Matthijs, E. Alofs and B. Segaert (eds.), *Changing Family Dynamics and Demographic Evolution – The Family Kaleidoscope* (Edward Elgar, 2016), pp. 25–26.

[16] Eurostat, *Share of Live Birth Outside Marriage*, online at http://ec.europa.eu/eurostat/tgm/table.do?tab=table&init=1&language=en&pcode=tps00018&plugin=1 (last access 9 February 2019).

[17] Toulemon, 'Fifty Years', p. 37.

[18] Ibid.

[19] R. Collier, 'Law and the Making of Fatherhood in Late Modernity: Reflections on Family Policy in England and Wales 1997–2010', in M. Oechsle, U. Müller and S. Hess (eds.), *Fatherhood in Late Modernity – Cultural Images, Social Practices and Structural Frames* (Verlag Barbara Budrich, 2012), p. 301.

[20] T. Johansson and J. Andreasson, *Fatherhood in Transition – Masculinity, Identity and Everyday Life* (Palgrave Macmillan, 2017), p. 60. Existing research seems, however, to illustrate that living in gender-equal circumstances before divorce helps parents to maintain stable and positive relationships with their children after. See C. Yodanis, 'Divorce Culture and Marital Gender Equality', *Gender and Society*, 19(5) (2005), pp. 644–659.

responsibilities will thus typically perform them while living in a different household, possibly sharing the role of social father with the mother's new partner and, in case they have re-partnered, perhaps cohabitating with and taking care of the children of their new partner. Following divorce or – more generally – family breakdown, therefore, 'fragmented fatherhood' resonates with a very practical kind of fragmentation, where the work of fathering is split between two or more men.

The third catalyst of family change lies in the transition from the male breadwinner norm to the dual-earner family model and, although at a slower pace, to a more equal distribution of childcare responsibilities between men and women. Over the last two decades, women's increasing participation in the labour market has upset the traditional organisation of labour along gendered lines and, as a consequence, men have lost their role as the exclusive providers and breadwinners for their families. In this context, therefore, the fragmentation of fatherhood reflects the practical sharing of breadwinning responsibilities – that have been conventionally performed by fathers – between mothers and fathers.

Fourth, and finally, the progressive opening of the family avenue to homosexual individuals and couples possibly represents the demographic shift with the highest disruptive effects on the 'dominant ideology of the family'. In the domain of homosexuality, the conventional continuum between sex, marriage and parenthood is, indeed, often broken in multiple ways. Heterosexuality remaining a prerequisite of marriage in most jurisdictions, neither sex nor parenthood is likely to take place within a marital union. Moreover, the extensive resort to ARTs or adoption as a means to have children implies that homo-parenthood does not always follow from biology. As a result of an increased presence – or, at least, visibility – of homosexual families, various aspects of fatherhood that used to be bundled are, therefore, separated and undertaken by different men. Fatherhood is thus fragmented in the sense that the work of fathering is likely to be carried out by a man who is neither biologically related to the child nor married to the child's mother.

This brief outline of social changes demonstrates, first of all, that the 'dominant ideology of the family' is out of step, to a greater or lesser extent depending on the country considered, with European family realities. It further reveals that, if accurate answers are to be provided, the question 'who, in law, is a father?' – that used to have a relatively simple and straightforward answer – now needs to be broken down into multiple sub-questions, including: Who should be named on the birth certificate? Who should be granted contact rights and parental responsibility? Who should be responsible for financially providing for the child?[21] Vis-à-vis social transformation and its fragmentary effects on fatherhood, legal systems have therefore been forced to ask themselves what makes someone a father, and – when formulating their answers – to broaden their horizons and to provide for enough flexibility to accommodate the 'diversity of fathers and the fluidity of fatherhood'.[22]

2 THE LAW'S REACTION: NEW AND OLD WAYS OF CONNECTING FATHERS TO CHILDREN

In the same way as families have been transformed, family laws, too, could not remain unchanged.[23] The fragmentation of parenthood and, more specifically, of fatherhood on the ground has therefore entailed a shifted attitude also in the law. A crucial part of this process has been to acknowledge that the relationships between children and their fathers (and, more generally, their parents) today are much more intricate and heterogeneous than they used to be in the last century. A further premise has been, therefore, to realise that deciding who should be a child's father or granted paternal rights and responsibilities is no longer a simple task. This is especially so because the factors historically relied on by the law to attach men to children are no longer able to provide a definitive answer or, indeed, any answer at all. The evolution of family laws has therefore been driven by the need for alternative logics of relatedness and, further, by the search of new concepts and techniques – sometimes, reflecting old mechanisms – to sort out how to (re)define fatherhood and the broader legitimacy of family ties.[24]

While there exist significant differences between the legal reactions of European jurisdictions to the changing social context outlined in the previous section, family laws are nonetheless unfolding in similar directions.[25] This convergence is, first of all, the product of institutional forces.[26] The guiding principles that have informed family law reform over the last decades all have

---

[21] Sheldon, 'The Regulation of Reproductive Technologies', 530.
[22] N. E. Dowd, 'From Genes, Marriage and Money to Nurture: Redefining Fatherhood', *Cardozo Women's Law Journal*, 10 (2003–2004), 134.
[23] Smart and Neale, *Family Fragments?*, p. 184.
[24] L. A. Sharp, 'Blood Ties, Bioethics, and the Bright-line of the Law', in B. Feuillet-Liger, T. Callus and K. Orfali (eds.), *Reproductive Technology and Changing Perceptions of Parenthood Around the World* (Bruylant, 2014), p. 17.
[25] For an overview of common developments concerning specific family law topics, see J. M. Scherpe (ed.), *European Family Law – Family Law in a European Perspective*, vol. III (Edward Elgar, 2016).
[26] J. M. Scherpe (ed.), *European Family Law – The Impact of Institutions and Organisations on European Family Law*, vol. I (Edward Elgar, 2016).

their place in human rights discourse and the ECtHR certainly represents one of the most influential actors in bringing about legislative and jurisprudential convergence across Europe.[27] At the same time, however, using the evocative language of Scherpe, common approaches have 'organically grown' out of similar societal developments that, in turn, have confronted the law with similar dilemmas in redefining and regulating the modern family.[28]

One of the common trends that has concerned fatherhood more specifically consists in breaking away from the two-parent paradigm according to which only two persons may hold full parental responsibility (and, therefore, should a new person acquire parental responsibility, he or she could only do so at the expense of a person already holding parental responsibility).[29] Family laws have slowly come to terms with the widespread sub-division of fatherhood by gradually beginning to appreciate a wider variety of routes to fatherhood as equally legitimate and the role played by each father figure as equally fundamental.[30] While it remains the case that a child can have no more than one legal father registered on the birth certificate, legal systems have, at least in part, responded to the demographic changes noted earlier by accepting that a child can nonetheless have a legal connection with more than one man and that, accordingly, the rights and responsibilities of fatherhood can be shared or fragmented through the allocation of parental responsibility and/or contact rights.

These attempts to attach children to more than one father indicate a potentially significant departure from the past. At the same time, however, law's openness to multi-fatherhood has often developed along conventional lines. In other words, apart from showing a remarkable delay when it comes to catching up with demographic shifts, any update of the law tends to come as a response to the dominant ideology.[31] In particular, in recent times, we have witnessed a shift towards a 'geneticisation'[32] of fatherhood: in other words,

---

[27] H. Keller, 'Article 8 in the System of the Convention', in A. Büchler and H. Keller (eds.), *Family Forms and Parenthood: Theory and Practice of Article 8 ECHR in Europe* (Intersentia, 2016), p. 3.

[28] J. M. Scherpe (ed.), *European Family Law – The Present and the Future of European Family Law*, vol. IV (Edward Elgar, 2016), p. 40; Krause, 'Comparative Family Law', p. 1101. Of a similar view, Smart argues that changes in the way people organise their family life and their desire to have their relationships legally recognised have driven the liberalisation of family law. It is not, by the same token, the law that has become more pluralistic to accommodate diversity. C. Smart, 'Making Kin: Relationality and Law', in A. Bottomley and S. Wong, *Changing Contours of Domestic Life, Family and Law – Caring and Sharing* (Hart, 2009), p. 7.

[29] Scherpe, *The Present and the Future of European Family Law*, pp. 107–110.

[30] Sheldon, 'The Regulation of Reproductive Technologies', 530.

[31] McGlynn, *Families and the EU*, p. 27.

[32] Collier and Sheldon, *Fragmenting Fatherhood*, pp. 225–226.

biological ties have assumed increased relevance in defining the legal position of fathers with respect to their children.[33] This is not surprising at a time when, due to its decline from a demographic perspective, the institution of marriage can no longer serve as the sole or primary ground whereby granting paternal status, as well as the rights and responsibilities that traditionally accompany that status. All the more so in light of DNA technology that makes it possible to easily identify the biological parent of every child, thus casting doubts on the validity of presumptions regarding fatherhood, *in primis*, the marital presumption.

This enhanced focus on biological ties can thus be seen, at least in part, as a reaction to the proliferation of non-marital families. In the face of increasing numbers of children born out of wedlock, family laws have moved away from treating fathers – and, as a consequence, children – differently, depending on the status of their relationship with the child's mother.[34] Legal fatherhood has come also to include unmarried fathers through a series of reforms that have often sought to secure and reinforce men's (legal) connections with their non-marital children by insisting on biological relatedness.[35] The legal recognition of unmarried fathers, however, has often responded to deep-rooted beliefs about the symbolic importance of fathers or the pragmatic need to ensure financial support, rather than to concerns with ensuring the involvement of a social father.[36]

A desire to involve unmarried fathers in the life of their biological children can also be seen in circumstances where the child's mother is in a relationship with a different man who is actively engaged in the role of social father.[37] In recent times, when dealing with requests for paternity testing, domestic courts have shown an increasing openness to the idea that having access to one's biological origins does not necessarily undermine the child's ties with his social father. National judges seem therefore less concerned with protecting the nuclear family from external incursions and more inclined to order paternity testing, even when this would introduce an additional paternal

---

[33] In relation to US law, see Dowd, 'From Genes', 132–145.
[34] K. Boele-Woelki, F. Ferrand, C. González-Beilfuss, M. Jänterä-Jareborg, N. Lowe, D. Martiny and W. Pintens (eds.), *Principles of European Family Law Regarding Parental Responsibilities* (Intersentia, 2007), p. 65.
[35] In the UK, for instance, legislative efforts of this kind have culminated in the compulsory requirement of joint birth registration for unmarried parents (Welfare Reform Act 2009, s. 56).
[36] In relation to compulsory joint registration in the UK, see, inter alia, J. Wallbank, '"Bodies in the Shadows": Joint Birth Registration, Parental Responsibility and Social Class', *Child and Family Law Quarterly*, 21(3) (2009), 282.
[37] J. Fortin, 'Children's Right to Know Their Origins – Too Far, Too Fast?', *Child and Family Law Quarterly*, 21(3) (2009), 352; Sheldon, 'The Regulation of Reproductive Technologies', 529.

figure, under the conviction that the child needs to know the truth about her origins.

The 'geneticisation' of fatherhood is by no means uniquely a fact of unmarried families. The trend has often been towards supporting biological fathers' continued responsibility for their children also in post-divorce settings. The presumption that children will benefit from contact with both biological parents[38] and, especially, with non-residential fathers, has prompted a transition from a paradigm in which mothers were regarded as primary caregivers and fathers tended to spend time with their children every other weekend and during school holidays (seen more like visiting parents) to a more diversified and egalitarian model, where parents split custody and other childcare responsibilities more equally.[39] These reforms have often intersected with invasive mechanisms to collect child support that rely on the biological link to enforce men's responsibility towards their children also after the end of the parental relationship and, eventually, 'reconstruct the gendered complementarity of the traditional family through the imposition of the economically viable male'.[40] Within national legal systems, therefore, de facto relationships and divorce have sometimes resonated more with the beginning of biology-based – and, to some extent, financial – relationships than with the end of the marital family.[41]

The 'geneticisation' of fatherhood therefore incorporates, at the same time, change and continuity. On the one hand, the increased importance attached to biological ties signals family laws' move towards a more child-centric vision of the parent–child relationship[42] and, more importantly, towards the understanding of fatherhood as direct and no longer contingent upon the nature of

[38] Legal actors could also rely on an extensive body of social science research that has emphasised the vital and lifelong importance of children's relationship with both parents. For instance, S. Gilmore, 'Contact/Shared Residence and Child Well-Being: Research Evidence and Its Implications for Legal Decision-Making', *International Journal of Law, Policy and the Family*, 20 (2006), 344; P. Amato and J. Gilbreth, 'Non-Resident Fathers and Children's Well-Being: a Meta-Analysis', *Journal of Marriage and the Family*, 61(3) (1999), 557; J. Dunn, H. Cheng, T. O'Connor and L. Bridges, 'Children's Perspectives on Their Relationships with Their Non-Resident Fathers: Influences, Outcomes and Implications', *Journal of Child Psychology and Psychiatry*, 45(3) (2004), 553; F. Furstenberg and C. Nord, 'Parenting Apart: Patterns of Childrearing After Marital Dissolution', *Journal of Marriage and the Family*, 47 (1985), 893.
[39] Johansson and Andreasson, *Fatherhood in Transition*, p. 137. Also Fathers' rights activism has played a significant role in bringing about such legislative shift. See, inter alia, R. Collier and S. Sheldon (eds.), *Fathers' Rights Activism and Law Reform in Comparative Perspective* (Hart, 2006).
[40] M. A. Fineman, *The Autonomy Myth: A Theory of Dependency* (New Press, 2004), p. 203.
[41] Sheldon, 'The Regulation of Reproductive Technologies', 528.
[42] Scherpe, *The Present and the Future of European Family Law*, p. 101.

the father's relationship with the child's mother. This 'new' focus on vertical as opposed to horizontal relationships, however, harks back to biology as the – new, but, at the same time, old – vehicle to connect men with children and, therefore, as a decisive determinant of paternal rights and responsibilities. Whilst biological relatedness per se might not be either indispensable or sufficient to obtain the rights associated with fatherhood, it now tends to be accepted as a valid starting point on the basis of which fathers might claim their right to develop a relationship with their child. Despite the rethinking of the place of fatherhood triggered by a changing social context, therefore, there is a danger that paternal ties remain mostly biological, legal and financial.[43]

3 INTRODUCING THE KEY CONCEPTS

Prior to engaging with the specific role played by the ECtHR in redefining fatherhood, it is necessary to introduce the conceptual framework against which the Court's performance will be assessed. The key concepts, which resonate with different models of fatherhood and will guide the case-law analysis enclosed in the following chapters, are three: 'conventional fatherhood', 'fragmenting fatherhood' and 'new fatherhood'. While 'fragmenting fatherhood' and 'new fatherhood' constitute pre-existing notions, 'conventional fatherhood' offers a new paradigm through which the relationship between legal understandings of fatherhood and social change can be fruitfully explored.

'Conventional Fatherhood'

The term 'conventional' is defined as 'based on or in accordance with what is generally done or believed'.[44] It is therefore used herein because it renders visible the often-blurred boundaries between law, culture and society, thus testifying to the influence of the dominant culture on the legal regulation of fatherhood. In this vein, 'conventional fatherhood' refers to the individual who has those characteristics (both physical and behavioural) that, in line with dominant societal perceptions and expectations, have for a long time been and, to some extent, continue to be ascribed to the father figure. It is important to note that, apart from describing what allegedly used to be the most

---

[43] Fineman, 'Fatherhood, Feminism and Family Law', *McGeorge Law Review*, 32 (2000–2001), 1036.
[44] Oxford Dictionaries, online at www.oxforddictionaries.com/definition/english/conventional (last access 9 February 2019).

widespread reality of fatherhood, 'conventional fatherhood' tends also to express a normative vision of the 'proper' father and, indirectly, of the appropriately constituted family. To the extent that it has permeated the formulation and the application of the law, therefore, the conventional paradigm of fatherhood has had concrete repercussions on the life of fathers, mothers and children: it has indeed contributed to delineating what father–child relationships have a legal existence or deserve greater legal entitlements and, at the same time, to sanctioning those who do not comply with the 'norm' with lack of recognition and support.[45]

The features of 'conventional fatherhood' can be drawn from McGlynn's conceptualisation of the 'dominant ideology of the family' and include: a biological tie with his child; a marital or marriage-like relationship (opposite-sex couple living in a sexual relationship) with the child's mother; breadwinning; heterosexuality and, more generally, compliance with heteronormativity.[46] A fifth characteristic can be added or, simply, made explicit: it lies in the unitary nature of 'conventional fatherhood' and, accordingly, in the coexistence of all those attributes within one and the same individual. It follows that a 'conventional father' is, at the same time, the biological progenitor of the child, the heterosexual husband of the child's mother and the family breadwinner. According to a similar definition of fatherhood, therefore, the father's interest and actual engagement in his child's life constitute irrelevant considerations in determining who should enjoy the status of legal father and/or the rights that accompany that status. In other words, paternal care is neither a feature of nor a prerequisite for obtaining legal fatherhood.

'Fragmenting Fatherhood'

In contrast with the paradigm of 'conventional fatherhood', Collier and Sheldon have observed that, as a consequence of the evolving social context outlined earlier, fatherhood has become increasingly fragmented and ambiguous both as a concept and as a practice.[47] 'Fragmenting fatherhood' embodies, therefore, the father-specific effects of the wider structural changes affecting families and, as such, captures dimensions of the sub-division of

---

[45] Fineman, 'The Sexual Family', p. 46.
[46] 'Heteronormativity' is defined by Berlant and Warner as 'the institutions, structures of understanding, and practical orientations that make heterosexuality seem not only coherent (...) but also privileged'. See L. Berlant and M. Warner, 'Sex in Public', *Critical Inquiry*, 24(2) (1998), 548.
[47] Collier and Sheldon, *Fragmenting Fatherhood*, p. 87; Sheldon, 'The Regulation of Reproductive Technologies', 527.

the model of 'conventional fatherhood' that, in the past, had been held together by a body of laws around marriage, parenthood and the heterosexual family. This process of disintegration can be detected at a variety of levels. From a subjective perspective, for instance, 'fragmenting fatherhood' might resonate with men's beliefs regarding fatherhood, with their perceptions of what being a father means and entails and, even beyond, with aspects of their lived experience of fathers themselves.[48]

For our purposes, however, the dimensions of 'fragmenting fatherhood' that are most relevant are the legal as well as the practical one. Starting from the latter, in its possibly most immediate connotation, this sub-division of fatherhood involves the split of conventional paternal features and roles among two or more individuals.[49] In an era like ours, which is characterised by the proliferation of non-traditional families, it is not surprising that children might live and be nurtured in more than one household during their childhood and adolescence, thus establishing bonds with more than one father figure and that, more generally, two or more men might have distinct contributions to make to the life of the same child. As illustrated in Section 2, this very concrete kind of fragmentation has triggered specific legal responses. The legal dimension of 'fragmenting fatherhood' thus depicts how legal systems have slowly evolved towards the recognition of diversity and heterogeneity in men's family practices.

'New Fatherhood'

The third key concept is that of 'new fatherhood'. Over the past decades, we have witnessed the heightened visibility of a revisited cultural imaginary of what being a 'good father' entails: it is no longer enough to be a breadwinner and there is great awareness of the importance of spending time with children. As early as 1987, Pleck described the ideal father as more than the breadwinner of the family but someone who combines full-time work with daily childcare[50] – using Crowley's words, 'just like any other modern mother'.[51] In more recent times, a similar definition has been provided by Collier and Sheldon, according to

---

[48] Collier and Sheldon, *Fragmenting Fatherhood*, p. 5. See also the research undertaken by J. Ives on focus groups with fathers in the UK: *Becoming a Father/Refusing Fatherhood: How Paternal Responsibilities and Rights are Generated*, PhD thesis submitted to the University of Birmingham (July 2007), p. 179.

[49] Collier and Sheldon, *Fragmenting Fatherhood*, p. 5.

[50] J. Pleck, 'American Fathering in Historical Perspective', in M. Kimmel (ed.), *Changing Men: New Directions in Research on Men and Masculinity* (Sage, 1987).

[51] J. Crowley, 'Taking Custody of Motherhood: Fathers' Rights Activists and the Politics of Parenting', *Women's Studies Quarterly*, 37(3) 2009, 223.

whom a 'new father' is a 'man who is not (or, at least, not just) seen as a primary breadwinner but is also, increasingly, a "hands-on" carer, an individual who is (or who should be) emotionally engaged and involved in the day-to-day care of his children'.[52] As Caracciolo di Torella puts it, the 'new father' is someone who is willing to move away from the traditional division of life between the private/domestic sphere and the public sphere.[53] Despite being called 'new' and announcing a wind of change, therefore, this third model of fatherhood does not totally break with the past, but combines (expectations of) greater participation and nurture with conventional characteristics, in particular, breadwinning.[54]

This mix of and tension between change and continuity is also reflected in fathering practices. Despite men's increased participation in childcare and domestic work, the emergence of a more engaged vision of fatherhood has entailed men struggling with the concept of fatherhood. One of the complexities of refashioning fatherhood lies in the fact that many fathers attempt to masculinise care, namely, to construct tasks and roles that are not traditional for men as masculine with the purpose of alleviating the threat to their masculinity.[55] Care, as redefined by some Norwegian fathers, consists, for instance, in being a friend to the child, teaching independence while continuing to be heavily involved in the labour market.[56] Other studies have pointed out that engaged fathers show a greater involvement in instrumental functions (as opposed to expressive functions), such as discipline, protection, income provision and encouraging responsibility, which are known as the traditional functions of fathers.[57] Empirical research thus shows that 'new fatherhood' is more about processes and slowly shifting attitudes rather than entirely new practices:[58] fathers have not abandoned their traditional roles, but they have simply attempted to re-envision them by adding on new features.[59]

---

[52] Collier and Sheldon, *Fragmenting Fatherhood*, p. 209.

[53] E. Caracciolo di Torella, 'Brave New Fathers for a Brave New World? Fathers as Caregivers in an Evolving European Union', *European Law Journal*, 20(1) (2014), 95.

[54] Ibid.

[55] N. E. Dowd, *The Man Question – Male Subordination and Privilege* (New York University Press, 2010), p. 112. Empirical evidence is provided by, inter alia, T. Maurer and J. Pleck, 'Fathers' Caregiving and Breadwinning: A Gender Congruence Analysis', *Psychology of Men and Masculinity*, 7(2) (2006), 101; A. Doucet, *Do Men Mother? Fathering, Care and Domestic Responsibility* (Toronto University Press, 2006), p. 219.

[56] B. Brandth and E. Kvande, 'Masculinity and Child Care: the Reconstruction of Fathering', *Sociological Review*, 26(2) 1998, 310.

[57] G. Finley and S. Schwartz, 'Parsons and Bales Revisited: Young Adult Children's Characterisation of the Fathering Role', *Psychology of Men and Masculinity*, 7(1) (2006), 52.

[58] Johannson and Andreasson, *Fatherhood in Transition*, p. 7.

[59] B. Catlett and P. McKenry, 'Class-Based Masculinities: Divorce, Fatherhood and the Hegemonic Ideal', *Fathering*, 2(2) (2004), 1–20; Dowd, *The Man Question*, p. 114. It is,

4 THE AIM AND STRUCTURE OF THE ANALYSIS

The aim of this book is twofold. First, it identifies shifts and inconsistencies in the ECtHR's understandings of what it means to be a 'father' and what rights and obligations should accrue to that status. Second, it examines to what extent the emerging definition(s) of fatherhood has (have) doctrinal and/or moral underpinnings. In other words, by delving into the reasoning developed by the Court in each relevant case, the following analysis clarifies whether the Court's use of its doctrines of interpretation has been 'productive of' or 'subservient to' its moral views[60] on who should be considered a child's legal father and/or enjoy parental rights with respect to his child.

To achieve the aims mentioned earlier, the book is structured as follows. This chapter has attempted to locate the upcoming case-law analysis in a context of social change that, apart from affecting the realities of family life in Europe, has prompted a partially shifted attitude to fatherhood also in the law. Chapter 2 is devoted to the protagonist of the book, the ECtHR. It explores the potential and limits of the Court's role in modernising its legal approach to fatherhood by introducing the core Convention provisions – namely, Articles 8 and 14 – as well as the doctrines of interpretation that have thus far played a role in the development of the Strasbourg jurisprudence pertaining to family relationships.

In appraising the Court's definition(s) of fatherhood and its underpinnings, the jurisprudence is divided around the four demographic transformations introduced in Section 1. By examining paradigmatic cases arising from artificial insemination, IVF and surrogacy, Chapter 3 - which marks the beginning of the case-law analysis - traces change and continuity in the Court's understanding of fatherhood in the domain of ARTs. As noted already, in this context, questions on what kinds of tie are most decisive in making someone a father have been starkly posed as a consequence of the fragmentation of fatherhood triggered by the use of these techniques. In Chapter 4, the focus of the analysis shifts to the more variegated domain of unmarried and post-separation fatherhood. Here, the vast case-law arising out of paternity proceedings and contact and residence disputes involving unmarried fathers provides a fruitful terrain for investigating the Court's reaction to the decline of marriage as a father–child connector.

---

therefore, not surprising that doubts as to whether involved fatherhood represents a real change or simply a reconstruction of hegemonic masculinity have been raised. See, inter alia, L. Plantin, S. Mansson and J. Kearney, 'Talking and Doing Fatherhood: On Fatherhood and Masculinity in Sweden and England', *Fathering*, 1(1) (2003), 3–26.

[60] P. Johnson, *Homosexuality and the European Court of Human Rights* (Routledge, 2013), p. 88.

Chapter 5 takes us to the context of family–work reconciliation. By focusing on cases arising from the exclusion of fathers from childcare-related measures, it examines whether the Court has seized the occasion offered by women's increased participation in paid employment to move beyond a gendered division of labour and, more specifically, to redefine the role of fathers as more than mere economic provision. Finally, in Chapter 6, the construction of fatherhood endorsed by the Court is considered in the context of homo-parenthood. Here, the principal focus of contestation has concerned the legal position of homosexuals – both gays and lesbians – in relation to single-parent and second-parent adoption. The ensuing case-law will therefore offer the opportunity to test the persistence of heterosexuality – and other connected conventional traits – as an essential feature of 'conventional fatherhood' and, more generally, of parenthood. The jurisprudential analysis is followed by a concluding chapter, which provides an up-to-date picture of fatherhood as reconstructed by the Court, and discusses the roles played by doctrines in this process.

2

The ECtHR and Fatherhood: Limits and Potential

INTRODUCTION

This book focuses on a series of paradigmatic judgments through which the Court has sketched the contours of the rights and responsibilities of legal fatherhood, relying particularly on the right to respect for private and family life under Article 8, taken alone or in conjunction with Article 14. In the ECtHR jurisprudence, fatherhood is a subject that cuts across a variety of different legal issues and, therefore, takes shape across disparate contexts. With some exceptions, however, the applicant tends to be an unconventional (potential) father who is denied the allocation of paternal status or rights as a result of national measures that are premised on a conventional understanding of fatherhood.

The aim of this chapter is to illustrate the main doctrinal elements at the Court's disposal when dealing with such cases and their potential contribution to shaping the understanding of fatherhood emerging from the jurisprudence. After a general overview of the Court's role as an interpreter of the Convention in the context of family relationships (Section 1), Section 2 introduces the ECHR provisions through which the Court's legal approach to fatherhood has come to the fore: namely, the right to respect for private and family life protected by Article 8 and the prohibition of discrimination enshrined in Article 14. Section 3, in contrast, elaborates on the intricate relationship between the Court's interpretative repertoire and its jurisprudence, thus offering a basis against which the genesis of the Court's construction of fatherhood can be critically assessed. More specifically, it illustrates that the role of doctrines vis-à-vis the Court's approach to fatherhood can be twofold. They might contribute to delineate the contours of legal fatherhood in line with their 'updating' or 'conservative' potential or – in the opposite scenario – be employed to support a predetermined moral position on fatherhood and, as such, as a vehicle to pursue a specific moral agenda. Finally, Section 4 outlines the case-law selection criteria.

1 FAMILY RELATIONSHIPS: BETWEEN RESTRAINT AND INNOVATION

At over 60 years of age, the European Court of Human Rights is considered one of the most successful international human rights treaty bodies.[1] Nonetheless, its role as an interpreter has given rise to heated debates and legitimacy concerns. The Court regularly attracts the criticism that it has failed to deliver full human rights as guaranteed in the Convention[2] or, conversely, that it has gone too far in developing human rights standards thus interfering with prerogatives of national legislatures.[3] This last concern is not surprising if attention is given to the origins and institutional features of the ECHR system. The adoption of the ECHR by the Member States of the Council of Europe was premised on the assumption that they would retain their full prerogatives as sovereign states and, therefore, full autonomy of their respective societies, with the sole – but important – exception of the core fundamental rights enshrined in the Convention.[4] The ECHR system is therefore the product of a 'tidy arrangement',[5] which is preserved by the principle of subsidiarity: national authorities are free to choose the measure they deem appropriate to meet the requirements of the Convention, while the Court is (only) responsible for reviewing the compatibility of national choices with the Convention standards.

At the same time, the general formulation characterising ECHR provisions has been read as revealing that a certain degree of judicial creativity on the side of the Court is not only welcome, but practically necessary.[6] The

---

[1] A. Føllesdal, B. Peters and G. Ulfstein, 'Introduction' in A. Føllesdal, B. Peters and G. Ulfstein (eds.), *Constituting Europe – The European Court of Human Rights in a National, European and Global Context* (Cambridge University Press, 2013), p. 1; F. Bruinsma and S. Parmentier, 'Interview with Mr Luzius Wildhaber, President of the European Court of Human Rights', *Netherlands Human Rights Review*, 21(2) (2003), 193; A. Bradley, 'Introduction: The Need for Both International and National Protection of Human Rights – The European challenge' in S. Flogaitis, T. Zwart and J. Fraser (eds.), *The European Court of Human Rights and its Discontents – Turning Criticism into Strength* (Edward Elgar Publishing, 2013), p. 2.

[2] See, inter alia, E. Benvenisti, 'Margin of Appreciation, Consensus and Universal Standards', *New York University Journal of International Law and Politics* 31(4) (1999), 843.

[3] See, inter alia, T. Zwart, 'More Human Rights than Court: Why the Legitimacy of the European Court of Human Rights in the Need of Repair and How it Can be Done' in *The European Court of Human Rights and its Discontents – Turning Criticism into Strength* (Edward Elgar, 2013), pp. 72–78.

[4] J. H. H. Weiler, *The Constitution of Europe – "Do the New Clothes Have an Emperor?" and Other Essays on European Integration* (Cambridge University Press, 1999), pp. 102–107.

[5] Ibid, p. 104.

[6] C. Nikolaidis, *The Right to Equality in European Human Rights Law – The Quest for Substance in the Jurisprudence of the European Courts* (Routledge, 2015), p. 52; P. Mahoney,

Convention – just like other international human rights treaties and constitutions – enshrines a set of abstract rights that individuals hold against governments and it faces the problem of how the passage of time impacts its interpretation and application.[7] In its interpretative capacity, the Court is therefore confronted with the challenge of ensuring due regard to changing conditions in Europe that could not be foreseen at the time of drafting or accession, in order to maintain a meaningful and effective system of human rights protection.

The tension between the need to provide a contemporary reading of a dated instrument while obeying the principle of subsidiarity has become particularly visible in the context of Article 8 and, as it will be shown, it has navigated also the ECtHR's approach to fatherhood. Despite the existence of international provisions,[8] the institution of the family has been traditionally conceived as a matter 'private' to States and, as such, to be regulated within their domestic jurisdiction.[9] Accordingly, family law has been generally understood as

'Judicial Activism and Judicial Self-Restraint in the European Court of Human Rights: Two Sides of the Same Coin', *Human Rights Law Journal*, 11 (1–2) (1990), 63.

[7] M. Andenas and E. Bjorge, 'National Implementation of ECHR Rights' in A. Føllesdal, B. Peters and G. Ulfstein (eds.), *Constituting Europe – The European Court of Human Rights in a National, European and Global Context* (Cambridge University Press, 2013), pp. 191–192; G. Letsas, 'The ECHR as a Living Instrument: Its Meaning and Legitimacy' in A. Føllesdal, B. Peters and G. Ulfstein (eds.), *Constituting Europe – The European Court of Human Rights in a National, European and Global Context* (Cambridge University Press, 2013), p. 107; B. Rainey, E. Wicks and C. Ovey, *Jacobs, White and Ovey: The European Convention on Human Rights* (Oxford University Press, 2014), p. 66.

[8] All major human rights instruments include provisions applicable to the family. For instance, both the Universal Declaration of Human Rights and the International Covenant on Civil and Political Rights provide that 'the family is the natural and fundamental group unit of society and is entitled to protection by society and the State'. Article 16(3), Universal Declaration of Human Rights (10 December 1948); Article 23, International Covenant on Civil and Political Rights (16 December 1966, entry into force 23 March 1976).

[9] G. Van Bueren, *International Law on the Rights of the Child* (Kluwer, 1998), p. 72. It is therefore not surprising that, in the European Union, for instance, States have retained their competence in the field of substantive family law and, therefore, parenthood does not fall within its original legislative competences. See, inter alia, E. Caracciolo di Torella, 'Brave New Fathers for a Brave New World? Fathers as Caregivers in an Evolving European Union', *European Law Journal*, 20 (1) (2014), 89; C. McGlynn, *Families and the European Union: Law, Policy and Pluralism* (Cambridge University Press, 2006), pp. 79–80. Even within national jurisdictions, direct State intervention in the family and the home has for a long time been considered improper. This very traditional view of the role of the State has been largely criticised for its significant repercussions on the lives of women. See, inter alia, C. Chinkin, 'A Critique of the Public/Private Dimension', *European Journal of International Law*, 10(2) 1999, 387–395; H. Charlesworth, C. Chinkin and S. Wright, 'Feminist Approaches to International Law', *American Journal of International Law*, 85 (1991), 613–645; E. Brems, 'Protecting the Rights of Women' in G. Lyons and J. Mayall (eds.), *International Human Rights in the 21st Century – Protecting the Rights of Groups* (Rowman & Littlefield, 2003), pp. 100–137.

a 'national' type of law: embedded in national laws, national legal cultures, national traditions and national societies. The progressive emergence of common patterns notwithstanding,[10] family law continues to be an introverted subject as it remains particularly open to influence by moral, cultural, religious, political and psychological factors.[11] This explains why, although the relationship between law and fatherhood has become a subject of international interest,[12] the pronounced moral dimension of the concepts of 'family', *in primis*, and subsequently 'fatherhood' as well as the great variations in fathering practices across countries and sociocultural milieus have eventually made any reconsideration of these concepts State and context specific, at the cultural as much as at the legal level.[13] At the same time, family life is also one of the fastest changing domains in society. Since the drafting of the ECHR, the Court has indeed been faced with unpredictable societal and technological shifts, from the advent of ARTs to the proliferation of homosexual unions, that – as explained above – have transformed the way in which personal and social relationships are created and developed.

It can therefore be argued that the protection of family rights has been caught in between two prima facie opposing, and yet complementary, needs: to guarantee a greater match with modern family realities, while respecting State-specific variations in family laws and sociocultural notions of what constitutes a 'family'. In other words, to interpret Article 8 in accordance with 'contemporary needs' whilst being cautious not to override the 'will of the States'.[14] To settle

[10] J. M. Scherpe (ed.), *European Family Law – The Present and the Future of European Family Law*, vol. IV (Edward Elgar, 2016), p. 2.
[11] W. Müller-Freienfels, 'The Unification of Family Law', *American Journal of Comparative Law* 16(1/2) (1968), 175. Of a similar view is Judge Morenilla, dissenting, in *Kroon and Others v the Netherlands*, 27 October 1994, Series A no. 297-C. By referring to the tension between dynamic interpretation and the need to respect policy decisions taken by elected bodies, he held that: '[T]he dilemma is even greater in matters such as marriage, divorce, filiation or adoption, because they bring into play the existing religious, ideological and traditional conceptions of the family in each community.'
[12] R. Collier, 'The Responsible Father in New Labour's Legal and Social Policy' in J. Bridgeman, H. Keating and L. Craig (eds.), *Regulating Family Responsibilities* (Ashgate, 2011), p. 47.
[13] R. Collier, *Men, Law and Gender: Essays on the 'Man' of Law* (Routledge, 2010), chapter 5; S. Ruddick, 'The Idea of Fatherhood' in H. L. Nelson (ed.), *Feminism and Families* (Routledge, 1997), p. 207; R. Day and M. Lamb (eds.), *Conceptualizing and Measuring Father Involvement* (Lawrence Erlbaum Associates, 2004), pp. 2–3.
[14] A. Mowbray, 'Between the Will of the Contracting Parties and the Needs of Today – Extending the Scope of Convention Rights and Freedoms Beyond What Could Have Been Foreseen by the Drafters of the ECHR' in E. Brems and J. Gerards (eds.), *Shaping Rights in the ECHR – The Role of the European Court of Human Rights in Determining the Scope of Human Rights* (Cambridge University Press, 2013), pp. 36–37.

this – 'more apparent, than real'[15] – tension, the Court has relied on a set of distinctive doctrinal tools. One of the most prominent is the doctrine of the margin of appreciation. The latter is premised on the idea that each signatory State is entitled to a certain amount of discretion in settling the inherent conflicts between individual rights and national interests or between competing individual rights. In the context of Article 8, the application of this doctrine has therefore supported the Court's efforts to ensure that morals, traditions and historical context – that exercise significant influence on the regulation of private and family law matters – are taken into consideration and that legal diversity is recognised.

As a 'counterweight' to the doctrine of the margin, the Court has long deemed the Convention to be a 'living instrument' that must be interpreted in light of present-day conditions. In the family domain, dynamic or evolutive interpretation has been variously employed to adapt the text of Article 8 to new technologies and social change, 'to justify a higher standard of protection' as well as 'to derive new rights from those expressly enshrined'.[16] Article 8 has, in fact, been effectively described as the 'nursery in which new rights are born'.[17] A series of rights connected to parenthood – such as the right to respect for the decision to become a genetic parent, or the right to become a parent through ARTs – that were not conceivable at the time of drafting have, for instance, found protection under the concept of 'private and family life'. The interpretation of the Convention as a 'living instrument' has also been the impetus behind the development of positive obligations.[18] The interpretation of 'respect' in active terms – rather than as a passive concept – has enabled the Court to develop the spectrum of obligations arising from Article 8, in accordance with the needs of the applicants assessed against the background of contemporary European families.[19]

Before setting new standards, however, the Court has generally proved quite thoughtful by anchoring its interpretation of Article 8 to State practice

---

[15] Mahoney, 'Judicial Activism', 59.
[16] J.-P. Costa, 'On the Legitimacy of the European Court of Human Rights' Judgments', *European Constitutional Law Review*, 7(2) (2011), 178.
[17] M. Burbergs, 'How the Right to Respect for Private and Family Life, Home and Correspondence Became the Nursery in Which New Rights Are Born' in E. Brems and J. Gerards (eds.), *Shaping Rights in the ECHR – The Role of the European Court of Human Rights in Determining the Scope of Human Rights* (Cambridge University Press, 2013), pp. 315–329.
[18] D. Feldman, *Civil Liberties and Human Rights in England and Wales* 2nd edn (Oxford University Press, 2002), p. 55.
[19] A. Mowbray, *The Development of Positive Obligations under the European Convention on Human Rights by the European Court of Human Rights* (Hart, 2004), p. 229.

primarily. In other words, to avoid perceptions of arbitrariness, the Court has generally waited for a European common ground on the matter at issue to be established before opting for a dynamic reading of Article 8. Conversely, vis-à-vis a substantive discrepancy in the legal regulation of a particular issue in Europe, Strasbourg judges have been consistent in stating that national authorities should be granted a wide margin of appreciation. European consensus has, therefore, helped the Court to set a balance between judicial restraint and judicial innovation by working – at least formally – as a 'means of mediation'[20] between evolutive interpretation and the doctrine of the margin of appreciation.

If transposed into the more specific context of fatherhood, European consensus might therefore either empower or discourage the Court from reconsidering its understanding of fatherhood. Being a 'tool of judicial self-restraint',[21] resorting to the doctrine of the margin is likely to contribute to entrenching the status quo and, as such, to prevent any significant departure from conventional fatherhood. Being a tool for expanding the application of the Convention, evolutive interpretation has instead the potential to make the Court's approach apt for modern family realities and, therefore, to smooth the way for a redefinition of fatherhood beyond its conventional boundaries, in line with social and scientific developments. In practice, however, the relationship between doctrines and the Court's understanding of fatherhood has proved far from linear and straightforward.

2 CORE PROVISIONS

In the Strasbourg jurisprudence, the construction of fatherhood endorsed by the Court emerges primarily from the interpretation of two provisions: Article 8, which provides for the right to respect for private and family life and is often called upon in conjunction with the prohibition of discrimination enshrined in Article 14. The aim of the following sections is to illustrate the relevance of each provision to molding the Court's understanding of fatherhood. Starting from Article 8, emphasis is placed on the contribution of each stage of review – in accordance with the provision's bifurcated nature[22] – to identify the

---

[20] K. Dzehtsiarou, *European Consensus and the Legitimacy of the European Court of Human Rights* (Cambridge University Press, 2015), p. 138.
[21] Mahoney, 'Judicial Activism', 78.
[22] L. Lavrysen, 'The Scope of Rights and the Scope of Obligations – Positive Obligations' in E. Brems and J. Gerards (eds.), *Shaping Rights in the ECHR – The Role of the European Court of Human Rights in Determining the Scope of Human Rights* (Cambridge University Press, 2013), p. 163.

model(s) of fatherhood that is prima facie and *definitively* accorded protection,[23] as well as on the positive obligations that have arisen in the context of private and family life. Moving onto Article 14, its 'magnifying effects'[24] and the adoption of an anti-stereotyping approach are identified as the main doctrinal developments that have the potential to guide and influence the Court's reconstruction of fatherhood.

2.1 Article 8 and Fatherhood

Two Stages of Review

The Court does not openly discuss the concept of fatherhood in its jurisprudence. Rather, it generally conveys its definition(s) by approaching the question from the perspective of whether the relationship at stake falls within the notion of private and family life and, if so, whether the applicant's right to respect for private and family life has been violated and/or a differential treatment contrary to Article 14 can be found.[25] In line with the bifurcated structure of Article 8,[26] the Court's assessment of complaints brought under this provision is therefore made of two stages.[27] The first concerns the applicability of Article 8: herein, the Court examines whether the situation of the applicant enters the scope of 'private and family life' and, therefore, whether there has been an interference with the applicant's right to respect for private and family life. Only if the complaint is considered to engage one of the interests protected by Article 8(1), the Court will continue its investigation to determine whether the interference could pass the legality, legitimacy and proportionality tests enclosed in

---

[23] Ibid, p. 164.
[24] O. M. Arnardóttir, 'Discrimination as a Magnifying Lens – Scope and Ambit under Article 14 and Protocol No. 12' in E. Brems and J. Gerards (eds.), *Shaping Rights in the ECHR – The Role of the European Court of Human Rights in Determining the Scope of Human Rights* (Cambridge University Press, 2013), pp. 331–349.
[25] S. Choudhry and J. Herring, *European Human Rights and Family Law* (Hart, 2010), p. 170.
[26] Article 8 provides that: '1. Everyone has the right to respect for his private and family life, his home and his correspondence. 2. There shall be no interference by a public authority with the exercise of this right except such as is in accordance with the law and is necessary in a democratic society in the interests of national security, public safety or the economic well-being of the country, for the prevention of disorder or crime, for the protection of health or morals, or for the protection of the rights and freedoms of others.'
[27] G. van der Schyff, 'Interpreting the Protection Guaranteed by Two-Stage Rights in the European Convention on Human Rights' in E. Brems and J. Gerards (eds.), *Shaping Rights in the ECHR – The Role of the European Court of Human Rights in Determining the Scope of Human Rights* (Cambridge University Press, 2013), p. 66.

Article 8(2) and eventually conclude whether Article 8 – alone or in conjunction with Article 14 – has been violated.

Both stages of review contribute to bringing to the fore the definition of fatherhood endorsed by the Court. The first clarifies what factors make the relationship between a father and his child worthy of protection under Article 8 and, more importantly, whether these factors reflect or depart from the paradigm of 'conventional fatherhood'. As such, it points to the model of fatherhood that is, prima facie, afforded protection in the Court's jurisprudence. The second stage of adjudication, in contrast, reveals the conditions under which the establishment of private and family life between a father and his child brings along a set of rights in favour of the applicant; or, to the contrary, the missing conditions that have justified the conclusion that the refusal to grant the legal status and/or parental rights to the applicant father is compatible with the Convention. In so doing, this second stage sheds light on the model of fatherhood that is *definitely* afforded protection by the Court after taking into account the possibility of limitations.

Starting from the first stage of analysis, the Court has generally adopted a pluralistic and inclusive approach to the question of what constitutes a family, thus allowing for a modernisation of the concept of 'family life' that takes into account social, legal and technological developments across the Council of Europe.[28] In the ECtHR's jurisprudence, the existence or absence of family life has become, in essence, a question of fact depending upon 'the real existence in practice of close personal ties' between the individuals concerned.[29] It is therefore the nature and purpose of the relationship at stake, rather than its form per se, that is paramount.

This 'functional'[30] approach has proved particularly beneficial to unconventional parent–child relationships. It is now a well-established principle that, from the moment of the child's birth and by the very fact of it, there exists a tie between the child and his/her parents amounting to family life,[31] even if the parents are not living together or are separated. This further implies that the breakdown of the couple's relationship – for instance, through divorce – does not put an end to the family life between the child and the non-

---

[28] H. Stalford, 'Concepts of Family Law under EU Law – Lessons From the ECHR', *International Journal of Law, Policy and the Family*, 16 (2002), 413; Mowbray, 'Between the Will', pp. 26–29.

[29] *K. and T. v Finland* [GC], no. 25702/94, § 150, ECHR 2001-VII; *Lebbink v the Netherlands*, no. 45582/99, § 36, ECHR 2004-IV.

[30] Choudhry and Herring, *European Human Rights*, p. 168.

[31] *Berrehab v the Netherlands*, 21 June 1988, § 21, Series A no. 138; *Keegan v Ireland*, 26 May 1994, § 44, Series A no. 290.

residential parent – who, in most cases, is the child's father. In other words, once established, family ties between parents and children cannot be severed, save in exceptional circumstances.[32] Moreover, the Court has considered that intended family life might, exceptionally, fall within the ambit of Article 8.[33] The concept of 'family life' has therefore come to include also the potential relationship that can develop between a child born out of wedlock and his/her natural father, provided that the absence of a pre-existing relationship was not attributable to the applicant.[34] In such cases, relevant factors that might indicate the real existence in practice of close personal ties include the nature of the relationship between the natural parents and a demonstrable interest in and commitment by the father to the child both before and after birth.[35]

Despite an increased relevance attached to the substance of relationships to the advantage of 'unconventional' family arrangements, an examination of the Court's jurisprudence on Article 8 reveals that there is still a hierarchy of relationships, whose top position continues to be occupied by the traditional heterosexual married couple.[36] In other words, when approaching the question of whether family life has been established, the Court will first consider the form of the relationship at stake[37] and, in particular, whether it reflects the 'conventional ideology of the family'. The existence of a public undertaking, *in primis* marriage, continues therefore to be interpreted as the ultimate evidence of the intention to create family life and, further, as an undisputed point of reference for establishing parenthood.[38] It follows that, even if the recognition of family life as a direct consequence of birth has implied – at least, in principle – a certain disconnection between the relationship between the parents and the parent–child relationship, de facto, the nature of the relationship from which a child is born is likely to have a bearing on whether the father–child tie is considered to enjoy the status of 'family life'.

Although the scope of Article 8 can extend to intended family life, the Court has clarified that the protection of the right to respect for family life is premised

---

[32] J. Liddy, 'The Concept of Family Life under the ECHR', *European Human Rights Law Review* 1 (1998), 18.
[33] *Anayo v Germany*, no. 20578/07, § 57, 21 December 2010; *Schneider v Germany*, no. 17080/07, § 81, 15 September 2011; *Kautzor v Germany*, no. 23338/09, § 61, 22 March 2012; *Ahrens v Germany*, no. 45071/09, § 58, 22 March 2012.
[34] Ibid.
[35] Ibid.
[36] B. Rainey, E. Wicks and C. Ovey, *Jacobs, White and Ovey: The Convention on Human Rights* (Oxford University Press, 2017), p. 373.
[37] Choudhry and Herring, *European Human Rights*, p. 169.
[38] *Burden v the United Kingdom* [GC], no. 13378/05, § 65, ECHR 2008; *Van der Heijden v the Netherlands* [GC], no. 42857/05, § 69, 3 April 2012.

on the existence of a 'family' and, therefore, it does not safeguard the mere desire to found a family. The repercussions of failing to establish family life might, however, not be significant: in cases where the pre-requisites of family life are not met, the protection afforded to private life 'often serves as a catch-all'.[39] That explains why, vis-à-vis pre-birth claims, the Court considered the decision to become/not to become a parent to give rise to an issue of 'private life'.[40] In the same vein, in cases concerning access to adoption, the Court tends to examine the matter from the perspective of private life,[41] except where concrete family ties already exist. The Court has – on several occasions – considered that the notion of 'private life' covers also a man's right to have his paternity established[42] or to challenge his presumed paternity.[43]

The Court has therefore given a generous interpretation to the scope of Article 8 by extending protection to a wide range of parent–child relationships and related interests. Yet, the fact that Article 8 is found applicable in most cases pertaining to fatherhood is not necessarily indicative of the Court's support for the claims of the fathers (who are mostly unconventional) involved. Being a qualified right, the 'scope' of Article 8 must indeed be kept distinct from its 'limit' or review of justification.[44] In other words, the establishment of 'private and family life' does not automatically result in concrete protection for the Article 8's rights of the fathers involved because their scope might be limited, and how far national authorities can go in justifiably restricting the afforded protection is ultimately decided as part of the second stage of review. Therefore, at least in principle, it is (only) in this adjudicative phase that considerations on the width of the margin of appreciation and other doctrinal factors influencing decision making come into play.[45] It follows that the second stage of analysis is most decisive to clarify the genesis of the (re-)definition of fatherhood emerging from the ECtHR case-law and, in particular, the role played by doctrines in this process.

---

[39] A. Büchler, 'The Right to Respect for Private and Family Life – The Case Law of the European Court of Human Rights on Parenthood and Family Forms' in A. Büchler and H. Keller (eds.), *Family Forms and Parenthood: Theory and Practice of Article 8 ECHR in Europe* (Intersentia, 2016), p. 30.

[40] *Evans v the United Kingdom* [GC], no. 6339/05, ECH 2007-I. However, in *Dickson v the United Kingdom* ([GC], no. 44362/04, ECHR 2007-V), the right to respect for the decision to become genetic parents has been considered to fall within the notion of both private and family life.

[41] *Fretté v France*, no. 36515/97, ECHR 2002-I; *E.B. v France* [GC], no. 43546/02, 22 January 2008.

[42] *Ahrens v Germany*, § 60 and § 71; *Kautzor v Germany*, § 63 and § 73.

[43] *Rasmussen v Denmark*, 28 November 1984, § 33, Series A no. 87; *Paulík v Slovakia*, no. 10699/05, § 42, ECHR 2006-XI (Extracts).

[44] G. van der Schyff, 'Interpreting the Protection', p. 66.

[45] J. Gerards and H. Senden, 'The Structure of Fundamental Rights and the European Court of Human Rights', *International Journal of Constitutional Law*, 7 (2009), 650.

Positive Obligations

Traditionally, international law has attempted to safeguard the privacy of the family, with no intention to control the quality of family relationships.[46] Along the same lines, the main concern underlying the adoption of Article 8 ECHR was to protect individuals against arbitrary interference (by the public authorities) with their domestic affairs.[47] Yet, with the time, the 'shaping' role played by the ECtHR has resulted in the creation of position obligations,[48] which add up to the primarily negative undertakings ensuing from Article 8. Since its ground-breaking judgment in *Marckx v Belgium*, the Court has indeed increasingly required Contracting States to take positive steps to ensure an effective respect for private and family life.[49] In the context of parent–child relationships, the doctrine of positive obligations has served two main purposes: to promote the legal recognition of existing family ties and to protect their integrity.[50] Both obligations exhibit the doctrine's potential for extending the protection of the right to respect for private and family life to the advantage of unconventional father–child relationships.

Article 8 has been interpreted as requiring positive action to ensure that ties between family members can develop, as early as in 1979. Under Belgian law, unmarried mothers had to initiate legal proceedings in order to obtain official recognition of their maternal affiliation with their children. In the case of *Marckx v Belgium*, the applicants – an unmarried mother and her daughter – claimed that this requirement breached their right to respect for private and family life under Article 8, taken alone and in conjunction with Article 14. Having established that the natural ties between the applicant and her biological daughter constitutes 'family life' within the meaning of Article 8, the Court argues that the notion of 'respect' does not simply compel the State to abstain from interference.[51] Rather, national authorities are further required to 'act in a manner calculated to allow those concerned to lead a normal family life'.[52] In the Court's view, this entails, inter alia, the provision of legal safeguards that enable the child's integration in his/her family from the moment of birth.[53]

---

[46] Van Bueren, *International Law*, p. 72.
[47] Case 'Relating to Certain Aspects of the Laws On the Use of Languages in Education in Belgium' (Merits), 23 July 1968, p. 29, § 7, Series A no. 6.
[48] Lavrysen, 'The Scope of Rights', p. 162.
[49] *Marckx v Belgium*, 13 June 1979, § 31, Series A no. 31.
[50] U. Kilkelly, 'Protecting Children's Rights Under the ECHR: The Role of Positive Obligations', *Northern Ireland Legal Quarterly* 61(3) (2010), 245–261.
[51] *Marckx v Belgium*, § 31.
[52] Ibid. See also *Johnston and Others v Ireland*, 18 December 1986, § 45, Series A no. 112.
[53] *Marckx v Belgium*, § 31.

Applying this principle to the situation of the applicants, the Court found that the failure to provide automatic recognition to their relationship breached Article 8.

The Court has built on its own approach in *Marckx* to establish a duty upon States to create legal mechanisms enabling the prompt determination of a person's paternity. In the landmark case of *Kroon and Others v the Netherlands*, the applicants – the mother, the biological father and the child – were unable to obtain recognition of the second applicant's paternity of the third applicant due to the presumption of paternity existing under Dutch legislation in favour of the husband of the mother at the time of registration of the birth.[54] The Court agreed that the irrebutable presumption of paternity prevented the child's father from being recognised and, therefore, breached the right to respect for family life of all three applicants. In reaching this conclusion, the Court held that national authorities were placed under an obligation to allow complete legal family ties to be formed between the child and his biological father as expeditiously as possible.[55] More specifically, it specified that 'respect' for family life requires that 'biological and social reality prevail over a legal presumption which, as in the present case, flies in the face of both established fact and the wishes of those concerned without actually benefiting anyone'.[56] This jurisprudence demonstrates, therefore, that the creation and regulation of family status is an issue that – despite typically belonging to the prerogatives of the State – engages the notion of 'private and family life' within the meaning of Article 8 and gives rise to positive duties.[57]

The doctrine of positive obligations has also proved useful to protecting the integrity of family relationships. The Court has indeed recognised that Article 8 includes a right for the parent 'to have measures taken with a view to his or her being reunited with child' and, therefore, that States are under an obligation to take such measures.[58] Although originally developed in the context of public care,[59] this positive obligation has been subsequently extended to cases where contact and residence disputes concerning children arise between parents and/or other family members. Its basic rationale, however, remains the same: to counter the potentially detrimental effects of the passage of time

[54] *Kroon and Others v the Netherlands*.
[55] Ibid, § 36.
[56] Ibid, § 40.
[57] Kilkelly, 'Protecting Children's Rights', p. 251; L. Lavrysen, *Human Rights in a Positive State – Rethinking the Relationship Between Positive and Negative Obligations under the European Convention on Human Rights* (Intersentia, 2016), p. 103.
[58] *Hokkanen v Finland*, 23 September 1994, § 55, Series A no. 299-A.
[59] *Eriksson v Sweden*, 22 June 1989, Series A no. 156; *Olsson v Sweden (No. 2)*, 27 November 1992, Series A no. 250.

upon the durability of the relationship between a separated child and his/her parent.[60]

One specific case-law domain in which this obligation has therefore the potential to certainly advance the claims of fathers is that of post-separation. The Court has indeed established that, once family life is found between parent and child, their right to respect for family life encompasses their right to enjoy one another's company, even if the relationship between the parents has broken down.[61] Apart from obliging States to abstain from hindering such enjoyment, therefore, the principle of 'mutual enjoyment' might also require State action to aid the continuity of contacts between the non-residential parent and the child. However, this obligation is not absolute[62] and, when scrutinising the legality of the measures taken by national authorities – especially following particularly complex family break-ups – the Court has adopted a rather cautious approach.[63] It has clarified that the reunion of a parent with children who have lived for some time with the other parent or in a foster family might require some preparatory steps and certainly the understanding and cooperation of all individuals involved.[64] It follows that, despite the State's duty to bring about such cooperation, the use of coercion in this area must be limited as the rights and interests of all those involved, and more particularly the best interests of the child, must be taken into account.[65]

Apart from reading positive obligations of substantive nature, the Court has 'added a procedural layer'[66] to the scope of Article 8 and, in particular, requires the State to ensure a careful decision-making process.[67] The Court tends to examine whether the decision-making process was fair and whether due respect was given to the interests of the individuals concerned in a range of areas, including childcare measures and the withdrawal of parental responsibility,[68] determination of residence and contact rights[69] and, albeit

---

[60] *Elsholz v Germany* [GC], no. 25735/94, § 49, ECHR 2000-VIII; *Sommerfeld v Germany* [GC], no. 31871/96, § 63, ECH 2003-VIII (Extracts); *Görgülü v Germany*, no. 74969/01, § 42, 26 February 2004.
[61] *McMichael v the United Kingdom*, 24 February 1995, § 86, Series A no. 307-B.
[62] *Hokkanen v Finland*, § 62; *Ignaccolo-Zenide v Romania*, no. 31679/96, § 94, ECHR 2000-I.
[63] Mowbray, *The Development of Positive Obligations*, p. 169. For example, see *Glaser v UK* (Application no. 32346/96, 19 September 2000).
[64] *Hokkanen v Finland*, § 62; *Ignaccolo-Zenide v Romania*, § 94.
[65] Ibid.
[66] E. Brems, 'Procedural Protection – An Examination of Procedural Safeguards Read Into Substantive Convention Rights' in E. Brems and J. Gerards (eds.), *Shaping Rights in the ECHR – The Role of the European Court of Human Rights in Determining the Scope of Human Rights* (Cambridge University Press, 2013), p. 138.
[67] Lavrysen, *Human Rights in a Positive State*, p. 75.
[68] *B.B. and F. B. v Germany*, nos. 18734/09 and 9424/11, § 47, 14 March 2013.
[69] *Sahin v Germany* [GC], no. 30943/96, § 68, ECHR 2003-VIII; *Elsholz v Germany*, § 52.

more sporadically, paternity proceedings.[70] Although the specific requirements vary depending on the context and on the type of decision under examination, the Court has emphasised, inter alia, the need for authorities to provide parents with relevant information on the basis of which a decision has been reached,[71] the need to order an independent psychological report[72] as well as to ensure that children are able to express their views.[73]

2.2 Article 14 and Fatherhood

In addition to Article 8, fatherhood cuts across another Convention provision, that of Article 14. An important peculiarity of this provision is that it prohibits only those forms of discrimination that hinder the equal enjoyment of rights enshrined in the Convention. Whilst it is true that, on its face, Article 14 is an accessory guarantee, in practice, the Court has – especially over the last decade – made great strides in attaching an autonomous, substantive meaning to the prohibition of discrimination protected by Article 14.[74] To that effect, it has moved beyond assessing whether or not similarly situated individuals are treated equally in their entitlements under the Convention. Article 14 – as interpreted by the Court – has come to embrace the wider goal of enabling individuals to pursue their life options in an autonomous manner, namely 'free from (...) prejudice, stereotyping and lack of reasonable accommodation' relating to their personal characteristics.[75] It is interesting to note that the 'beginning of substance' – using Nikolaidis' words – has taken place exactly in the jurisprudence on Article 8 taken alone and in conjunction with Article 14.[76]

Among the several paths undertaken by the Court to create a right to substantive equality in its jurisprudence, two are particularly relevant as they have the potential to influence the Court's approach to fatherhood: the employment of Article 14 as a 'magnifying lens'[77] and anti-stereotyping.

---

[70] *Tsvetelin Petkov v Bulgaria*, no. 2641/06, § 57, 15 July 2014.
[71] *McMichael v the United Kingdom*, § 92; *K. and T. v Finland* [GC], § 173.
[72] *Elsholz v Germany*, § 53.
[73] *Saviny v Ukraine*, no. 39948/06, § 51, 18 December 2008.
[74] Nikolaidis, *The Right to Equality*, p. 50; D. Harris, M. O'Boyle, E. Bates and C. Buckley, *Harris, O'Boyle, and Warbrick: Law of the European Convention on Human Rights* (Oxford University Press, 2014) p. 787; R. O'Connell, 'Cinderella Comes to the Ball: Article 14 and the Right to Non-Discrimination in the ECHR', *Legal Studies* 29(2) 2009, 228.
[75] Nikolaidis, *The Right to Equality*, p. 52.
[76] Ibid, p. 57.
[77] Arnardóttir, 'Discrimination as a Magnifying Lens', pp. 335–338. See also R. Wintemute, '"Within the Ambit": How Big is the "Gap" in Article 14 European Convention on Human Rights? Part 1', *European Human Rights Law Review*, 4 (2004), 366–382.

Starting from the former, case-law demonstrates that Article 14 does not always act as the 'parasite' sometimes alleged,[78] but might actually function as a lens magnifying the interests protected by other Convention rights.[79] There are two main ways in which the magnifying effects of Article 14 might result in expanding the scope of Article 8, thus potentially enhancing the protection afforded to the claims of the applicant fathers.

The first is when Article 8 is applicable, but Article 14 results in a further violation or operates as an aggravating factor.[80] The judgment in *Sahin v Germany* – which will be analysed at length in Chapter 4 – is a good example of this doctrinal development.[81] The applicant father complained of the impossibility to obtain contact rights with respect to his biological child born out of wedlock. Although contact falls within the scope of Article 8, the Court invoked the margin of appreciation enjoyed by national authorities and concluded that the refusal to grant the applicant contact rights did not violate Article 8. However, since national legislation allowed for differential treatment between unmarried fathers and divorced fathers, the Court found a violation of Article 14 taken in conjunction with Article 8.

The second kind of magnifying effect consists in relying on the ground of discrimination in order to make a claim fall within the ambit of Article 8.[82] An example is provided by the case of *E.B. v France*, in which a lesbian was rejected the authorisation to adopt on the grounds of her sexual orientation.[83] It was not disputed that Article 8 encompasses neither the right to adopt nor the right to found a family and that there was, therefore, no interference with Article 8 taken on its own.[84] Yet, the Court decided to consider the claim under Article 14 on the ground that the prohibition of non-discrimination 'applies also to those additional rights, falling within the general scope of any Convention Article, for which the State has voluntarily decided to provide'.[85] Since French authorities had gone beyond their obligations under Article 8 in

---

[78] D. J. Harris, M. O'Boyle and C. Warbrick, *Law of the European Convention on Human Rights* (Butterworths, 1995), p. 463. A. McColgan, 'Principles of Equality and Protection from Discrimination in International Human Rights Law', *European Human Rights Law Review*, 2 (2003), 164.

[79] Apart from Arnardóttir, see also, S. Livingstone, 'Article 14 and the Prevention of Discrimination in the European Convention on Human Rights', *European Human Rights Law Review* 1 (1997), 25–34.

[80] Arnardóttir, 'Discrimination as a Magnifying Lens', p. 335.

[81] *Sahin v Germany* [GC], no. 30943/96, ECHR 2003–VIII.

[82] Arnardóttir, 'Discrimination as a Magnifying Lens', 337. See also Nikolaidis, *The Right to Equality*, pp. 64–65.

[83] *E.B. v France* [GC], no. 43546/02, 22 January 2008.

[84] Ibid., § 41.

[85] Ibid., § 48.

creating a right to adopt, they could not grant that right in a discriminatory manner.[86] A violation of Article 14 taken in conjunction with Article 8 was consequently found. As a result of this second type of magnifying effect, the discriminatory element makes claims brought by fathers – that would not otherwise fall within the scope of Article 8 (or other Convention provisions) – reviewable in their merits by the Court.

Connected to this second kind of magnifying effect, the Court has – although only recently and in a rather piecemeal fashion – started to develop an anti-stereotyping approach in its case-law under Article 14.[87] Stereotypes ascribe specific features and roles to an individual only by virtue of his/her membership in a particular group. Apart from limiting the ability of individuals to shape their personal identities in accordance with their preferences, stereotypes might penetrate the formulation of the law, thus reinforcing discrimination and inequality. Although its engagement in anti-stereotyping analysis remains quite prudent, especially if compared to its American counterpart,[88] the ECtHR has – also in the context of Article 8 – shown an increased sensitivity and awareness of the implications of stereotyping on the enjoyment of human rights.[89] Whilst in earlier cases the Court has tended to endorse an anti-stereotyping attitude only implicitly – i.e., by refusing to accept general assumptions as valid justifications for differential treatment without, however, openly speaking of 'stereotypes'[90] – its eagerness to address stereotyping has become more vocal throughout the time. In more recent case-law, the Court has in fact proved ready to 'name' harmful stereotypes in its reasoning, thus uncovering hidden discriminatory beliefs underlying national legislation and jurisprudence and exposing what harms these beliefs do.[91]

---

[86] Ibid, § 49.
[87] L. Peroni and A. Timmer, 'Gender Stereotyping in Domestic Violence Cases – An Analysis of the European Court of Human Rights' Jurisprudence' in E. Brems and A. Timmer (eds.), *Stereotypes and Human Rights Law* (Intersentia, 2016), p. 39; A. Timmer, 'Toward an Anti-Stereotyping Approach for the European Court of Human Rights', *Human Rights Law Review* 11(4) 2011, p. 713; S. Gurol, 'Challenging Gender Stereotyping before the ECtHR: Case of Carvalho Pinto v Portugal', *EJIL: Talk!*, online at https://www.ejiltalk.org/challenging-gender-stereotyping-before-the-ecthr-case-of-carvalho-pinto-v-portugal/ (last access on 11 February 2019).
[88] E. Brems and A. Timmer, 'Introduction' in E. Brems and A. Timmer (eds.), *Stereotypes and Human Rights Law* (Intersentia, 2016), p. 6.
[89] *Alajos Kiss v Hungary*, no. 38832/06, 20 May 2010; *Kiyutin v Russia*, no. 2007/10, ECHR 2011; *Konstantin Markin v Russia* [GC], no. 30078/06, ECHR 2012 (Extracts); *Carvalho Pinto de Sousa Morais v Portugal*, no. 17484/15, 25 July 2017.
[90] *Mizzi v Malta*, no. 26111/02, § 134, ECHR 2006-I (Extracts); *Zaunegger v Germany*, no. 22028/04, §§ 56–57, 3 December 2009; *Schneider v Germany*, § 89 and § 100; *Nazarenko v Russia*, no. 39438/13, § 66, ECHR 2015 (Extracts).
[91] R. Cook and S. Cusack, *Gender Stereotyping – Transnational Legal Perspectives* (University of Pennsylvania Press, 2010), p. 39.

In the case-law pertaining to fatherhood, the stereotypes at play are essentially three: the so-called 'man-breadwinner/woman-homemaker' stereotype, according to which caregiving is women's primary role while fathers are responsible for economic provision; the belief that unmarried fathers are generally irresponsible and uninterested in their children; and, finally, the generalised view that gay are unsuited to parenting. All these assumptions contribute, each by restating the primacy of a specific conventional feature (breadwinning, marriage and heterosexuality), to support the preservation of a conventional understanding of fatherhood in the law and, as such, operate to deny the full enjoyment of their right to respect for private and family life to 'unconventional' fathers. In the context of fatherhood, therefore, anti-stereotyping analysis brings the advantage of enabling the Court to advance a new definition of fatherhood that, rather than reflecting general assumptions about what being a father entails and should entail, is based on an objective assessment of the facts of the case and, therefore, is likely to allow consideration for the 'unconventional' element of care. The Court's efforts (or its lack of) to combat harmful stereotypes as structural forces underpinning the disadvantaged position of (certain) fathers might therefore constitute an important indicator of its willingness to depart from 'conventional fatherhood'.

3 DOCTRINES AND DECISION MAKING

This section illustrates that doctrines of interpretation and decision making might interact in various ways, and their relationship can range between two 'extreme' patterns: the former can be 'productive of' or 'subservient to' the latter.[92] Focusing on the specific context of family relationships, Subsection 1 will explain how the doctrine of the margin of appreciation can play a decisive role in shaping the Court's approach to fatherhood by impacting the strictness of review undertaken by the Court. According to the first pattern, therefore, the Court's judgments and, in particular, the vision of fatherhood therein displayed are the outcome of the consistent application of the doctrinal methods relied on by the Court.

By drawing from existing studies concerning other fields of case-law, Subsection 2 will then explain how doctrines might be used as a vehicle to advance the Court's moral positions on a given subject. According to a second pattern, therefore, it is the Court's a priori substantive choice that determines the variable use of doctrines and, therefore, its judgments can be said to be grounded in the Court's moral interpretations of the Convention. This

---

[92] P. Johnson, *Homosexuality and the European Court of Human Rights* (Routledge, 2013), p. 88.

categorisation of patterns is not meant to say that the relationship between doctrines and decision making is an 'either/or'. Rather, as it will be shown, the abovementioned two patterns might coexist within the same judgment and, therefore, the definition of fatherhood endorsed by the Court might be, simultaneously, the outcome of both doctrinal and moral forces.

3.1 The Doctrine of the Margin and Strictness of Review

This subsection aims to elucidate how the doctrine of the margin of appreciation can be 'productive of'[93] the Court's construction of fatherhood by determining the strictness of review undertaken by the Court. In concrete terms, in order to understand the actual role played by this doctrine in moulding the contours of fatherhood as understood by the Court, attention is to be given, first, to the variables taken into consideration in defining its width and, second, to the actual impact of the margin on the intensity of the scrutiny that is applied to the contested measure.

Starting from the latter, there is a general consensus in the literature as to the roughly inverse relationship that exists between the doctrine of the margin of appreciation and the doctrine of proportionality. The former can be considered – as Gerards puts it – a 'tool for differentiation of the intensity of the assessment'.[94] As a rule, the wider is the margin of appreciation enjoyed by State, the less restrictive is the scrutiny carried out by the Court. Therefore, when States are granted a wide margin of appreciation, the Court is left with a limited margin of manoeuvre to carry out the proportionality test and, as a result, sufficient reasons might be enough to justify an interference. By contrast, in cases where States are considered to enjoy a narrow margin of appreciation, the interference complained of will be subject to a stricter scrutiny and, therefore, the Court will require weightier justifications on the part of the State.

Taking one step back, the width of the margin of appreciation tends to be influenced by a variety of factors, pointing in the direction of a more or less strict scrutiny. In the specific domain of family relationships, these influencing factors tend to give reasons to grant a wide margin and, therefore, to perform a lenient scrutiny. A typical situation in which national authorities are granted broad parameters of discretion is when the case under examination raises particularly sensitive ethical and moral issues. The so-called 'moral margin'[95]

---

[93] Ibid.
[94] J. Gerards, *Judicial Review in Equal Treatment Cases* (Martinus Nijhoff, 2005), p. 169.
[95] C. Ryan, 'Europe's Moral Margin: Parental Aspirations and the European Court of Human Rights', *Columbia Journal of Transnational Law*, 56 (2018), 473.

has consistently been invoked – according to some, almost exclusively[96] – in matters concerning reproductive choices and family formation. The *rationale* for this approach pertains to, inter alia, considerations of both local legitimacy and judicial efficiency in fact finding.[97] By virtue of their direct contact and first-hand knowledge of the particular culture, tradition, morality and religion in their societies, national authorities are deemed better equipped than international judges to deal with delicate moral and ethical issues.

Where such issues are involved, the Court proves also keener to examine whether there is a common ground among Contracting States as to the relative importance of the interest at stake or as to the best way of protecting it. These two influencing factors are therefore often considered together and, in the context of family relationships, have proved of particular significance in cases dealing with the consequences of ARTs, homosexuality and transsexuality on family life.[98] In assessing the issue whether homosexuals should be given access to adoption, for instance, the Court concluded that 'since the delicate issues raised in the case (...) touch on areas where there is little common ground amongst the member States of the Council of Europe and, generally speaking, the law appears to be in a transitional stage', national authorities enjoyed a wide margin of appreciation.[99] Consensus among the Contracting States has yet to be established also on the lawfulness of surrogacy agreements and the legal recognition of parent–child relationships resulting from surrogacy carried out abroad.[100] Neither is there any common standard on the legal position of biological vis-à-vis legal fathers and the possibility of the former to challenge paternity.[101] With respect to those matters, the Court tends therefore to accept a wider range of possible implementations of Article 8 and to carry out a rather lenient scrutiny.

Another element that is often taken into account when determining the width of the margin in the context of private and family life is the seriousness of the interference. The Court has clarified that, 'where a particularly important facet of an individual's existence or identity is at stake',[102] the margin granted to

---

[96] Ibid.
[97] Y. Arai-Takahashi, *The Margin of Appreciation Doctrine and the Principle of Proportionality in the Jurisprudence of the ECHR* (Intersentia, 2002), p. 207.
[98] Choudhry and Herring, *European Family Law*, pp. 24–25.
[99] *Fretté v France*, § 41. Other examples are *X, Y and Z v the United Kingdom*, 22 April 1997, § 52, Reports of Judgments and Decisions 1997-II; *S.H. and Others v Austria* [GC], no. 57813/00, § 90, ECHR 2011.
[100] *Mennesson v France*, no. 65192/11, § 78, ECHR 2014 (Extracts).
[101] *Shavdarov v Bulgaria*, no. 3465/03, § 56, 21 December 2010; *Ahrens v Germany*, § 70; *Kautzor v Germany*, § 72.
[102] *Evans v UK*, § 77.

the State will be restricted. Cases where the legal parent–child relationship is concerned, for instance, are considered to touch upon an essential aspect of the identity of individuals.[103] Hence, despite surrogacy giving rise to ethical and moral issues on which there is generally no European consensus, national authorities have been awarded a narrow margin with respect to the refusal to grant recognition to the biological parentage of a child born through surrogacy abroad.

At the same time, when deciding on the removal of a child from her parents, the Court has generally granted a wide margin of appreciation on the ground that national authorities, especially welfare authorities, are better placed than an international court to assess the needs and interests of children, thanks to their direct experience and access to the circumstances of the case.[104] In this specific range of cases, however, it is not always possible to draw a correlation between the width of the margin and the intensity of review.[105] Indeed, although the Court is likely to refer to the better position of the domestic judiciary (in striking a fair balance) thus allowing for a wide margin of appreciation, the decision-making process that led to the decision complained of has become subject to some scrutiny.[106]

The width of the margin tends to be influenced also by the nature of the rights at stake. The Court has recognised that national authorities enjoy a wide margin of appreciation when deciding on custody matters. However, a stricter scrutiny is called for any restrictions placed on contact rights or on any legal safeguards designed to secure the mutual enjoyment by parent and child of one another's company.[107] In general, therefore, in situations where the very essence of the right to respect for private and family life is at stake and, therefore, there exists the danger that the family relationship between a child and one or both parents would be effectively curtailed,[108] the Court will apply strict scrutiny.

Finally, when Article 8 is taken in conjunction with Article 14, another variable that might affect the width of the margin and, thus, the level of scrutiny is the badge of differentiation.[109] In the case-law pertaining to fatherhood, complaints of discrimination under Article 14 are brought in relation to

[103] *Mennesson v France*, § 80.
[104] Arai-Takahashi, *The Margin of Appreciation*, pp. 64–65.
[105] Ibid, p. 65.
[106] Choudhry and Herring, *European Family Law*, p. 21.
[107] *Johansen v Norway*, 7 August 1996, § 64, *Reports of Judgments and Decisions* 1996-III; *Sahin v Germany*, § 65; *Görgülü v Germany*, § 50.
[108] *Elsholz v Germany*, § 49; *Sommerfeld v Germany*, § 63.
[109] J. Schokkenbroek, 'The Prohibition of Discrimination in Article 14 of the Convention and the Margin of Appreciation' *Human Rights Law Review* 19(1) (1998), 22; O. M. Arnardóttir,

the following personal characteristics: sex, sexual orientation and 'illegitimacy' – all of which have been treated by the Court as 'suspect'.[110] When a 'suspect' ground is involved, national authorities are generally accorded a narrow margin and the assessment of proportionality tends to manifest itself in its stringent version.[111] The Court held that 'very weighty reasons' are needed to justify, for instance, discrimination between unmarried and divorced fathers with respect to contact rights[112] or the exclusion of fathers from parental leave entitlements.[113] In such cases, as the arguments put forward to justify the treatment complained of are strictly scrutinised, the Court is more likely to find a violation of Article 14.

Whilst the above account identifies how the doctrine of the margin of appreciation should operate in the Court's reasoning, there seems to be a 'gap between the normative ideal and the Court's practice'.[114] The Court is not always precise when defining the scope of the margin.[115] The variables listed above are mostly hard to measure and the exact content of each of them is not entirely clear.[116] Hence, they cannot be said to eliminate any subjectivity from the determination of the scope of the margin.[117] Moreover, a variety of these factors might concur simultaneously within the same case and point to diametrically opposed directions as to the width of the margin.[118] The Court is

---

Equality and Non-Discrimination under the European Convention on Human Rights (Martinus Nijhoff, 2003), pp. 141–155; Gerards, *Judicial Review*, pp. 84–90.

[110] Gerards defines 'suspect' those grounds that 'immediately raise a suspicion of unreasonableness and prejudice'. See J. H. Gerards, 'Discrimination Grounds' in S. Schiek, L. Waddington and M. Bell (eds.), *Cases, Materials and Text on National, Supranational and International Non-Discrimination Law* (Hart, 2007), p. 36. See also S. Haverkort-Speekenbrink, *European Non-Discrimination Law – A Comparison of EU Law and the ECHR in the Field of Non-Discrimination and Freedom of Religion in Public Employment with an Emphasis on the Islamic Headscarf Issue* (Intersentia, 2012), pp. 167–171; O. M. Arnardóttir, 'The Differences that Make a Difference: Recent Developments on the Discrimination Grounds and the Margin of Appreciation under Article 14 of the European Convention', *Human Rights Law Review*, 14 (2014), 649.

[111] For discrimination based on sex, see *Abdulaziz, Cabales and Balkandali v the United Kingdom*, 28 May 1985, § 78, Series A no. 94. In relation to 'illegitimacy', see *Inze v Austria*, 28 October 1987, § 41, Series A no. 126. For differential treatment based on sexual orientation, the first explicit reference is *E.B. v France*, § 91.

[112] *Hoffmann v Germany*, no. 34045/96, § 56, 11 October 2001.

[113] *Petrovic v Austria*, 27 March 1998, § 37, *Reports of Judgments and Decisions* 1998-II.

[114] J. Gerards, 'Margin of Appreciation and Incrementalism in the Case Law of the European Court of Human Rights', *Human Rights Law Review*, 18 (2018), 500.

[115] Ibid, 502–504.

[116] Dzehtsiarou, *European Consensus*, p. 136.

[117] M. Delmas-Marty, *The European Convention for the Protection of Human Rights. International Protection versus National Restrictions* (Kluwer, 1992), p. 333.

[118] Arai-Takahashi, *The Margin of Appreciation*, p. 206.

therefore often called to draw a balance between them"[119] and this might provide further scope for judicial discretion.

Different from what might be expected, the Court does not always spell out how and with what effects the doctrine of the margin was applied to the particular circumstances of a case.[120] In its case-law, the Court has sometimes proved satisfied with making a quick reference to the margin without actually deferring to the appreciation of national authorities.[121] In some cases, the margin of appreciation is only mentioned in the conclusions, where the Court holds that a restriction is or is not justified and necessary and, therefore, falls within or exceeds the State's margin. In other cases, the doctrine has been instead invoked as 'mere gesture'[122] and, therefore, the Court has nonetheless closely scrutinised the merits of the case. All in all, therefore, the doctrine of the margin of appreciation is not consistently used as an indicator for the degree of deference conferred on national authorities.[123]

Nevertheless, what can be reasonably expected is a certain correlation between the strictness of review undertaken and the Court's critical attitude towards 'conventional fatherhood'. Considering that the case-law herein analysed generally originates from national laws or practices that are premised on a conventional model of fatherhood, a lenient scrutiny tends to be indicative of the Court's acceptance of such conventional approach. Conversely, the undertaking of a strict assessment reveals – at least, in principle – the Court's willingness to question a conventional understanding of fatherhood and, possibly, to propose a new definition that attaches weight to paternal care.

3.2 *The Variable Use of Doctrines and the Court's Moral Views*

The Court's application of its methods of interpretation has often been criticised for lacking coherence and consistency. This type of criticism can be defined as 'procedural': rather than concerning the normative value of doctrines and their appropriateness in human rights adjudication, it pertains to the way in which doctrines are deployed in the Court's reasoning.[124] In relation to European consensus, procedural concerns mainly target the

---

[119] Gerards, 'Judicial Review', p. 218.
[120] O. Gross and F. Ní Aoláin, 'From Discretion to Scrutiny: Revisiting the Application of the Margin of Appreciation Doctrine in the Context of Article 15 of the European Convention on Human Rights', *Human Rights Quarterly*, 23 (3) (2001), 635.
[121] Arai-Takahashi, *The Margin of Appreciation*, p. 16.
[122] Ibid.
[123] Gerards, 'Margin of Appreciation and Incrementalism', p. 501.
[124] I take this distinction between 'procedural criticism' and 'substantive criticism' from Dzehtsiarou, *European Consensus*, p. 115.

method of consensus identification and application.[125] Whilst it is true that, over the years, the methodology used by the Court to establishing the presence or absence of consensus has evolved and improved considerably, a number of commentators continue to perceive the Court's use of consensus as 'highly selective',[126] 'ad hoc'[127] and incoherent.[128] The Court has never clarified what makes a standard common or shared and, in practice, the establishment of commonly accepted standards has followed more or less loose and linear measurements,[129] thus sometimes raising doubt as to whether the Court is paying lip service to the idea of common ground. Even before, the Court sometimes fails to include relevant comparative data in the text of the judgment, thus making its findings concerning the presence or absence of European consensus appear unsubstantiated.[130]

Consensus being a frequent basis for granting a wide margin of appreciation or interpreting the Convention as a 'living instrument', the above procedural objections have obvious repercussions also on the way in which these two doctrines are used and perceived. The Court has not always managed to legitimise an evolutive interpretation with the support of empirical data in its own reasoning. Hence, it is sometimes disputed whether the Court's reading of the Convention actually reflects present-day conditions or rather attempts to shape and impose new conditions, thus becoming a tool of judicial activism.[131] Similarly, the lack of precise rules of application triggers a fear that the doctrine of the margin of appreciation might allow for overly broad judicial discretion on the part of the Court.[132] The doctrine of the margin

---

[125] Ibid, p. 207.
[126] Choudhry and Herring, *European Family Law*, p. 16. See cases on transsexuals.
[127] L. R. Helfer, 'Consensus, Coherence and the European Convention on Human Rights', *Cornell International Law Journal* 26(1) (1993), 154.
[128] P. Mahoney, 'The Comparative Method in Judgments of the European Court of Human Rights: Reference Back to National Law' in G. Canivet, M. Andenas and D. Fairgrieve (eds.), *Comparative Law before the Courts* (British Institute of International and Comparative Law, 2004), p. 149; P. G. Carozza, 'Uses and Misuses of Comparative Law in International Human Rights: Some Reflections on the Jurisprudence of the European Court of Human Rights', *Notre Dame Law Review*, 73 (1997–1998), 1225.
[129] D. McGoldrick, 'Religion in the European Public Square and in European Public Life – Crucifixes in the Classroom?, *Human Rights Law Review*, 11(3) (2011), 476–477; E. Brems, 'Margin of Appreciation Doctrine in the Case-Law of the European Court of Human Rights', *Zeitschrift für ausländisches öffentliches Recht und Völkerrecht*, 56(1–2) (1996), 284–286.
[130] *Fretté v France*, § 41; *Appleby and Others v the United Kingdom*, no. 44306/98, § 46, ECHR 2003-VI; *Shofman v Russia*, no. 74826/01, § 37, 24 November 2005.
[131] Johnson, *Homosexuality and the ECtHR*, p. 85.
[132] Gross and Ní Aoláin, 'From Discretion to Scrutiny', p. 629; R. S. Macdonald, 'The Margin of Appreciation' in R. Macdonald, F. Matscher and H. Petzold (eds.), *The European System for the Protection of Human Rights* (Kluwer, 1993), p. 85.

has been variously described as a 'black box',[133] 'a substitute for coherent legal analysis of the issues at stake',[134] a 'conclusory label',[135] which serves to obscure the Court's true reasoning. All these definitions reflect, inter alia, a concern that the margin of appreciation might be invoked to avoid the need to provide clear arguments as to why the Court interprets the Convention in a certain way.[136]

Despite their potential significance to preserve the stability of the ECHR system, the often variable and unpredictable use of doctrines by the Court has therefore contributed to create a suspicion that the Court bends interpretative doctrines to support its own moral standpoints. In his persuasive study on the Court's jurisprudence pertaining to homosexuality, Johnson shows that what determines the development of the human rights of gays and lesbians is not the methods of interpretation relied on by the Court, but rather its moral policy in respect of homosexuality.[137] In particular, he observes that – in this specific domain – there is a close relationship between the Court's moral approach to homosexuality and the application of the doctrine of the margin of appreciation.[138] He explains that, until early 1980s, the Commission proved particularly generous because it viewed homosexuality as contrary to social morality and public health. As soon as the Court began to understand homosexuality as an aspect of 'personality' that deserves Article 8's protection,[139] it also began to progressively reduce the margin available to States in respect of the criminalisation of private and consensual sexual practices.[140] Therefore, although the Court appears to precisely calculate its width by relying on methods, in Johnson's view, the margin is no more than 'an expression of the moral reasoning of the Court'.[141] The same has been argued with respect to the 'living instrument' doctrine that, as illustrated by Johnson, has been erratically employed to endorse both judicial activism and judicial conservatism, depending on the moral standing of the Court with respect to

[133] J. A. Brauch, 'The Margin of Appreciation and the Jurisprudence of the European Court of Human Rights: Threats to the Rule of the Law', *Columbia Journal of European Law*, 11(1) (2004–2005), 133.
[134] Lord Lester of Herne Hill, 'The European Convention in the New Architecture of Europe', *Public Law* Spring (1996), 5.
[135] R. Singh, 'Is There a Role for the "Margin of Appreciation" in National Law after the Human Rights Act?', *European Human Rights Law Review* 1 (1999), 20.
[136] J. Kratochvíl, 'The Inflation of the Margin of Appreciation by the European Court of Human Rights', *Netherlands Quarterly of Human Rights* 29(3) (2011), 336–337.
[137] Johnson, *Homosexuality and the ECtHR*, p. 66.
[138] Ibid, p. 71.
[139] *Dudgeon v the United Kingdom*, 22 October 1981, Series A no. 59.
[140] Johnson, *Homosexuality and the ECtHR*, p. 72.
[141] Ibid, p. 71.

the specific issue at stake. Although producing variable outcomes for applicants, the selective use of doctrines reflects – according to Johnson – a deliberate strategy of the Court: that is to advance its own moral judgment.[142]

This type of correlation between decision making and doctrines has been traced also in other case-law domains. Brems seems to suggest that the Court's different reactions to Islamophobia and rights-restrictive measures targeting Muslims and homophobia and rights-restrictive measures targeting LGB individuals is not doctrinally grounded, but rather depends on the Court's moral positions.[143] In these two fields, the Court reached opposite outcomes. It justified a 'very large margin of appreciation'[144] by reference to the lack of a European consensus and therefore upheld national face covering bans. Conversely, it found gay-propaganda legislation in violation of the Convention on the ground that, as a consequence of a 'clear European consensus'[145] about the recognition of the right of individuals to openly identify as belonging to a sexual minority and to promote their rights and freedoms, the margin enjoyed by States is narrow. However, Brems observes that – in fact – the same degree of consensus existed in relation to both issues.[146] At the time of *SAS v France*,[147] indeed, despite being discussed in several countries, nationwide face-covering bans had been adopted only in France and Belgium.[148] Similarly, in the field of gay propaganda, in addition to Russia, Lithuania has restrictive legislation in place.[149]

In Brems's view, therefore, the light scrutiny in the face-veil cases and the stricter scrutiny in the 'gay-propaganda' cases should not be considered the consequence of opposite findings pertaining to European consensus – like the text of judgments suggests – but rather a 'matter of choice'.[150] The different approaches adopted in these two fields demonstrate that the selective use of consensus might be 'determined by, and not determinative of, the Court's moral reasoning'.[151] Using Johnson's effective wording, European consensus might work as 'a device through which "reality" is selectively represented in

---

[142] Ibid, p. 81.
[143] E. Brems, 'Islamophobia at the ECtHR: A Test-Case for Positive Subsidiarity', unpublished draft paper presented at the ESIL-ECHR Conference European Convention on Human Rights and Migration, 6 October 2017.
[144] *Belcacemi and Oussar v Belgium*, no. 37798/13, § 55, 11 July 2017.
[145] *Bayev and Others v Russia*, nos. 67667/09, 44092/12 and 56717/12, § 66, 20 June 2017.
[146] Brems, 'Islamophobia at the ECtHR', 11.
[147] *S.A.S. v France* [GC], no. 43835/11, ECHR 2014 (Extracts).
[148] Brems, 'Islamophobia at the ECtHR', 11.
[149] Ibid.
[150] Ibid, p. 20.
[151] Johnson, *Homosexuality and the ECtHR*, p. 82.

order to add weight to moral reasoning'.[152] This does not mean that the Court 'makes up' consensus but that what is relevant to establish consensus is considerably influenced by the moral positions held by the judges sitting in each individual case.[153]

Of a similar view, Gülalp argues that the width of the margin of appreciation granted to States seems to vary according to the Court's 'implicit normative preferences' also in the case-law concerning the relationship between State and religions in Europe.[154] In particular, despite the Court's tendency to grant a wide margin of appreciation as a matter of principle, the width of the margin and, more generally, the actual reasoning appears to be informed by historically ingrained assumptions about the religion in question, not only about the division between Christianity and Islam, but also between western and eastern Christianity. Gülalp concludes therefore that, although the flexibility in widening and narrowing the margin might at first appear source of incoherence and inconsistency, it reveals in fact an 'implicit but consistent logic'[155]: that is the Court's preference for some models of secularism to others. Therefore, it is the 'meaning and the normative content'[156] that the Court intends to attach to notions of secularism, rather than doctrinal accuracy, that determines the Court's variable use of the doctrine of the margin and, as a consequence, its apparently inconsistent approach to questions concerning the relationship between State and religions.

Instances where the use of doctrines appears to be driven by moral considerations have been identified also in the context of family relationships. The Court has occasionally stated that its moral position on who constitutes a family is neutral. In the case of *Fretté v France*, concerning the possibility for a single homosexual man to adopt a child, the partly dissenting judges argued that 'it is not for the Court to take decisions (or pass moral judgment) instead of States in an area which is also a subject of controversy in many Council of Europe member States (...). Nor it is for the Court to express preference for any type of family model'.[157] Kilkelly's account of the development of positive obligations in the Court's jurisprudence under Article 8, however, seems to suggest otherwise.[158] Although the notion of 'family life' – as interpreted by the

---

[152] Ibid, pp. 77–78.
[153] Ibid, p. 78.
[154] H. Gülalp, 'Secularism and the European Court of Human Rights', *European Public Law* 16(3) (2010), 455.
[155] Ibid, 459.
[156] Ibid, 470.
[157] *Fretté v France*, Joint Partly Dissenting Opinion of Judge Bratza, Judge Fuhrmann and Judge Tulkens, § 2(c).
[158] Kilkelly, 'Protecting Children's Rights'.

Court – has come to cover a wide variety of unconventional family units, not all of them have de facto benefited from the same level of protection.

In other words, despite demonstrating a strong awareness of the importance of formally recognising family ties, the Court has failed to apply the positive obligations arising from Article 8 consistently to all types of relationships.[159] More specifically, Kilkelly seems to detect a tendency to water down the positive obligation to provide existing family ties with legal recognition when the family life in question departs from the image of the 'conventional family'.[160] This variable approach to positive obligations tends therefore to create the suspicion that the Court makes an instrumental use of its interpretative doctrines to support its own moral standpoints also with respect to fatherhood. Therefore, whilst it remains true that doctrines might work as an empowering tool to update the construction of fatherhood, if not consistently applied, they might also serve the opposite purpose of obscuring true reasoning and, in this context, to advance the wish of restating 'conventional fatherhood' at all costs.

4 CASE-LAW SELECTION

The structure of the case-law analysis is derived from the four major social changes introduced in Chapter 1, Section 1. The Court's approach to fatherhood is, therefore, traced in the following four areas: filiation and parental rights following the employment of ARTs (Chapter 3); parental rights of unmarried fathers following family breakdown, and paternity proceedings (Chapter 4); childcare-related allowances (Chapter 5); and, adoption and parental rights of homosexual individuals and couples (Chapter 6).

Apart from directly confronting the Court with the various factual consequences of 'fragmenting fatherhood', the abovementioned domains have been chosen due to the potential of each of them to shed light on one specific trait of 'conventional fatherhood' and to reveal its persisting decisiveness or diminished importance as a parameter of legal fatherhood. Whilst the employment of ARTs jeopardises the tenacity of biology as a defining attribute of legal fatherhood, marriage's role as a father–child connector is undermined by rising rates of extra-marital childbearing and family breakdown, in combination with an increasingly widespread resort to DNA testing. Similarly, the heightened participation of women in the labour market casts doubts on the endurance of the male breadwinner model and, therefore, on economic

---
[159] Ibid, 254.
[160] Ibid, 251–253.

provision as a uniquely paternal role; and, finally, as a consequence of the growing social and legal recognition of same-sex families, the relevance of heterosexuality as a feature of legal fatherhood has come under challenge. Although discussing 'conventional fatherhood' as a whole, each of the jurisprudential chapters provides therefore a more in-depth account on the specific conventional attribute under threat.

Within each of the case-law domains, however, the analysis does not aim at being exhaustive in its coverage but is rather limited to a number of carefully selected cases. Almost of all them can be considered as landmark or leading cases under different viewpoints. They are generally perceived as milestones in legal development by virtue of their intrinsic merits: they either confirm and strengthen preceding practices or openly depart from them; they establish new principles or settle new legal issues; in general, they are understood to offer important guidelines on how to approach future cases.[161] Most of the selected cases have also been the subject of extensive and critical legal scholarship and debates.[162] Even before, they have been selected and published in the Reports of Judgments and Decisions – replaced by the Selection of Key Cases as of 2016 – and, as such, they have been treated as highly significant by the Court itself.[163]

In the present case, however, case relevance is primarily defined by the research question that guides the case-law analysis. The focus is therefore placed on those cases – or series of cases – that are considered 'paradigmatic'[164] by virtue of their contribution to defining the Court's construction of fatherhood. Attention will therefore be brought to those judgments that show or reveal key elements of the phenomenon under study and, examined alone or in comparison with other judgments, make the Court's construction of fatherhood intelligible. The Court's attachment or departure from 'conventional fatherhood' has rarely been an explicit process. Blunt statements that emphasise the presence of specific factors as crucial for the determination of legal fatherhood are sporadic. Therefore, the envisaged investigation entails digging deep into the reasoning to unveil

---

[161] U. Sadl and Y. Panagis, 'What Is a Leading Case in EU Law? An Empirical Analysis', *European Law Review*, 40(1) (2015), 15.

[162] This criterion for selecting 'leading' cases is taken from E. Lim, 'Of "Landmark" or "Leading" Cases: Salomon's Challenge', *Journal of Law and Society* 41(4) (2014), 531.

[163] This criterion is suggested by L. Van den Eynde, 'Selecting Landmark Cases', *Strasbourg Observers*, 28 August 2015, online at https://strasbourgobservers.com/2015/08/28/selecting-landmark-cases/ (last access on 11 February 2019).

[164] The definition of 'paradigmatic case' is taken from G. Pavlich, 'Paradigmatic Case' in A. J. Mills, G. Durepos and E. Wiebe (eds), *Encyclopedia of Case Study Research* vol. II (Sage, 2010), pp. 645–647.

values and assumptions underpinning the Court's views regarding fathers and their role within the family. By bringing to the fore the Court's implicit understanding of what makes someone a legal father, this book contributes, inter alia, to help the Strasbourg judges to become more self-aware of the vision of fatherhood that they are supporting.

3

Fatherhood and Assisted Reproduction

1 THE IMPACT OF ARTS ON CONVENTIONAL FATHERHOOD

In this chapter, the ECtHR's understanding of fatherhood is traced in the context of assisted reproduction. Assisted reproductive technologies (ARTs) certainly represent one of the main forces responsible for the ongoing fragmentation of families and, more specifically, of fatherhood. By offering radical possibilities for disaggregating parenthood into different constituent parts, these techniques inevitably urge reflections and, ultimately, decisions upon what kind of tie – biological, marital (with the child's mother), intentional/social, gestational, etc. – is most decisive to make someone a legal parent. ARTs, therefore, constitute a significant threat to the persistence of 'conventional fatherhood': not only because different roles of the traditional father figure are less likely to be undertaken by one man, but also because they introduce the 'new' element of intention that, in view of determining who should enjoy the legal status, rights and responsibilities of fatherhood, might clash and compete with some of the conventional parameters.[1] The bioethical era brings, therefore, also precious opportunities to revise legalistic logics to better incorporate important affective understandings of care and nurture.[2]

ART-created fatherhood might break from the conventional paradigm in four major ways. First, the advent of ARTs has deprived biology of its 'status of a prior fact'[3] and, as such, has challenged the primacy of blood ties in defining

---

[1] On the importance of recognising the intention to parent as a ground for determining legal parenthood in the ARTs context, see K. Horsey, 'Challenging Presumptions: Legal Parenthood and Surrogacy Arrangements', *Child and Family Law Quarterly*, 22(4) (2010), 449–474.

[2] L. Sharp, 'Blood Ties, Bioethics and the Bright-line of the Law' in B. Feuillet-Liger, T. Callus and K. Orfali (eds.), *Reproductive Technology and Changing Perceptions of Parenthood Around the World* (Bruylant, 2014), p. 17.

[3] M. Strathern, *After Nature: English Kinship in the Late Twentieth Century* (Cambridge University Press, 1992), p. 194.

parenthood and granting legitimacy to family ties.[4] As a result of the possibility of outsourcing reproduction through the participation of third parties, a biological link with the child is indeed – at least, in factual terms – no longer indispensable to become a father. Processes that were previously unitary and, therefore, concentrated in one man can now be subdivided: in particular, biological reproduction can be split from the social and physical dimensions of interpersonal relationships.[5] It follows that – and this is the second point of departure from 'conventional fatherhood' – whenever male third parties are involved, fatherhood risks losing its unitary character. Even in one of the simplest reproductive situations, where a married couple create a child through sperm donation, two men might claim the paternal status: the sperm donor, on the grounds of his biological contribution, and the intentional/social father, by virtue of his marital relationship with the child's mother and/or his actual involvement in the child's life.

Third, ARTs also allow fatherhood outside the marital family. Hence, there is also the scenario where a man embarks on a course of treatment services with the child's mother – despite not being either the biological father or the mother's husband. In a similar case, therefore, in addition to biology, also marriage ceases to operate as a bright-line test to determine legal fatherhood. As such, the question of who should be considered the child's legal father and, on what grounds, is here put forward in a particularly stark way. More specifically, what relevance shall be attributed to the mother's marital status; to the intentions of one of the men involved to become a parent and to act as a social father; to the biological link existing between one man and the child; to the fact that the sperm originated from an anonymous sperm donor?[6]

Fourth, ARTs disrupt 'conventional fatherhood' by questioning its heterosexual nature and, more generally, its compliance with heteronormative schemes. The voices of homosexuals willing to become parents have become increasingly louder in several European States, which can also be traced to the 'desexualisation' of reproduction allowed by ARTs.[7] Lesbian couples can now

---

[4] At the same time, it has been argued that, instead of threatening, these techniques reproduce the conventional family by enabling infertile couples to have biologically-related children. See R. Rao, 'Assisted Reproductive Technology and the Threat to the Traditional Family', *Hastings Law Journal*, 47 (1996), 952.

[5] M. M. Shultz, 'Reproductive Technology and Intent-Based Parenthood: An Opportunity for Gender Neutrality', *Wisconsin Law Review*, (1990), 300.

[6] S. Sheldon, 'Fragmenting Fatherhood: The Regulation of Reproductive Technologies', *Modern Law Review*, 68(4) 2005, 523.

[7] B. Feuillet-Liger, 'Preface' in B. Feuillet-Liger, T. Callus and K. Orfali (eds.), *Reproductive Technology and Changing Perceptions of Parenthood Around the World* (Bruylant, 2014), p. 25. Despite offering the chance to become parents to a wide audience of either infertile or

fulfil their desire to become parents by employing sperm donation, while male couples are enabled to have a child through surrogacy.[8] This development has also triggered the issue of the interchangeable nature of parenthood, namely the option for one person to change from his/her legal status of father or mother to the other one following a gender reassignment.[9] In all these scenarios, the status of father is granted to a person, irrespective of his/her birth sex and sexual orientation; hence, the traditional continuum between heterosexuality and, more generally, heteronormativity and fatherhood is broken.[10]

One uncontroversial fact that emerges from the above account is the ability of ARTs to confuse and disrupt the ways fatherhood has been thus far understood and regulated.[11] Given the multiple possibilities of 'constructing kinship through choice',[12] ARTs have pushed legal actors to rethink fatherhood – more specifically, who has rights to the resulting child and who is excluded – beyond the conventional paradigm.[13] Apart from being at the core of national legal debates and jurisprudence, the rights and responsibilities of men in the reproductive context have been at the core of a number of applications brought before the ECtHR. The legal regulation of ARTs, therefore, emerges as a particularly valuable resource through which it is possible to reveal the values and the assumptions underlying the Court's views regarding fathers and their role within the family.[14] Moreover, given their 'relative' novelty and, certainly, being one of the technological developments not contemplated when the Convention was drafted, ARTs constitute a fruitful terrain where to test the Court's efforts to update its definition of fatherhood to bring it in line with present-day family realities.

---

homosexual couples and individuals, ARTs prescribe two major access limitations: high costs for services and the discretion of providers as to whom to treat. See J. Daar, 'Accessing Reproductive Technologies: Invisible Barriers, Indelible Harms', *Berkeley Journal of Gender, Law and Justice*, 23(1) (2013), 35–45.

[8] This is what science permits. In practice, however, national legislation is often less permissive. It is therefore not surprising that the Court has been called to decide on the application (held inadmissible) submitted by a lesbian couple who, due to their sexual orientation, were unable to conceive a child by means of artificial insemination. See *Charron and Merle-Montet v France* (Dec.), no. 22612/15, 8 February 2018.

[9] Feuillet-Liger, 'Preface', p. 25.

[10] R. Collier, *Masculinity, Law and the Family* (Routledge, 1995), p. 266.

[11] Sheldon, 'The Regulation of Reproductive Technologies', 524; M. Johnson, 'A Biomedical Perspective on Parenthood' in A. Bainham, S. Day Sclater, M. Richards (eds.), *What Is a Parent? A Socio-Legal Analysis* (Hart, 1999), p. 52.

[12] F. Swennen and M. Croce, 'Family (Law) Assemblages: New Modes of Being (Legal)', *Journal of Law and Society*, 44(4) (2017), 533.

[13] Sharp, 'Blood Ties', p. 17.

[14] Sheldon, 'The Regulation of Reproductive Technologies', 524.

The first significant engagement of the Court with ART-created fatherhood dates back to 1997, in the case of *X, Y and Z v UK*.[15] Here, the Court was faced with the challenging – especially at the material time – question of whether one must be born male to be recognised as a father. The relationship that was denied legal recognition, indeed, involved a post-operative female-to-male transsexual who acted as the social father of his child, born to his female partner through sperm donation. Ten years later, another extremely controversial case reached Strasbourg: that of *Evans v UK*,[16] arising from a conflict between ex-partners on the future of stored embryos created with their genetic material. This case, together with that of *Dickson v UK*[17] – where a prisoner and his wife were refused access to ARTs – allowed the Court a certain amount of creativity in imagining the ideal father figure, as the children were not yet conceived.

Last, the question of what makes someone a legal father returned to the Court with respect to surrogacy. The landmark case of *Mennesson v France*[18] stemmed from the refusal to grant legal recognition to the family relationships that had been legally established in the United States between twins born from surrogacy and their intended parents. In its latest judgment – *Paradiso and Campanelli v Italy*[19] – delivered in January 2017, by way of contrast, the Grand Chamber was called to assess the compatibility of the child's removal from the intended parents with Article 8. Despite dealing with distinct legal implications of surrogacy, both cases contribute to clarify what features remain indispensable for an intended father to be legally recognised as such and, even before, to continue living with his surrogacy-born child.

These five judgments, especially considering that they were issued over a period of twenty years, allow us to trace how the construction of fatherhood endorsed by the Court in the field of ARTs has evolved throughout the time. More specifically, has the Court accepted or rather attempted to contain the fragmentation of fatherhood resulting from ARTs, thus restating the primacy of the conventional paradigm? What conventional features have been abandoned or confirmed? And, to what extent have conventional grounds left space or come to coexist with the 'new' element of intentionality? Before addressing these questions by digging more deeply in each of the selected cases, however, the following section introduces the Court's broader reaction to ARTs and anticipates its repercussions on the emerging definition of fatherhood.

---

[15] *X, Y and Z v the United Kingdom*, 22 April 1997, *Reports of Judgments and Decisions* 1997-II.
[16] *Evans v the United Kingdom* [GC], no. 6339/05, ECHR 2007-I.
[17] *Dickson v the United Kingdom* [GC], no. 44362/04, ECHR 2007-V.
[18] *Mennesson v France*, no. 65192/11, ECHR 2014 (extracts).
[19] *Paradiso and Campanelli v Italy* [GC], no. 25358/12, 24 January 2017.

2 THE ECTHR AND ARTS: AN AMBIVALENT REACTION

ARTs have provided the Court with precious opportunities to adjust its understanding(s) of fatherhood to present-day family realities. The Court, however, has not fully seized the occasion yet and, thus far, its reaction can be described as ambivalent: while going far in extending the applicability of Article 8 to a vast array of procreative scenarios made possible by medical progress, it has proved rather hesitant to broaden the scope of State's obligations in this field. The expansion of the scope of Article 8 has occurred – as vividly described by Burbergs – in a tree-like fashion, 'where one "branch" is the base and support for other branches to grow'.[20] In other words, the Court has often used an already established right and, more generally, previous case-law to sustain further development of scope.[21] In this process, the landmark judgment in *Evans v UK* constitutes an important (jurisprudential) departure point whereby the Court has recognised several new interests as being covered by Article 8.[22]

In this case, the Court established for the first time that the notion of 'private life' encompassed also the right to respect for the decision to become or not to become a parent.[23] The same finding was reiterated in the judgment of *Dickson v UK*, which was issued some months later. Here, however, the right to respect for the decision to become a parent in the genetic sense was considered an expression of both private and family life.[24] The Court went a step further in the case of *S.H. and Others v Austria*: it clarified that the right of a couple to conceive a child and to make use of ARTs to that purpose was protected by Article 8, in both its 'private' and 'family life' limbs.[25] Finally, the right to respect for private and family life was further expanded in the judgment of *Costa and Pavan v Italy*, where it was considered to cover also 'the applicants' desire to conceive a child unaffected by the genetic disease of which they are healthy carriers and to use ARTs and pre-implantation genetic diagnosis to this end'.[26]

---

[20] M. Burbergs, 'How the Right to Respect for Private and Family Life, Home and Correspondence Became the Nursery in Which New Rights Are Born' in E. Brems and J. Gerards (eds.), *Shaping Rights in the ECHR – The Role of the European Court of Human Rights in Determining the Scope of Human Rights* (Cambridge University Press, 2013), p. 325.
[21] Ibid.
[22] J. M. Scherpe, 'Medically Assisted Procreation: This Margin Needs to Be Appreciated', *Cambridge Law Journal*, (2012), 277.
[23] *Evans v UK*, § 71.
[24] *Dickson v UK*, § 66.
[25] *S. H. and Others v Austria* [GC], no. 57813/00, § 82, ECHR 2011.
[26] *Costa and Pavan v Italy*, no. 54270/10, § 57, 28 August 2012.

If regard is given to the reinterpreted scope of Article 8, therefore, what can be maintained is that the Court has certainly taken a major stride towards bringing the content of that provision in line with medical advances thus adjusting to new ways of creating families and having children. However, if the focus is placed on the outcome of the above cases, it becomes clear that these 'updating' effects do not go beyond the Court's first stage of review – concerning the applicability of Article 8 – and, therefore, are not reflected in the content of the obligations imposed by that provision on States. To date, indeed, the Contracting States are far from being required to allow and make all types of reproductive technique available. Although claiming that the issue 'needs to be kept under review',[27] in *S.H. and Others v Austria*, for instance, the Grand Chamber held that the absolute ban on ova donation and sperm donation for in vitro fertilisation did not exceed the margin of appreciation accorded to the Respondent State at the material time.[28]

The same ambivalence can be traced with respect to the Court's approach to the more specific issue of ART-created fatherhood. Whilst feeling prepared to declare Article 8 applicable also to 'unconventional' father–child relationships and, more generally, to procreative scenarios potentially leading to unconventional ties, in its second stage of review, the Court has showed a certain willingness to contain the fragmentation of fatherhood resulting from ARTs. It is, indeed, not surprising that the only two cases in which the Court found a violation concerned a man who, in spite of IVF, would have become a father in the conventional sense[29] and a man who, despite resorting to surrogacy, was the biological father of his children and married to the intended mother.[30] The case-law that will be analysed, therefore, clearly supports a conventional vision of fatherhood: in particular, it confirms the relevance of biology, marriage, and of the compliance with heteronormativity as essential grounds for making someone a legal father.

Doctrinal considerations and, in particular, the award of a particularly wide margin of appreciation to national authorities, have definitely played an important role in maintaining a conventional understanding of fatherhood despite changed/ing family realities following medical advances.[31] ARTs remain, indeed, an area that gives rise to sensitive moral and ethical issues

---

[27] *S.H. and Others v Austria*, § 118.
[28] Ibid, § 115.
[29] *Dickson v UK*.
[30] *Mennesson v France*.
[31] A. Mulligan, 'Identity Rights and Sensitive Ethical Questions: The European Convention on Human Rights and the Regulation of Surrogacy Arrangements', *Medical Law Review*, 26(3) (2018), 6.

on which there is not yet clear European consensus and, therefore, the Court is generally hesitant to interfere with the policy choices of the Contracting States. It will however be shown that, apart from being influenced by doctrinal limits the Court is bound to, this prima facie shy attitude is – to varying degrees, depending on the case – also a matter of choice. The persistence of 'conventional fatherhood' in the ARTs domain, therefore, can be seen as, at the same time, an act of judicial self-restraint and a premeditated choice on the side of the Court to resist the revolutionary impact of ARTs on the regulation of fatherhood.

2.1 Transsexuality and Fatherhood

The first significant case that explores the concept of fatherhood in the ARTs domain is that of X, Y and Z v UK.[32] The father involved, X, was 'unconventional' in many respects: he was a post-operative female-to-male transsexual, not genetically linked to his child, Z, who was born to her female partner, Y, through donor insemination. Despite living together and acting as a social father towards Z, X was not allowed to be registered as the child's legal father. The provision – contained in the HFEA 1990 – according to which the male partner of a woman who gives birth to a child through donor insemination shall be treated as the child's legal father was considered inapplicable to X because, in the Registrar General's view, only a person who started life genetically as a man could be considered a father for the purposes of registration.[33] The applicants – the couple and the child – alleged that the refusal of national authorities to register X as the legal father of Z constituted a breach of their

---

[32] Prior to X, Y and Z v the United Kingdom, see J.R.M. v the Netherlands (no. 16944/90, Commission decision of 8 February 1993). The applicant in this case had accepted to act as a sperm donor for a lesbian couple, under the agreement that the latter would have exclusive custody of the child. However, after childbirth, he decided to become involved in the child's life and applied for contact rights, against the couple's will. His claim to be granted contact rights failed on multiple grounds: his initial agreement with the couple but also, and most importantly, his limited contact with the baby during his first months of life and, more generally, his lack of involvement in raising the child. The Commission declared Article 8 inapplicable on the ground that 'the situation in which a person donates sperm only to enable a woman to become pregnant through artificial insemination does not of itself give the donor a right to respect for family life with the child' ('The Law', § 1).

[33] At the material time, English law defined a person's sex on the basis of biological facts at birth and prohibited any reassignment. This also meant that transsexuals were not allowed to marry. A reform was introduced by the Gender Recognition Act 2004, which allows for the recognition of a person's new gender, under specific conditions. At present, X would therefore be able to become legally a man and, as such, would be in a position to be legally recognised as a father of Z.

right to respect for private and family life under Article 8 and discrimination contrary to Article 14.

This case – as it will be shown – brings a particularly rich contribution to our discussion as it provided the Court with the chance to depart from the paradigm of 'conventional fatherhood' under multiple dimensions.[34] Yet, this opportunity was largely missed and, as a consequence, the definition of fatherhood that emerges from the judgment of *X, Y and Z v UK* confirms the Court's attachment to the conventional paradigm at many levels. The absence of a biological connection was expressly identified as justifying the refusal to legally recognise X's and Z's social tie (as a result of the non-application of the positive obligation established in *Marckx*). Similarly, X's gender identity, his consequential departure from heteronormativity and, further, his impossibility to comply with the ideal of 'marital fatherhood' seem to have played a decisive role in dismissing the applicants' request to confer the status of Z's legal father to X.

In discussing the applicability of Article 8, the Court did not hesitate to acknowledge that the applicants' situation resembled, in all its basic features, to the life of a traditional heterosexual family and was, for practical considerations, indistinguishable from the traditional notion of family life. In particular, it was regarded as relevant that X and Y were – to all appearances – a male–female couple, who had cohabitated for a long time and had undertaken a parental project together; and that X had acted as Z's father since birth.[35] While care was attached weight over biology in the first stage of analysis and, therefore, with a view to establishing family life between X and Z, the concreteness of the emotional bond existing between them did not prove sufficient to reach the threshold of legal fatherhood. In other words, X's non-adherence to the image of 'conventional fatherhood' eventually made a difference in the second stage of adjudication and, more specifically, it led to holding the refusal to recognise X's paternal status compatible with Article 8.

What prevented the Court from finding a violation of Article 8 and, therefore, from reconsidering legal fatherhood outside its conventional boundaries is the Court's approach to positive obligations and, in particular, its departure from its previous case-law. In assessing compliance with Article 8, the Court began by reiterating the principle set out in *Marckx*, according to which the establishment of family life triggers the State's positive obligation to enable

---

[34] A. Bainham, 'Sex, Gender and Fatherhood: Does Biology Really Matter?', *Cambridge Law Journal*, 56 (1997), 514.

[35] *X, Y and Z v the United Kingdom*, § 37.

existing ties to develop and to provide legal safeguards that ensure the child's integration in his family from the moment of birth.[36] However, the Court then argued that the unconventional nature of the father–child tie at stake required a more careful consideration of the scope of that positive obligation.[37] More specifically, it concluded that Article 8 could not, in this context, be interpreted as implying a positive obligation on the State to legally recognise as the father of a child someone who is not his/her biological father.[38]

The Court's departure from its approach in *Marckx* is, in turn, attributable to the interaction between doctrinal and moral considerations pertaining to the nature of the relationship between X and Z. In its reasoning, the Court found it important to stress that, while its earlier case-law where Article 8 was read to require States to actively protect family life concerned ties existing between biological parents and their offspring, 'Z was conceived by AID and is not related, in the biological sense, to X, who is a transsexual'.[39] As pointed out by Kilkelly, the Court's attitude seems to reflect a broader tendency to water down positive obligations when the family life at issue involves unconventional relationships[40] and, as such, it reveals the Court's willingness to support a conventional understanding of fatherhood.

The feature that is most decisively restated is the existence of a biological link between the father and his child. If, on the one hand, the Court seems to reject the indispensability of biology by qualifying the social ties existing between X and Z as 'family life', on the other hand, when it comes to the conferral of legal fatherhood, care is no longer sufficient and biology is reaffirmed as an element that makes someone a legal father. Following the Court's reasoning, its hesitancy to extend the precedent in *Marckx* to the case of *X, Y and Z* rests also on the fact that X is a post-operative transsexual. Besides biology, therefore, what seems to have hindered the finding of a violation of Article 8 is the disconnection between X's assigned sex and his gender identity that, according to a heteronormative vision of fatherhood, ought to be 'naturally' aligned.[41]

Another element that had an important bearing on the outcome of this case is the alleged lack of a European shared approach with regard to both the

---

[36] Ibid, § 43.
[37] U. Kilkelly, 'Protecting Children's Rights under the ECHR: The Role of Positive Obligations', *Northern Ireland Legal Quarterly* 61(3) (2010), 252.
[38] *X, Y and Z v the United Kingdom*, § 52.
[39] Ibid, § 43.
[40] Kilkelly, 'Protecting Children's Rights', 251–253.
[41] A. Mowbray, *The Development of Positive Obligations under the European Convention on Human Rights by the European Court of Human Rights* (Hart, 2004), p. 154.

conferral of parental rights on transsexuals and the wider question of how to legally recognise the tie between an ART-conceived child and his/her social parent.[42] As a consequence, the majority 'did not wish to force a change in law'[43] to allow X to be recognised as the legal father of Z and, therefore, to adopt what could be perceived as an unpopular vision of fatherhood. Rather, it opted for a more 'prudent'[44] or 'non-interventionist'[45] approach: it took note of the transitional and heterogeneous state of the law in Contracting States and, accordingly, granted a wide margin of appreciation and conducted a lenient review.[46]

The Court was of the view that, although several adverse consequences stemmed from the non-recognition of X's paternal status, X was not restrained in any way from acting as a social father[47] and there were alternative ways through which he could have acquired some of the legal attributes of fatherhood. It was noted, inter alia, that the absence of any automatic right of inheritance in case of X's death could have been practically circumvented by making a will.[48] X, moreover, could have applied – together with Y – for a joint residence order thus obtaining full parental responsibility for Z and contributing to Z's sense of personal identity and security within her family.[49] Hence, the Court did not feel prepared to hold the UK in violation of its obligation to respect the private and family lives of the applicants.

While the influence exercised by the non-existence of a common European standard on the width of the margin and, as a consequence, on the strictness of review is consistent with the Court's practice, the problematic passage lies in the failure to support the asserted lack of European consensus with real evidence. Rather than embarking on a rigorous analysis of national laws and practices, the Court referred to 'the information available to the Court'[50] – presumably, the submissions of the parties and the Commission's assessment – as the only basis to substantiate its findings.

This lack of clarity as to the comparative data relied on casts some doubts on the actual legitimacy of the Court's decision to grant a wide margin, the more

---

[42] X, Y and Z v the United Kingdom, § 44.
[43] C. Lind, 'Perceptions of Sex in the Legal Determination of Fatherhood – X, Y and Z v UK', Child and Family Law Quarterly, 9(4) (1997), 406.
[44] X, Y and Z v the United Kingdom, Concurring Opinion of Judge Pettiti.
[45] U. Khaliq, 'Transsexuals in the European Court of Human Rights: X, Y and Z v UK', Northern Ireland Legal Quarterly, 49(2) (1998), 200.
[46] X, Y and Z v the United Kingdom, § 44.
[47] Ibid, § 50
[48] Ibid, § 48.
[49] Ibid, § 50.
[50] Ibid, § 44.

so since the Commission had arrived at the opposite conclusion. As reported by the Grand Chamber itself, the Commission had indeed observed 'a clear trend'[51] among the Contracting States towards the legal recognition of gender reassignment;[52] and, consequently, it had argued in favour of a presumption of legal recognition to the advantage of a post-operative transsexual who lived as part of a family relationship. The finding reached in X, Y and Z appears even shakier if regard is given to the subsequent decision in *Goodwin v UK*,[53] where the Court chose to attach less importance to the absence of a common European approach than to the 'clear and uncontested evidence of a continuing international trend in favour not only of increased social acceptance of transsexuals but of legal recognition of the new sexual identity of post-operative transsexuals'.[54]

To conclude, this judgment contributes to identify the underpinnings of the Court's approach to fatherhood in the ARTs domain in two respects. It certainly exhibits the facilitative role played by the doctrine of the margin of appreciation in preserving a conventional understanding of fatherhood embedded in national legal practice. More interestingly, however, it also shows that the extent to which the Court engages in reconstructing fatherhood is also contingent upon its own perception as to the state of European consensus on the issues at stake. It follows that, as much as European consensus can work as an empowering tool in the Court's enterprise to update its approach to fatherhood, in the absence of a clear methodology of identification, it becomes a way to mask an inherently deceptive reasoning and, ultimately, to legitimise the Courts' persistent attachment to a conventional ideology.

2.2 Not-Yet Conceived Children and the Ideal Father

Two landmark judgments followed in 2007: both of them concerning national measures interfering with the applicant's decision to become a genetic parent. In *Evans v UK*, the issue was whether the requirement for ongoing bilateral consent to the use and storage of frozen embryos – as provided by the Human

---

[51] Ibid, § 40.
[52] A similar view is shared by the Partially Dissenting Judges Casadevall, Russo and Makarczyk. Although acknowledging that the subject is clearly a controversial and divisive one, they found that 'it is no less certain than more and more States (at present nearly half the members of the Council of Europe) are taking steps to adapt and harmonise their legislation with a view to full legal recognition of the new identity of those who have had sex-change operations (...) so as to alleviate, as far as possible, the distress some human beings are suffering' (§ 2).
[53] Kilkelly, 'Protecting Children's Rights', 253.
[54] *Christine Goodwin v the United Kingdom* [GC], no. 28957/95, § 85, ECHR 2002-VI.

Fertilisation and Embryology Act 1990 ('HFEA') – amounted to a violation of the applicant's right to respect for her decision to become a mother in the genetic sense, protected under Article 8. Few months later, in the case of *Dickson*, the Grand Chamber was called to consider another UK policy: one that granted access to artificial insemination (AI) facilities to prisoners only in 'exceptional circumstances', and its compatibility with the applicants' right to respect for private and family life.

The Court reached two opposite verdicts: the HFEA consent rules were considered to strike a fair balance between the competing private and public interests, while the policy contested in *Dickson* failed the proportionality test and was therefore found in breach of Article 8. As a result, while in *Evans*, the wish of a potential genetic father not to become a genetic father prevailed over the applicant's desire to become a genetic mother, in *Dickson*, the parental project of a married heterosexual couple was considered worthy of realisation by enabling them to access AI facilities. Despite their opposite outcomes, these two judgments are evidence of a certain consistency in the Court's engagement with legal fatherhood. They both convey a conventional vision of what being a father means – essentially, being biologically linked to the child and, at the same time, in a relationship with the child's mother – whilst defining fatherhood as a relationship that ought to be freely chosen.

The facts of *Evans v UK* are well known. Prior to the surgical removal of her ovaries due to cancer, the applicant and her then partner, J., had undergone IVF treatment. Six embryos created with both their gametes were frozen in view of implantation at a later stage. Not long after, however, the couple split and J. withdrew his consent to the storage and use of the embryos, in accordance with the HFEA rules. In essence, therefore, the 'dilemma'[55] at the core of *Evans* lies in the tension between two conflicting reproductive rights,[56] both falling under the notion of 'private life' protected by Article 8: the applicant's right to respect for her decision to become a genetic mother and J.'s right to respect for his decision not to become a genetic father.[57] Further complexity is added by the mutually exclusive nature of each person's interest: if the applicant were permitted to use the embryos, J. would have been 'forced to become a father', whereas if J. were allowed to withdraw his consent, the

---

[55] *Evans v the United Kingdom* [GC], § 73.
[56] On this specific dimension of the judgment, see E. Brems, '*Evans v UK* – Three Grounds for Ruling Differently' in S. Smet and E. Brems (eds.), *When Human Rights Clash at the European Court of Human Rights – Conflict or Harmony?* (Oxford University Press, 2017), p. 75.
[57] *Evans v the United Kingdom* [GC], § 71.

applicant was prevented – once for all – from fulfilling her desire to become a genetic mother.[58]

In *Dickson v UK*, the applicants are a married couple who met through a prison correspondence scheme while serving prison sentences. Considering Mr Dickson's release date and Mrs Dickson's age, artificial insemination represented the only realistic hope for the applicants of having a child together. Nonetheless, their application to access such facilities was refused by the secretary of state. The grounds given for refusal included not only the risk of undermining public confidence in the prison system, but also the fact that the mother and the child would have only had a limited support network and that the child would have been without a father for an important part of her childhood.[59]

Whilst the Grand Chamber found the destruction of the embryos not to violate Ms Evans's right to respect for private life,[60] in *Dickson*, the refusal of AI facilities was deemed in breach of Mr and Mrs Dickson's Article 8's rights.[61] More precisely, in *Evans*, it was ruled that the legislature's decision to enact a bright-line rule was justified by the need to promote legal certainty and to avoid arbitrariness and inconsistency inherent in weighing, on a case-by-case basis, 'entirely incommensurable interests'.[62] In *Dickson* – which, it must be noted, did not even concern a blanket rule – instead, the Grand Chamber found that the national policy as structured prevented a balancing of the competing private and public interests and, therefore, the required examination of the proportionality of the restriction by domestic authorities, in any individual case.[63]

---

[58] Ibid, § 73.
[59] *Dickson v the United Kingdom* [GC], § 62.
[60] The applicant had also complained of discrimination contrary to Article 14 taken in conjunction with Article 8. She contended that, under the HFEA, a woman who could procreate without assistance was subject to no control over the embryos developed from the moment of fertilisation, while she or any other woman conceiving via IVF was subject to the will of the sperm donor. The Grand Chamber considered that no separate analysis was needed because the reasons underlying the finding of no violation of Article 8 could also provide for a justification under Article 14. Some commentators have argued that the best way for the applicant to challenge the UK legislation was possibly to argue that she was discriminated against on the basis of her sex. See C. Lind, '*Evans v UK* – Judgments of Solomon: Power, Gender and Procreation', *Child and Family Law Quarterly*, 18(4) (2006), 586, 587.
[61] The applicants had also complained of a violation of their right to found a family under Article 12 ECHR. The Court considered that no separate issue arose under Article 12 and therefore did not find it necessary to examine the applicants' complaint under that provision.
[62] *Evans v the United Kingdom* [GC], § 89 (referring to the Court of Appeal's decision).
[63] *Dickson v the United Kingdom* [GC], § 82.

These two judgments reveal the Court's attachment to 'conventional fatherhood' in various and complementing ways. *Evans* suggests, first of all, that fatherhood ought to be intended as a unitary status. By stating that the implantation of the embryos in the applicant's uterus would have necessarily forced J. to become a father, the Court does not seem to accept a potential disconnection between the biological, the social and the legal dimensions of fatherhood. That explains why the scenario in which J. was permitted to withdraw his consent to be treated as the child's father, while still allowing Evans to make use of the embryos without his involvement was never contemplated, neither at the domestic nor at the Strasbourg level. The Grand Chamber seems, therefore, to oppose any situation where conventional paternal features and care – or, at least, caring intentions – do not coexist within the same individual and, therefore, various ways of grounding paternal rights, obligations or status can be advanced on behalf of different men.

Both cases are, moreover, emblematic of the longstanding obsession with the idea that there should be a genetic link between those who raise children and the latter[64] and, in particular, confirm biology as an important basis on which the rights and responsibilities associated with fatherhood are granted.[65] In *Dickson*, given the personal circumstances of the first applicant, biological fatherhood seems, at least prima facie, to be regarded as sufficient to get a parental project started. In response to Mr Dickson's inability to immediately act as a father and its consequences on the welfare of any conceived child, it was indeed noted that Mrs Dickson was at liberty and therefore able to take care of the child, in anticipation of the husband's release.[66] At least in the short term, therefore, the Court seems to accept a traditional division of labour, which does not require the biological father to be present as a caretaker.

However, a more exhaustive reading of the judgment, especially in light of *Evans*, points to the supportive role that the marital link existing between the applicants might have played in favour of their claims.[67] On the one hand, the

---

[64] C. Lind, 'Evans v UK', 586.
[65] R. Collier and S. Sheldon, *Fragmenting Fatherhood: A Socio-Legal Study* (Hart, 2008), p. 96.
[66] *Dickson v the United Kingdom* [GC], § 76.
[67] Also, Cano Palomares seems to suggest that the different family situations of the applicants were attached some importance by the Court, but in relation to another aspect. He claims that, in *Dickson*, the right to respect for the decision to become a genetic parent was considered to fall within both notions of 'private life' and 'family life' (and not only 'private life', as in *Evans*) because the applicants were a couple and both wanted to have a child through AI. See G. Cano Palomares, 'Right to Family Life and Access to Medically Assisted Procreation in the Case Law of the European Court of Human Rights' in M. Gonzales Pascual and A. Torres Perez (eds.), *The Right to Family Life in the European Union* (Hart, 2017), p. 99.

dissolved relationship between Ms Evans and J. might have been interpreted as further discouraging the continuation of a parental project, which, at least in the eyes of the Court, appeared incomplete as involving a poor version of fatherhood. On the other hand, Mr and Mrs Dickson constituted a heterosexual married family and their promising family package might have therefore contributed to a more robust interpretation of the right to respect for the decision to become a genetic parent. In both cases, therefore, the Court tends to construct fatherhood as a corollary of his relationship with the child's mother, thus proving attached to a marital or pseudo-marital understanding of fatherhood. Therefore, a unitary conception of fatherhood ultimately emerges also from *Dickson*: biology, marriage, caring intentions – and, possibly, care after child's birth – are to be provided by the same man.

At the same time, however, the Court shows itself no longer satisfied with mere 'conventional fatherhood' by taking into consideration and valuing the intentions of the potential fathers involved. In addition to the abovementioned conventional features, the Court appears, indeed, to accord a great deal of trust to the mere intention of Mr Dickson to become a father and, similarly, to take J.'s wish to resist fatherhood seriously when deciding on Ms Evans's claim. Therefore, while difficult to talk about 'new fatherhood' in full terms as the children were unborn or not even conceived, it seems possible to detect the Court's attachment to a milder form of 'new fatherhood', where care – in anticipation of the child's birth – is replaced by caring intentions.

Apart from displaying a similar approach to fatherhood, these two judgments share the same doctrinal starting point: the granting of a wide margin of appreciation to national authorities on the ground of the lack of a uniform European approach[68] and, in *Evans*, also on the ethical and moral nature of the issues at stake.[69] However, the reasoning that follows and, in particular, the impact of the doctrine of the margin on the intensity of review in each case differ significantly. In *Evans*, the conferral of a wide margin led to a lenient scrutiny. In the majority's reasoning, the opinion of national authorities exercised a crucial – almost exclusionary – influence on the assessment of proportionality.[70] The Court did no more than underlining the comprehensive nature of the debates preceding the entering into force of HFEA 1990 and

---

[68] *Dickson v the United Kingdom* [GC], § 81 (on whether conjugal visits are allowed for prisoners); *Evans v the United Kingdom* [GC] (as to the point at which a sperm donor should be allowed to withdraw his consent and prevent the use of his genetic material), § 69.
[69] *Evans v the United Kingdom* [GC], § 69.
[70] On the link between the Court's degree of reliance on the national authorities' opinions and strictness of review, see O. M. Arnardóttir, 'Rethinking the Two Margins of Appreciation', *European Constitutional Law Review*, 12(1) (2016), 42–45.

restating the legitimate considerations that informed the formulation of the rules on consent, in line with the State's submission.[71] Notably, in *Dickson*, the decision complained of was – in spite of the wide margin – subject to a rather strict review. As a result, while the blanket rule at the core of *Evans* was considered proportionate, a non-blanket rule was considered unable to accommodate the nuances of individual cases in *Dickson*.

These variable effects of the doctrine of the margin of appreciation lend support to the suspicion that, in *Dickson*, it was rather the Court's position on fatherhood that influenced the way that doctrine was used, and not vice versa. In other words, the fact that the applicant father – as emphasised above – resembled the model of 'conventional fatherhood' in a significant way might have contributed to push the Court to undertake a strict scrutiny despite a wide margin enjoyed by the State. These two judgments confirm therefore that the relationship between the doctrine of the margin and the Court's approach to fatherhood is not necessarily one way. In cases like *Evans*, the former is productive of the latter. More explicitly, it is the doctrine of the margin that, by influencing the strictness of review, eventually determines the degree of departure from 'conventional fatherhood' as embedded in national laws. In cases like *Dickson*, in contrast, the persisting attachment to 'conventional fatherhood' appears more a matter of choice: it is the Court's moral position on fatherhood that guides its reasoning and, therefore, the inconsistent use of the doctrine of the margin contributes to legitimise a predetermined conclusion.

2.3 Surrogacy and Intended Fatherhood

Another controversial terrain where the Court has had the opportunity to reflect on the scope of the right to become a parent and, more specifically, on what being recognised as a legal father requires is that of surrogacy. Despite being a relatively new issue, situations in which the intended parents of a child born via surrogacy abroad are not legally recognised as such in their country of origin or, even before, are not allowed to de facto assume parental responsibilities have reached the Strasbourg Court already on several occasions.[72]

---

[71] *Evans v the United Kingdom* [GC], §§ 86–87. The weight attached to the opinion of national authorities was particularly problematic in this case because, as stressed by Brems, balancing had been undertaken only at the abstract level, but not at the level of the specific circumstances of the applicants. See Brems, '*Evans v UK*', 75.

[72] In addition to the cases analysed in this section, new applications aimed at the recognition of a filiation link between the child and each member of the couple who resorted to surrogacy abroad are pending before the Court: *Braun v France* (no. 1462/18), *Saenz and Saenz Cortes v France* (no. 11288/18) and *Maillard and Others v France* (no. 17348/18).

Despite recognising that family ties created through surrogacy may enjoy family life for the purposes of Article 8, the ECtHR has clarified that this recognition is not unlimited but, rather, is conferred along conventional lines. In relation to fatherhood, in particular, the Court has made it clear that the existence of a biological link between the intended father and the child remains an essential ground for allocating the paternal status.[73]

All cases thus far decided by the Court originate from national mechanisms introduced to limit or even to deprive international surrogacy arrangements of any legal effect, with the ultimate aim of restraining cross-border reproduction in Europe. The first case involved a Belgian couple who were denied travel authorisation for their child – born through surrogacy in Ukraine – due to the lack of evidence concerning the genetic relationship between at least one of the parents and the child.[74] *Mennesson v France* takes its cue from the refusal to fully transcribe in the French civil registries the birth certificates issued in the United States pursuant to a contract of surrogacy. In the most recent case, *Paradiso and Campanelli v Italy*, a couple attempted to circumvent national adoption legislation by resorting to surrogacy in Russia. The reaction of domestic authorities was even more drastic: the child was taken away from the intended parents and placed for adoption.

In all these cases, the intended parents – also on behalf of the child (apart from in *Paradiso and Campanelli*)[75] – argued that national authorities had acted in breach of their right to respect for private and family life. The Court reached different outcomes. The application in *D. and Others v Belgium* was dismissed as manifestly unfounded. In the cases against France, the failure not to recognise the family ties lawfully established abroad was considered to violate the surrogacy-born children's right to respect for private life, but not the intended parents' right to respect for family life. Finally, in *Paradiso and Campanelli*, the Grand Chamber found the child's removal compatible with Article 8.

Despite pointing to different conclusions, these judgments converge in supporting a biological understanding of fatherhood. In *D. and Others v Belgium*, the DNA tests provided by the applicants to show the existence of a biological link between themselves and the child were considered of no probative value as taken

---

[73] This has been reiterated also in the Court's (first) Advisory Opinion of 10 April 2019 (concerning the recognition in domestic law of a legal parent-child relationship between a child born through a gestational surrogacy arrangement abroad and the intended mother), Request no. P16-2018-001 by the French Court of Cassation, § 35.

[74] *D. and Others v Belgium* (dec.), no. 29176/13, 8 July 2014. Whilst in Italy and France, surrogacy is explicitly prohibited, Belgian law is silent on the issue.

[75] *Paradiso and Campanelli v Italy*, no. 25358/12, §§ 48–50, 27 January 2015. The Chamber dismissed the couple's complaints on behalf of the child on the ground that they had been considered to have no legal relationship with him by the Italian courts.

from an internet site.[76] As a consequence, the couple had to return to Belgium without the child – who was left in Ukraine to be cared for by a nanny – for a period of three months. In holding this application inadmissible, the Court stated that Article 8 does not oblige States to authorise the entry of surrogacy-born children into their territories without having conducted prior legal checks.[77] In the case at stake, Belgian authorities were therefore allowed to put in place legal verifications to prove the genetic relationship between the child and at least one of the intended parents before authorising the child's entrance to the country. This decision – even if not engaging in the merits – seems therefore to suggest that, when there is no biological link between the intended parents and the child, the resulting separation in different countries due to immigration restrictions does not breach their right to respect for private and family life.[78] Hence, biological relatedness emerges as a parameter against which the legitimacy of parent–child relationships ensuing from surrogacy – in particular, to what extent they are considered worthy of development and legal recognition – is tested.

The relevance of biology in according protection to surrogacy-created fatherhood transpires even more clearly in *Mennesson*. In this judgment, the fact that the refusal by the French authorities to recognise a parent–child relationship lawfully established abroad concerned the children's biological father played a decisive role in finding a violation of Article 8.[79] Before embarking on its proportionality analysis, the Court stressed that States enjoyed – at least in principle – a wide margin of appreciation in making decisions related to the delicate ethical issues raised by surrogacy. On the basis of a comparative-law survey, no consensus in Europe was found to exist either on the lawfulness of surrogacy arrangements or on the legal recognition of the parent–child relationships lawfully established abroad as a consequence of these arrangements.[80] However, given that an essential component of the identity of the individuals involved was at stake, the Court stated that, in the cases under examination, the margin needed to be reduced.[81]

With regards to the applicants' right to respect for family life, the Court reiterated its approach in *X, Y and Z v UK*: it did not contest the existence of de facto family ties between the couple and the children, but did not expect the State to undertake a positive obligation to legally recognise them. Despite

---

[76] *D. and Others v Belgium*, § 12.
[77] Ibid, § 59.
[78] C. Fenton-Glynn, 'International Surrogacy before the European Court of Human Rights', *Journal of Private International Law*, 13(3) (2017), 549.
[79] Ibid, 554; Cano Palomares, 'Right to Family Life', p. 107.
[80] *Mennesson v France*, § 78.
[81] Ibid, § 80.

acknowledging the difficulties encountered by the applicants as a result of a lack of legal recognition,[82] the Court observed that they were not prevented from enjoying their family life: they were all able to settle in France shortly after the birth of the children, 'to live together in conditions broadly comparable to those of other families' and there was nothing to suggest a risk of separation.[83] Therefore, once again, the unconventional nature of the family relationships at stake contributed to watering down the extent to which positive obligations are applicable and, consequently, to finding no violation of the applicants' right to respect for family life.[84]

On the contrary, when approaching the issue from the children's perspective, the Court found a violation of Article 8 and the importance of granting legal recognition to biological ties formed the cornerstone of the Court's reasoning. It was noted that the children were in a position of legal uncertainty[85] and, as a result, their right to respect for private life – according to which everyone shall be able to establish details of his/her identity, including their legal parentage – was significantly compromised.[86] In the Court's view, these issues acquired a 'special dimension' in the case at stake given that the intended father was also the children's biological father.[87] In particular, it held that:

> (g)iven the importance of biological parentage as part of one's identity, one cannot claim that it is in the interests of a child to deprive him of a legal relationship of this nature while the biological reality of this link is established, and the child and parent concerned demand full recognition.[88]

It was therefore concluded that, by preventing the establishment and recognition of the children's legal tie with their biological father, France had overstepped its margin of appreciation, thus violating the children's right to respect for private life.[89]

A biological understanding of fatherhood runs also through the Grand Chamber's decision in *Paradiso and Campanelli*.[90] Apart from being relied

---

[82] Ibid, §§ 87–91.
[83] Ibid, § 92.
[84] Kilkelly, 'Protecting Children's Rights', 251–253.
[85] *Mennesson v France*, § 96.
[86] Ibid, § 99.
[87] Ibid, § 100.
[88] Ibid.
[89] Ibid. The same ruling was issued in the case of *Labassee v France*, no. 65941/11, 26 June 2014, that was concomitantly heard as well as in two subsequent cases, *Foulon and Bouvet v France*, nos. 9063/14 and 10410/14, 21 July 2016; and *Laborie v France*, no. 44024/13, 19 January 2017.
[90] L. Bracken, 'Assessing the Best Interests of the Child in Cases of Cross-Border Surrogacy: Inconsistency in the Strasbourg Approach?', *Journal of Social Welfare and Family Law*, 39(3) (2017), 369.

on by domestic courts to justify the child's removal, the lack of a biological connection between the child and the couple was attached weight also in the Court's reasoning. In the first stage of review, the purely social – or intentional – nature of the ties at stake constituted one – or possibly, the main – obstacle to declaring the 'family life' limb of Article 8 applicable.

After acknowledging the existence of a parental project and the development of close emotional bonds between the couple and the child in the first stages of his life,[91] the Court placed decisive emphasis on the short duration of their cohabitation. It was noted that the applicants and the child had lived together for six months in Italy, starting from his third month of life and, before then, the intended mother had already spent some weeks with the child in Russia.[92] Despite admitting that family life had been found to exist vis-à-vis only two months of cohabitation in the previous case of *D and Others v Belgium*, the Court stressed that – in that case – the child was genetically linked to the intended father and that, once valid DNA evidence was submitted, cohabitation had resumed.[93] Therefore, the absence of a biological link, coupled with the brief length of cohabitation, and the uncertainty of the ties from a legal standpoint prevailed over the applicants' caring intentions and actual care, and led to the conclusion that the requirements for establishing the existence of de facto family life had not been met.[94] Yet, having regard to the couple's genuine intention and various attempts to become parents, the facts of the case were considered to fall within the notion of 'private life'.[95]

The influence of biological relatedness does not stop at the first stage of review, but goes as far as to impact the width of the margin of appreciation and, eventually, the outcome of the case. Before embarking on its proportionality assessment, the Grand Chamber held that Italian authorities had to be granted a wide margin of appreciation. It explained that, apart from touching upon ethically sensitive issues – adoption, the taking of children into care, and surrogacy[96] – the case under examination – unlike in *Mennesson* – did not involve the choice to become a genetic parent, an area in which the margin is narrowed. Moreover, the child not being a party to the proceedings, his identity was not at stake.[97] As a result, although much more extreme, the decision of the Italian courts was subject to a more lenient scrutiny as

---

[91] *Paradiso and Campanelli v Italy* [GC], § 151.
[92] Ibid, § 152.
[93] Ibid, § 154.
[94] Ibid, § 157.
[95] Ibid, § 163.
[96] Ibid, § 194.
[97] Ibid, § 195.

compared to the refusal of the French authorities to register the birth certificate of the twins born in the United States.

In assessing the compatibility of the child's removal with Article 8, the Grand Chamber noted that national authorities had been guided by the primary concern of putting an end to an illegal situation,[98] whilst attaching little weight to the applicants' interest in continuing to develop their relationship with the child. In so doing, they had struck a fair balance between the different interests at stake: according to the Court, consenting to let the child stay with the couple would have – indeed – been tantamount to legalising an unlawful situation put in place by them in breach of national law.[99]

Despite the finding of no violation, this judgment does not signal a change in direction. Rather, by placing a strong emphasis on the lack of a biological link, it reinforces the previous rulings and the inability of States to oppose the recognition of father–child relationships where surrogacy has involved the gametes of the intended father.[100] This strand of case-law seems, therefore, to suggest biological relatedness as necessary – or even sufficient – to make an intended father worthy of being attributed paternal status. This construction of fatherhood appears the product of moral and doctrinal considerations, inextricably interwoven. It reflects the Court's moral views in as much as it attaches a priori importance to biological parentage as a component of a child's identity and it considers the existence of a biological link as a relevant factor in the assessment of family life. The nature – biological or social – of the parental ties at stake is also what determined the width of the margin left to the State and, therefore, the intensity of review. Differently from previous case-law, however, the Court's moral views on fatherhood have not required an instrumental use of doctrines to gain support in the Court's reasoning. In these cases, the relevance of biology has rather been incorporated in the Court's practice as an element that guides the consistent application of the doctrine of the margin of appreciation.

3 CONCLUSIONS

While exemplifying the concrete impact of scientific developments on contemporary fatherhood realities, the above jurisprudence reveals that, in the ECtHR domain, the advent of ARTs has been a partially missed opportunity

---

[98] Ibid, § 204.
[99] Ibid, § 215.
[100] Fenton-Glynn, 'International Surrogacy', 561; Mulligan, 'Identity Rights', 16.

for rethinking the parameters of legal fatherhood. The Court has, in fact, attempted to contain or even to contrast the revolutionary impact of ARTs by repositioning fatherhood within its conventional boundaries. Despite taking into account – more or less explicitly – the intentions of the potential fathers and, in case of post-birth claims, their actual participation in the child's life, the Court has not attached unconditional recognition to these 'new' elements. The above jurisprudence shows, indeed, that intentionality and actual care are valued only if they are expressed and/or take place in a 'conventional' context.

This approach finds expression in the judgment of *Paradiso and Campanelli*, where the couple's parental project and the quality of their ties with the child succumbed in front of, inter alia, the lack of a biological link and, eventually, did not prove sufficient to establish 'family life'. Even before, the refusal to recognise X's social and emotional bonds with Z was considered compatible with Article 8 because of the father's transsexualism and, as a consequence, the lack of a biological link with the child and his non-formalised relationship with the child's mother. On the contrary, the Court supported Mr Mennesson's claim to have his paternal status recognised and Mr Dickson's desire to become a genetic father because both applicants reflected a present reality or a plan of 'conventional fatherhood'. Along the same lines, in *Evans*, J.'s wish to resist fatherhood was taken seriously because the child would have been born and raised by a single mother and, as such, in an unconventional family unit.

In sum, the Court supports those intentions – to become as well as not to become a father – and caring practices that reflect or aim at creating 'conventional fatherhood'.[101] In the emerging construction of fatherhood, therefore, change and continuity coexist. Fatherhood is restated in its biological, marital and heteronormative dimensions, whilst emerging as a relationship that ought to be freely chosen and, whenever possible, practised. This trend suggests that the Court is slowly embracing the ideology of 'new fatherhood' that, rather than signalling a departure from the conventional paradigm, combines it with care or, in a milder form, caring intentions.

While adopting a more engaged vision of fatherhood, the Court does not take any step toward 'fragmenting fatherhood'. Rather, it attempts to keep all components of 'conventional fatherhood' tied in the same individual and, as a result, fatherhood continues to be conceptualised as a status that is not susceptible to disaggregation. This unitary understanding of fatherhood

---

[101] In a similar vein, see E. Haimes, 'Recreating the Family? Policy Considerations Relating to the "New" Reproductive Technologies' in M. McNeil, I. Varcoe and S. Yearly (eds.), *The New Reproductive Technologies* (Macmillan, 1990), p. 169.

explains why the complaints of Mr Mennesson and Mr Dickson were successful, while no violation was found in *X, Y and Z* and *Paradiso and Campanelli*. While the first two applicants were, at the same time, biologically related to the child and married to the child's mother, attributing legal fatherhood to X and Mr Paradiso would have instead amounted to accept a split of conventional paternal features among two or more individuals. In both cases, indeed, the biological contribution had been provided by another man and, therefore, one important piece of the puzzle of 'conventional fatherhood' was missing.

ARTs is an area in which, given the delicate moral and ethical issues triggered by the employment of these techniques, coupled with the lack of a common European approach, the Court has proved quite generous in granting a wide margin of appreciation to the Contracting States. Hence, one could expect the underpinnings of the emerging definition of fatherhood to be essentially doctrinal. The wider is the margin, the more lenient is the scrutiny undertaken by the Court and, therefore, the lower are the chances to challenge the largely conventional understanding of fatherhood embedded in national legal legislation and practice. In reality, however, the relationship between doctrines and the Court's understanding of fatherhood has proved far from straightforward and univocal in the above jurisprudence.

In *X, Y and Z*, although the Court grounds its approach to positive obligations on both doctrinal and moral forces, the failure to provide comparative data to substantiate the alleged absence of a European consensus triggers doubts as to the actual genesis of the Court's attachment to conventional fatherhood. These doubts become even more substantial in the pre-birth cases, where the award of a wide margin of appreciation has led to divergent doctrinal paths, but eventually pointing to the same substantive direction: the 'tenacious hold'[102] of a marital, biological and unitary conception of fatherhood, and more generally of the conventional family model. It seems therefore possible to contend that, if not in *X, Y and Z*, certainly in *Dickson*, the emerging definition of fatherhood is rather a matter of choice, on the basis of which the Court has then constructed the necessary supportive doctrinal path. Also in the field of surrogacy, the Court's moral views – i.e., its restrictive understanding of the concept of identity[103] and the importance attached to biology – can be considered to have a bearing on the effects of doctrines: what made the scrutiny stricter in *Mennesson* – compared to *Paradiso and*

---

[102] S. Sheldon and J. McCandless, 'The Human Fertilisation and Embryology Act (2008) and the Tenacity of the Sexual Family Form', *Modern Law Review*, 73(2) (2010), 177.

[103] Mulligan, 'Identity Rights', p. 22. He argues for a wider approach to identity that is not confined to biology, but encompasses also the child's relationship with the intended parents and the gestational mother.

Campanelli – was indeed the biological nature of the relationship between the applicant father and the surrogacy-born children. In these cases, however, the line between doctrines and morals is even more blurred as the endorsement of a biological understanding of fatherhood is not connected to a variable use of the margin of appreciation, but has rather become integral part of its consistent application.

4

Post-Separation and Unmarried Fatherhood

1 FATHERHOOD AND THE 'CRISIS' OF MARRIAGE

In this chapter, the Court's construction of fatherhood is examined in the contexts of post-separation and unmarried fatherhood. Marriage has long played a crucial function in connecting men to their children and, as a consequence, the father–child relationship has been conventionally understood as mediated by men's relationships with women.[1] In practical terms, men's serial parenting is a clear illustration that fatherhood is seldom 'practised in isolation', but is rather correlated to their relationship with their partner as well as whether they live with their partner.[2] Fathers tend to parent by household and, therefore, they are more likely to nurture the children they live with.[3] Fatherhood has been traditionally perceived as part of a 'package deal',[4] in which the father–child tie depends on the inter-parental relationship, also in the law. Marriage was and, to some extent, continues to be the institution through which the law confers a status on both men and children. Its primary role in the legal determination of fatherhood is, possibly at best, exemplified by the so-called 'marital presumption', which identifies the mother's husband as the biological father of any child born in wedlock and, as such, keeps the biological and marital dimensions of fatherhood within the same individual.

---

[1] N. E. Dowd, *Redefining Fatherhood* (New York University Press, 2000), p. 182; B. Simpson, J. Jessup and P. McCarthy, 'Fathers after Divorce' in A. Bainham (ed.), *Children and Their Families: Contact, Rights and Welfare* (Hart, 2003), p. 210.
[2] Dowd, 'Redefining Fatherhood', p. 24.
[3] N. E. Dowd, *The Man Question – Male Subordination and Privilege* (New York University Press, 2010), p. 108. Instances where fathers engage in multiple and simultaneous nurturing relationships are rare, although increasing. See N. E. Dowd, 'Multiple Parents/Multiple Fathers', *Journal of Law and Family Studies*, 9 (2007), 231.
[4] N. Townsend, *The Package Deal: Marriage, Work, and Fatherhood in Men's Lives* (Temple University Press, 2004).

In present times, however, the conventional dyad marriage–parenthood is increasingly at risk of separation. Social shifts as diverse as the decline of marriage as a long-term commitment to one partner and a striking rise in the rate of extra-marital births have – in metaphorical terms – loosened or untied the 'Herculean knot'[5] binding men and their children, thus seriously compromising the possibility of relying on marriage as the primary vehicle for grounding legal fatherhood and allocating parental rights to fathers.[6] Whilst in cases of parental separation and divorce, the end of the marital tie literally resonates with the termination of marriage, in the context of unmarried fatherhood, the 'crisis' of marriage is *in primis* symbolically represented by the couple's choice not to formalise their union and, subsequently, by the potential breakdown of their relationship. In both situations, therefore, the law has to look for alternative ways to recognise, regulate and maintain alive the link between unmarried and separated/divorced fathers, and their biological children.

The steadily diminishing pre-eminence of marriage has been further accelerated by scientific progress. The presumption of biological kinship within marriage originates from an era when no certain means existed of establishing genetic paternity and the law made it difficult for a married man to exclude paternity. Today, however, it is relatively easy to determine who the child's genetic father is with a high degree of accuracy through DNA testing. As a result, recent years have witnessed a growing judicial willingness to order paternity tests, even in scenarios where this would open the way to another father figure external to the social unit where the child is raised.[7]

Apart from jeopardising the role of marriage as an 'adequate securer of paternity',[8] the above social shifts might entail the fragmentation of fatherhood. This is particularly visible in the case-law on paternity proceedings that often involves a biological father contesting the paternity attributed to the mother's husband and social father or, in cases of disestablishment, a legal father that wishes to disavow his paternity pointing to the existence of a distinct biological father. The same split between the traditionally coexistensive features of marriage and biology and the ensuing existence of multiple (potential) father figures occurs in post-separation scenarios, where – next to the biological father – the social role of fatherhood might be undertaken by the mother's new partner or husband. In such cases, the resulting family arrangement no

---

[5] Sir Thomas More, quoted by Simpson et al., 'Fathers after Divorce', p. 201.
[6] R. Collier and S. Sheldon, *Fragmenting Fatherhood: A Socio-Legal Study* (Hart, 2008), p. 101.
[7] S. Sheldon, 'Fragmenting Fatherhood: The Regulation of Reproductive Technologies', *Modern Law Review*, 68(4) (2005), 528.
[8] R. Collier, *Masculinity, Law and the Family* (Routledge, 1995), p. 205.

longer fits into the conventional bi-parental structure and, more specifically, the law is directly confronted with the social reality of 'fragmenting fatherhood'.

Within the ECtHR context, the process of rethinking fatherhood in extra-marital terms has taken place in three distinct, but closely connected areas of case-law: parental rights of unmarried fathers after family breakdown; non-consensual adoption; and, paternity proceedings. In the first domain, which will be analysed in Section 2.1, the applicants are unmarried fathers who, after the end of their relationship with the child's mother, seek to acquire parental responsibility, contact or custody rights with respect to their biological children. Section 2.2, by way of contrast, deals with situations in which unmarried fathers oppose the placement of their biological children for adoption without their prior consent or even knowledge. Finally, the paternity proceedings, to which Section 2.3 is devoted, can be distinguished between those who are initiated by unmarried fathers seeking to be recognised as their biological child's legal fathers and those brought by divorced or otherwise legal fathers willing to contest their legal position vis-à-vis a child born within wedlock.

Apart from attesting to the diversity of father–child relationships, this jurisprudence tells us a great deal about current experiences and perceptions of fatherhood. On the one hand, cases in which men, who have erroneously believed to be the genetic fathers of their children, walk away after learning of misattributed paternity are indicative of the gap existing between aspirational and engaged visions of fatherhood and the reality of fathering.[9] On the other hand, however, alongside men who are concerned with contesting their paternity to avoid financial obligations, there are men who resort to paternity testing as a means of embracing fatherhood. Although possibly revealing that fatherhood is still primarily experienced as a function of genetic, this 'new' way of using paternity testing as well as the numerous requests of unmarried fathers seeking to remain involved in their children's lives even after the end of their relationship with the child's mother as well as their attempts to oppose secret placement for adoption are also symptomatic of a more engaged vision of what fatherhood entails by fathers themselves.

The case-law that follows tells us a great deal also about the conception of fatherhood endorsed by the Court and, more specifically, how far it has moved from the conventional paradigm in three main respects. First, it gives us the chance to identify the factor(s) to which the Court resorts, in the absence of marriage. Is the relationship between the biological parents still taken into

---

[9] W. Wiegers, 'Fatherhood and Misattributed Genetic Paternity in Family Law', *Queen's Law Journal*, (2010–2011), 669.

consideration? If so, to what extent and what are the implications? Shall we talk of a mere 'revisitation' of the concept of marriage or has the focus on horizontal relationships gone once and for all? Second, this case-law constitutes a fertile ground on which to test the tenacity of biology, especially vis-à-vis a divergent reality of social fatherhood. Are we witnessing a 'geneticisation of fatherhood',[10] namely an enhanced significance of the biological tie – rather than marriage or a social relationship with the child – as a way of establishing legal fatherhood? Is the existence of a biological link sufficient to become a legal father or to be granted parental rights? And/or have the abovementioned social changes generated an increased emphasis within ECtHR jurisprudence on the social bonds between fathers and their children, thus resulting in a more direct, unmediated understanding of fatherhood? Finally, the jurisprudence that follows is a useful platform for assessing the Court's openness to the reality of 'fragmenting fatherhood'. When faced with two alternative father figures, does the Court show itself mostly concerned with choosing who between the biological and the social father is to be given preference? Or, provided that they both make distinct contributions, does the Court attempts to accommodate them both within the child's life?

2 THE ECTHR, THE 'CRISIS' OF MARRIAGE AND FATHERHOOD

The ECtHR has unequivocally established that the lack of a marital bond does not preclude the existence of family life for the purposes of Article 8.[11] Family life is mostly intended as a question of fact where close personal ties exist between the individuals involved and, therefore, might include also de facto cohabitation and filiation out of wedlock.[12] Despite its focus on the substance of relationships and the opening of 'family life' to same-sex couples, the Court has showed some willingness to accept a certain degree of legal privileging of the marital family.[13] The automatic recognition of heterosexual married families as qualifying as 'family life' within the meaning of Article 8 is one

---

[10] Collier and Sheldon, *Fragmenting Fatherhood*, pp. 225–6.
[11] *Marckx v Belgium*, 13 June 1979, § 31, Series A no. 31; *Johnston and Others v Ireland*, 18 December 1986, § 55, Series A no. 112; *Keegan v Ireland*, 26 May 1994, § 44, Series A no. 290.
[12] *K. and T. v Finland* [GC], no. 25702/94, § 150, ECHR 2001-VII; *Lebbink v the Netherlands*, no. 45582/99, § 36, ECHR 2004-IV.
[13] C. O'Mahony, 'Irreconcilable Differences? Article 8 ECHR and Irish Law on Non-Traditional Families', *International Journal of Law, Policy and the Family*, 26(1) (2012), 34; S. Choudhry and J. Herring, *European Human Rights and Family Law* (Hart, 2010), p. 167; B. Rainey, E. Wicks, and C. Ovey, *Jacobs, White and Ovey: The European Convention on Human Rights* (Oxford University Press, 2014), p. 337.

clear example of this.[14] Given that the concept of fatherhood has historically developed through reference to the legal institution of marriage, it is unsurprising that also 'conventional fatherhood' has, to some extent, benefited from the 'special' position reserved by the Court to marriage.

In the case-law that follows, the legacy of marriage transpires, first of all, from the Court's persisting focus on the nature of the relationship between the biological parents as a relevant factor demonstrating the existence of family life between the applicant and his child born out of wedlock. When the applicant is an unmarried father, the Court pays attention to, inter alia, the duration of the relationship, whether it entailed cohabitation, the existence of a joint family project and, therefore, whether the pregnancy was planned or, rather, a casual occurrence.[15] Therefore, despite in principle favourable to de facto families, the Court seems to demand proofs of stability and long-term planning before declaring the 'family life' limb of Article 8 applicable to the case at stake. As such, fathers' relationships with their children born out of wedlock continue to be constructed as an extension of the relationship between the adults, also in the absence of marriage or in case of family breakdown.

At the same time, however, attention is also brought to the 'demonstrable interest in and commitment by the father to the child both before and after birth'.[16] Apart from being examined as the mother's former partner, therefore, unmarried fathers tend to be assessed as individuals on the basis of their behaviour towards the child.[17] Among the elements accorded weight, it is worth mentioning the acknowledgment of paternity,[18] attendance of medical examinations together with the mother,[19] presence at birth,[20] frequency of

[14] Moreover, when faced with complaints of discrimination, the Court has often recalled that marriage remains an institution that is widely accepted as conferring a special status on those who entered it and, as such, reserving privileges to married couples does not necessarily breach Article 14. See *Burden v the United Kingdom* [GC], no. 13378/05, § 63, ECHR 2008; *Van der Heijden v the Netherlands* [GC], no. 42857/05, § 69, 3 April 2012. In the latter, the Court specified: 'Rather than the length or the supportive nature of the relationship, what is determinative is the existence of a public undertaking, carrying with it a body of rights and obligations of a contractual nature' (§ 69).

[15] *Keegan v Ireland*, § 45; *Kroon and Others v the Netherlands*, 27 October 1994, § 30, Series A no. 297-C; *Schneider v Germany*, no. 17080/07, § 88, 15 September 2011.

[16] *Nylund v Finland* (Dec.), no. 27110/95, § 2(a), ECHR 1999-VI; *Lebbink v the Netherlands*, § 36; *Różański v Poland*, no. 55339/00, § 64, 18 May 2006; *Anayo v Germany*, no. 20578/07, § 61, 21 December 2010; *Schneider v Germany*, § 89; *Kautzor v Germany*, no. 23338/09, § 61, 22 March 2012.

[17] O'Mahony, 'Irreconcilable Differences?', 36.

[18] *Sahin v Germany* [GC], no. 30943/96, § 88, ECHR 2003-VIII; *Schneider v Germany*, § 89.

[19] *Schneider v Germany*, § 89.

[20] *Lebbink v the Netherlands*, § 39.

contact,[21] cohabitation between the father and the child,[22] involvement in the physical care of the child,[23] promptness to seek the assistance of social services for arranging contact[24] and promptness to initiate legal proceedings to obtain contact arrangements[25] or the establishment of paternity in light of biological evidence.[26]

The above assessment of the father–child relationship, however, is not undertaken in all circumstances. The existence of a double-standard becomes particularly visible in the domain of paternity proceedings. Whilst in cases brought by willing-to-be legal fathers the conduct of the applicant – who tends to be an unmarried father – is subject to a rigorous examination, in cases of disestablishment – that are mainly initiated by (former) husbands – the Court does not seem concerned with determining whether family life exists and prefers to approach the case through the lens of private life.

This comparison would therefore suggest a certain ambivalence in the Court's attitude to unmarried fatherhood. On the one hand, by placing emphasis on the applicant's behaviour towards the child, the Court shows itself willing to free the construction of fatherhood from harmful assumptions and generalisations about unmarried fathers. The stereotypical depiction of unmarried fathers as irresponsible and uninterested in taking care of their children is, therefore, increasingly supplemented – or even replaced – by a different image: that of men who are often deeply committed and want to develop or preserve relationships with their children, yet are denied paternal status and rights as a consequence of discriminatory (application of) laws. On the other hand, however, if compared to divorced fathers, unmarried fathers are requested to demonstrate 'fitness' in order to be granted equal treatment.[27] In other words, the benefits of legal fatherhood are extended to unmarried fathers provided that they prove to be 'meritorious'. As such, a certain distinction in the legal treatment afforded to divorced and unmarried fathers, respectively, survives also in the Court's practice.

The same degree of ambiguity can be discerned with respect to the role played by doctrines in bringing about this reconceptualisation of fatherhood. First of all, there exists no systematicity in the Court's references to doctrines.

---

[21] *Söderbäck v Sweden*, 28 October 1998, § 32, *Reports of Judgments and Decisions* 1998-VII; *Lebbink v the Netherlands*, § 39; *Zaunegger v Germany*, no. 22028/04, § 57, 3 December 2009.
[22] *Zaunegger v Germany*, § 57.
[23] *Lebbink v the Netherlands*, § 39. The Court refers to the fact that the applicant changed the child's diaper 'a few times'.
[24] *Söderbäck v Sweden*, § 32.
[25] *Schneider v Germany*, § 89.
[26] *Kautzor v Germany*, § 44.
[27] Collier and Sheldon, *Fragmenting Fatherhood*, p. 196.

The advent of scientific progress coupled with changed values and perceptions about 'illegitimacy' in Europe would have, at least in principle, prepared the ground for a dynamic reading of Article 8.[28] Yet, this instrument is – at least, explicitly – seldom and, rather, erratically employed. Second, even if a doctrine is consistently invoked throughout the jurisprudence, the role is actually given varies considerably from case to case. The function attributed to the doctrine of the margin of appreciation, in particular, despite being referred to in a rather consistent manner, ranges from being used as a 'purely rhetorical device'[29] to exercising a decisive influence on the intensity of review. What is clear, however, is that doctrinal forces rarely operate alone. Rather, as it will be shown, it is the Court's understanding of fatherhood that – by impacting the ways doctrines are used in each case – ultimately assumes a leading role in shaping the intensity of review and, therefore, the development of the case-law.

2.1 Parental Rights after Family Breakdown

This section deals with cases brought by biological (in one case, alleged biological)[30] fathers who, after the end of their relationships with the child's mother, seek to preserve their relationship with their children born out of wedlock by acquiring parental responsibility, contact or custody rights. In the jurisprudence that follows, the exclusion of the applicant father from the life of his biological child is often the consequence of legal provisions that allow for restrictions – such as the lack of automatic attribution of parental responsibility or contact rights – to be applied to unmarried fathers, but not to mothers or married but separated fathers. If it is true that unmarried fathers might encounter legal and practical obstacles also in the course of their subsisting cohabitation with the child's mother, their position tends to become even more precarious when their relationship comes to an end. This is especially so when, according to the law, the unmarried father's acquisition of parental rights is invariably dependent on the mother's consent. Moreover, this stream of case-law is illustrative of how stereotyping might operate in the law-making process.[31] In the cases herein analysed, national authorities have often ascribed

---

[28] C. Draghici, *Legitimacy of Family Rights in Strasbourg Case Law: Living Instrument or Extinguished Sovereignty?* (Hart, 2017), p. 263.

[29] J. Gerards, 'Margin of Appreciation and Incrementalism in the Case Law of the European Court of Human Rights', *Human Rights Law Review*, 18 (2018), 500. See also Y. Arai-Takahashi, *The Margin of Appreciation Doctrine and the Principle of Proportionality in the Jurisprudence of the ECHR* (Intersentia, 2002), p. 16.

[30] *Schneider v Germany*.

[31] A. Timmer, 'Toward an Anti-Stereotyping Approach for the European Court of Human Rights', *Human Rights Law Review*, 11(4) (2011), 715–16.

a certain attitude to the applicant by virtue of his gender and marital status, regardless of how he acted towards the child when they lived together and, more generally, of his intentions and abilities.

In this specific domain, the approach of the Strasbourg organs to unmarried fatherhood has evolved throughout the time. Overall, it has shifted from a deferential inclination – premised on the idea that national authorities are 'better placed' to examine the interests of the parties involved owing to their direct access to the factual circumstances – to an increased willingness to subject the exercise of national discretion to the yardstick of proportionality.[32] In its early case-law, the Commission found the imposition of conditions on unmarried fathers for obtaining recognition of their parental role justified as it allowed for the necessary flexibility of response to differing family situations. As explained in *M.B. v UK*, father–child relationships can range from 'circumstances where a child is conceived casually, unintentionally or perhaps even violently to the situation where a child is born into a stable and established relationship between an unmarried man and woman'[33]. Hence, subjecting the applicant's acquisition of parental responsibility – that was automatically enjoyed by mothers – to the requirement for the mother's consent or, as an alternative, for a court order did not amount to discrimination contrary to Article 14.[34]

This initial attitude of judicial self-restraint has gradually left room for an anti-stereotyping analysis of the justifications put forward by the State. In other words, despite acknowledging that national authorities enjoy a privileged position, the Court has proved more prepared to undertake a stricter review when assessing the compatibility of restrictions placed on parental rights of unmarried fathers with the Convention. This shift, however, has gone through an intermediary phase, where the dismissal of the applicant's claim for 'abstract' reasons has been gradually accompanied by references to the particular circumstances of the case. This mixed trajectory emerges from the admissibility decision in *Balbontin v UK*.[35] The applicant complained that, because of his marital status, he did not qualify as having parental responsibility and, therefore, he was unable – unlike a married father – to obtain

---

[32] Arai-Takahashi, *The Margin of Appreciation*, p. 65.
[33] *M.B. v the United Kingdom* (Dec.), no. 22920/93, § 3, 6 April 1994.
[34] See also *Dazin v France* (Dec.), no. 28655/95, 12 April 1996. Despite declaring this application inadmissible, the Commission upheld a similar differential treatment arguing that the weaker position attributed to unmarried fathers and the practical difficulties ensuing from the exclusive attribution of parental responsibility to mothers were considered the consequence of the choice of the parents not to marry and, therefore, in the Court's view, could be easily overcome through marriage.
[35] *Balbontin v the United Kingdom* (Dec.), no. 39067/97, 14 September 1999.

a declaration that his child had been wrongfully removed.[36] According to the Court, the justification for the discrimination between married and unmarried fathers complained of lied in the different responsibilities borne by fathers who are caretakers and those who are not.[37] Refusing to place individuals, like the applicant, who 'simply have contact with their child'[38] on an equal footing with those who have the child in their care, did not therefore disclose an appearance of violation of Article 14 in conjunction with Article 8.

Despite remaining sympathetic to their concerns, in more recent case-law, the Court has begun to explicitly require national authorities to consider whether, in the particular circumstances of the case, granting parental rights to the unmarried father would serve the child's best interests. In the case of *Zaunegger v Germany*, the inability of a father of a child born out of wedlock to obtain joint custody without the mother's consent was found to violate Article 14 taken in conjunction with Article 8.[39] The Court accepted that, in light of the variety of family environments, there might be valid reasons to exclude an unmarried father from his biological child's life, for instance when tensions between the parents risk compromising the child's best interests.[40] Nonetheless, it found that 'such an attitude is not a general feature of the relationship between unmarried fathers and their children'[41] and, having regard to the circumstances of the case, there was no prima facie evidence that awarding joint custody against the mother's will would be detrimental to the child's best interests.[42] In particular, emphasis was placed on the fact that, apart from having his paternity certified from the beginning, he had cohabitated with the mother and the child until the latter was three and a half years old.[43] It was further observed that, after parental separation, he had lived with his daughter for more than two years and, also after she had moved to the mother's flat, he had continued to enjoy extensive contact with her and to provide for her daily needs.[44]

The Court relied on a similar factual account to dismiss stereotypical assumptions about unmarried fathers also in other cases brought against Germany. In *Sahin*, the Court found that requiring either the mother's

---

[36] According to Article 3 of the Hague Convention on the Civil Aspects of International Child Abduction, removal or retention is wrongful when it is in breach of custody rights under the law of the country of habitual residence prior to the removal.
[37] *Balbontin v the United Kingdom*, p. 6.
[38] Ibid.
[39] *Zaunegger v Germany*, no. 22028/04, 3 December 2009.
[40] Ibid, §§ 55–6.
[41] Ibid, § 56.
[42] Ibid, § 59.
[43] Ibid, § 39.
[44] Ibid.

consent or a court ruling for an unmarried father to enjoy contact with his child, while recognising automatic contact rights to divorced fathers, amounted to discrimination contrary to Article 14 taken in conjunction with Article 8.[45] The Court was not persuaded by the government's justification that 'in the past, fathers of children born out of wedlock had frequently shown no interest in their children',[46] especially because, as underlined by the Court itself, this general consideration did not resonate with the applicant's situation: the child was born while the applicant and his former partner cohabitated; he had acknowledged paternity and undertaken to pay maintenance; and, he had continued to show interest in contact with his daughter even after his separation from the child's mother.[47]

In *Schneider*, the Court excluded that 'the best interest of children living with their legal father but having a different biological father can be truly determined by a general legal assumption'.[48] In this case, the applicant was denied contact rights with his biological child because he did not fall within the group of people – such as the legal father or a person who has developed social ties with the child – who were entitled to contact under the Civil Code. In its assessment, the Court had regard to the fact that the child was born from a relationship that was not merely 'haphazard'[49] and the applicant had sufficiently demonstrated interest and commitment to his son: he had accompanied the mother to medical examinations, acknowledged paternity before birth and he had initiated proceedings to obtain contact and information concerning the child's development 'relatively speedily', namely, in less than six months after the child's birth.[50] Given the wide variety of family situations possibly concerned, the refusal to grant contact rights to the applicant without an examination of the child's best interests was considered to breach Article 8.

---

[45] *Sahin v Germany* [GC], no. 30943/96, ECHR 2003-VIII. See also *Sommerfeld v Germany* [GC], no. 31871/96, 11 October 2011 that was concomitantly heard. Differently, but according to the same fact-based assessment of the child's best interests, in *Elsholz v Germany* [GC], no. 25735/94, ECHR 2000-VIII, the Court did not find the refusal to grant contact rights to the applicant father in violation of Article 14 taken in conjunction with Article 8. In the Court's view, the decision of domestic courts was indeed clearly based on the danger to the child's development that would have derived from contact with the father against the mother's will. Vis-à-vis the same facts, therefore, a divorced father would have been treated equally.

[46] *Sahin v Germany* [GC], § 83.

[47] Ibid, § 88.

[48] *Schneider v Germany*, no. 17080/07, § 100 15 September 2011.

[49] Ibid, § 88. Although the child's biological parents had never cohabitated, the Court considered that they had a relationship that lasted for one year and four months.

[50] Ibid.

As these cases seem to suggest, the adoption of a critical attitude towards the justifications submitted by national authorities has been facilitated by a partial redefinition of fatherhood on the part of the Court. If it is true that the non-formalised nature of the relationship between the biological parents is no longer accepted as a priori justifying a weaker position accorded to unmarried fathers, other features of this relationship retain significance in the assessment of family life and/or, even further, in the undertaking of the proportionality analysis. The prima facie overcome of marriage as a ground for attributing parental rights to fathers can therefore be more accurately described as a mere 'revisitation' of the conception of marital fatherhood. A clear sign of departure from 'conventional fatherhood' is, however, visible in relation to biology. In the judgment of *Lebbink v the Netherlands*, where the applicant was rejected contact to his daughter born out of wedlock, the Court clarified that 'a mere biological kinship, without further legal or factual elements indicating the existence of a close personal relationship' does not suffice to attract the protection of Article 8.[51] It is therefore not surprising that, in this stream of case-law, the Court's references to the nature and length of the mother–father relationship tend to be complemented with instances of care or, at least, caring intentions pertaining to the father's direct relationship with his child. The emerging construction of fatherhood is, therefore, a mix of change and continuity: while being conceptualised as a mediated relationship, the emphasis on care attempts to free the definition of fatherhood from its conventional boundaries and to move it closer to the ideology of 'new fatherhood'.

Apart from being supported by a revised definition of fatherhood, the Court's anti-stereotyping approach has developed in reliance of a variety of doctrinal tools. One of those resonates with the development of a procedural understanding of Article 8 that, in cases about contact and residence, consists in considering the applicant's participation in the proceedings as part of the proportionality analysis.[52] In *Sahin*, before turning to the applicant's complaint under Article 14, the Court explained that it could not assess whether domestic courts had adduced sufficient reasons for refusing contact without examining whether the decision-making process had provided the applicant with adequate protection of his interests.[53] Given that the father had been able

---

[51] *Lebbink v the Netherlands*, no. 45582/99, § 37, ECHR 2004-IV.
[52] E. Brems, 'Procedural Protection – An Examination of Procedural Safeguards read into substantive Convention Rights' in E. Brems and J. Gerards (eds.), *Shaping Rights in the ECHR – The Role of the European Court of Human Rights in Determining the Scope of Human Rights* (Cambridge University Press, 2013), p. 138.
[53] See also *Elsholz v Germany* [GC], § 52; *Hoffmann v Germany*, no. 34045/96, §§ 44–6, 11 October 2001.

to put forward all arguments in order to obtain contact arrangements and he was also granted access to all relevant information that was relied on by the authorities, the Court was satisfied that the procedural requirements of Article 8 had been complied with.[54] The judgment in *Sahin* constitutes, therefore, an example of how procedural scrutiny can be used by the Court 'as a check on state discretion'[55] in contexts where the margin enjoyed by national authorities is wide.

The application of the 'very weighty reasons' test has further helped the Court to prepare the terrain for a stricter scrutiny. In *Sahin*, as well as in other cases where Article 14 was invoked, the Court has shown consistency in requiring States to put forward very weighty reasons for a difference in treatment on the grounds of sex or birth out of or within wedlock to be considered compatible with the Convention.[56] In the Court's view, the same principle extends to a situation – like that of the applicants – where the father of a child born from a relationship that entailed cohabitation outside marriage is treated differently from the father of a child born out of marital relationship.[57] Hence, the width of the margin enjoyed by States was considerably restricted as a consequence of the 'suspect' ground of discrimination at hand. In *Sahin*, moreover, the Court's undertaking of an anti-stereotyping analysis was also facilitated by the employment of Article 14 as a 'magnifying lens'.[58] Despite finding no violation of Article 8, Article 14 was considered applicable because the facts of the case clearly fell within the scope of Article 8 and, given that German law distinguished between fathers depending on whether their children were born within or outside wedlock, to have been breached. Therefore, the discriminatory dimension of the case ultimately operated as an aggravating factor and, together with the suspect ground of discrimination, prevailed over the 'better placed' argument as the factor determining the outcome of the complaint.

In *Zaunegger*, instead, in addition to the 'very weighty reasons' test, the Court has relied on a limited version of consensus analysis, with considerable effects on the width of the margin and the application of the 'living instrument' doctrine. It was held that, despite the lack of consensus as to whether

---

[54] *Sahin v Germany* [GC], § 71.
[55] Brems, 'Procedural Protection', p. 160.
[56] *Sahin v Germany* [GC], § 94. See also *Hoffmann v Germany*, § 56; *Zaunegger v Germany*, § 51; *Sporer v Austria*, no. 35637/03, § 75, 3 February 2011.
[57] Ibid.
[58] O. M. Arnardóttir, 'Discrimination as a Magnifying Lens – Scope and Ambit under Article 14 and Protocol No. 12' in E. Brems and J. Gerards (eds.), *Shaping Rights in the ECHR – The Role of the European Court of Human Rights in Determining the Scope of Human Rights* (Cambridge University Press, 2013), p. 335.

unmarried fathers have a right to apply for joint custody without the mother's consent, most Contracting States appeared to share a common point of departure when making custody determinations, namely the best interests of the child.[59] The Court further noted that, in case of tensions between the parents, the majority of national legislations provided that such decisions should be subject to the scrutiny of national courts.[60] In this case, therefore, rather than demanding convergence in terms of concrete legal provisions, the Court proved satisfied with the finding of consensus at the mere level of principles.[61]

This approach to consensus had an impact on the outcome of the case because, apart from limiting the typically wide margin of appreciation enjoyed by States when settling custody matters, it served also as a ground whereby advancing a dynamic interpretation of Article 8. In particular, the Court calls for an interpretation of Article 8 that takes into account 'the evolving European context in this sphere and the growing number of unmarried parents'.[62] In this judgment, therefore, the choice to identify common general directions, while disregarding the existence of diverging legal regulations as shown by the comparative survey included in the judgment, might resonate with a strategic use of European consensus in order to support a predetermined outcome. Requiring consensus at the level of rules would have, indeed, meant ascertaining a lack of a uniform approach and, therefore, accepting – like envisaged by Judge Schmitt in his dissenting opinion – that a variety of ways of solving the conflict between the interests at stake are compatible with the Convention.[63]

Similarly, not long after, the Court held in *Schneider* that, 'having regard to the realities of family life in the 21st century', it was not persuaded that the best interests of the child in the sphere of contact could be truly determined by a general legal assumption.[64] This constitutes a further instance of the deployment of the 'living instrument' doctrine to endorse judicial activism.[65] The comparative survey included in the judgment points, indeed, to the absence of a uniform approach in the Contracting States[66] and, therefore, the Court

---

[59] *Zaunegger v Germany*, § 60.
[60] Ibid.
[61] K. Dzehtsiarou, *European Consensus and the Legitimacy of the European Court of Human Rights* (Cambridge University Press, 2015), p. 14.
[62] *Zaunegger v Germany*, § 60.
[63] Ibid, Dissenting Opinion of Judge Schmitt, § 5.
[64] *Schneider v Germany*, § 100.
[65] P. Johnson, *Homosexuality and the European Court of Human Rights* (Routledge, 2013), p. 85.
[66] *Schneider v Germany*, §§ 38–46. In this case, consensus was assessed with regards to the question whether and, if so, under what circumstances a biological father has a right to contact with his child where a different legal father exists.

lacked evidence whereby legitimately advancing a creative interpretation of Article 8. However, in this judgment, the use of consensus might appear less 'agenda driven'[67] and its impact on the width of the margin less decisive because, different from *Zaunegger*, the restrictions complained of affected the applicant's contact rights and, therefore, called (already) for strict scrutiny.

To conclude, in this strand of case-law, the relationship between the definition of fatherhood endorsed by the Court and doctrines is not straightforward, but changes depending on the specific doctrinal tool at issue. On the one hand, the consistent application of the 'very weighty reasons' test to the cases brought under Article 14 exhibits the role of doctrines as 'productive of'[68] a more care-oriented understanding of fatherhood. On the other hand, the selective use of consensus in *Zaunegger* and the activist reading of comparative legal data in *Schneider* seem to suggest a (more) result-oriented way of proceeding. In other words, the inconsistent application of European consensus to legitimise a dynamic interpretation of Article 8 seems 'subservient to'[69] the moral position of the Court on fatherhood. Therefore, while in some cases the Court's reduced distance to 'new fatherhood' tends to come as a result of a consistent methodological path that demands the undertaking of a stricter review of national legislation and practice, in other cases, it appears a predetermined choice that is eventually supported by the most convenient doctrinal route available to the Court.

2.2 *Non-Consensual Adoption*

This section investigates the Court's position with respect to situations where the child born out of wedlock was placed for adoption, without the knowledge and consent of the biological father. This case-law displays a gradual departure from the conventional paradigm of fatherhood and, at the same time, a certain resistance to the fragmentation of legal fatherhood. A decreased (at least, explicit) emphasis on the mother–father relationship and/or on the biological tie between the child and the applicant seems to be accompanied by a heightened importance attached to the father's demonstrated interest and commitment to his child born out of wedlock as the most relevant factor to establishing family life and to finding a violation of Article 8. Vis-à-vis the existence of two competing father figures, the Court's major concern seems to

---

[67] Draghici, *Legitimacy of Family Rights*, p. 402.
[68] Johnson, *Homosexuality and the ECtHR*, p. 88.
[69] Ibid.

lie in identifying the most meritorious one, rather than in regulating their coexistence – for instance, through the award of parental responsibility to the adoptive father. Apart from assuming overall increasing relevance, care becomes the parameter against which the Court makes its own selection. At the same time, however, the mother–father relationship retains an essential role: first, by influencing the criteria against which care is assessed; and, second, by determining the extent to which applicants are owed positive – in addition to negative – obligations. Hence, while a move towards 'new fatherhood' is undeniable, this case-law is also evidence of a persisting legacy of 'marital fatherhood'.

In the case of *Keegan v Ireland*, non-consensual adoption of a child born out of wedlock was considered to breach the biological father's right to respect for family life.[70] The applicant instituted proceedings to be appointed guardian in order to be able to oppose the adoption of his biological daughter, born after the end of his relationship with the mother, and applied for custody rights. However, both his requests were dismissed because, with the passage of time, the child's attachment to the prospective adopters had grown stronger and, therefore, in case of replacement, the child was likely to suffer psychological trauma. As a first step, the Court established the existence of family life between the child and his biological father. Despite having relevant facts at its disposal,[71] the Court chose not to insist on the applicant's willingness to raise his daughter, but rather approached fatherhood as the by-product of the applicant's (failed) parental project with the child's mother.

Emphasis was placed on the length – two years – and the nature of the relationship between the biological parents – which included a period of cohabitation of one year – as well as on the couple's intention to have a child and get married.[72] Considering that the relationship between the biological parents had 'the hallmark' of family life, the tie existing between the applicant and his daughter also qualified as 'family life' since and by virtue of her birth.[73] As an extension of the finding in *Marckx*, the State was therefore considered under the positive obligation 'to act in a manner calculated to enable that tie to be developed' as well as to introduce 'legal safeguards (...) that render possible as from the moment of birth the child's integration in his family'.[74]

---

[70] *Keegan v Ireland*, 26 May 1994, Series A no. 290.
[71] As it has done in other cases, the Court could have observed, for instance, that the applicant had kept contact with the mother during pregnancy, visited her and the baby at the nursing home where she was born, and initiated custody proceedings (§ 6).
[72] *Keegan v Ireland*, § 45.
[73] Ibid.
[74] *Marckx v Belgium*, § 31.

Whilst being in accordance with Irish law and pursuing a legitimate aim, namely the protection of the rights and freedoms of the child,[75] the decision to place the child for adoption was not – in the Court's view – necessary in a democratic society. The crucial issue was that, by establishing new ties, the placement of a child with alternative carers compromised the nurturing of a bond between the biological father and the child.[76] Given that national authorities had failed to provide reasons related to the welfare of the child to justify its departure from the positive obligation of 'respect' arising from Article 8, a violation was found.[77] It seems therefore that, whilst a certain degree of resemblance with marriage might be sufficient to reach the threshold of family life, the allocation of residence rights must follow from an assessment of the best interests of the child. The Court, however, seems to adhere to a specific view of the best interests of the child, according to which the proper development of a biological father's ties with his child should be protected against 'irreversible' processes that place 'the applicant at a significant disadvantage in his contest with the prospective adopters for the custody of the child'.[78] Hence, in *Keegan*, biology appears to be constructed as naturally closer to the child's best interests.

The weight attached to the biological connection emerges even more clearly in the judgment of *Görgülü v Germany*. Although the applicant was considered 'in a position to care for his son together with his wife, who had already raised two children',[79] his request for custody was dismissed as contrary to the child's best interests, in light of the deep social and emotional ties he had developed with his foster family. Domestic courts also decided to suspend the applicant's contact right to preserve the child's psychological stability. Despite conceding that separating Christofer from his foster family might have produced negative consequences, the Court found a violation of Article 8 on the following basis:

> [B]earing in mind that the applicant is Christofer's biological parent and undisputedly willing and able to care for him, the Court is not convinced that the Naumburg Court of Appeal examined all possible solutions to the problem. [...] The Court recalls in this respect that the possibilities of reunification will be progressively diminished and eventually destroyed if

---

[75] *Keegan v Ireland*, § 53.
[76] Ibid, § 55.
[77] Ibid, § 55. The emphasis on positive obligations arising out of Article 8 also played a decisive role in finding a violation in the case of *Görgülü v Germany*, no. 74969/01, 26 May 2004.
[78] *Keegan v Ireland*, § 55.
[79] *Görgülü v Germany*, § 27.

the biological father and the child are not allowed to meet each other at all, or only so rarely that no natural bonding between them is likely to occur.[80]

As regards the suspension of contact rights, the Court recalled that it is in a child's interests to have his family ties preserved. Doing otherwise would entail 'cutting a child off from its roots',[81] which can be justified only in exceptional circumstances. Given the absence of similar justifications in the present case, coupled with the narrow margin of appreciation enjoyed when restrictions on contact rights are at stake, the Court found that domestic authorities had not fulfilled their positive obligation to take measures with a view to reuniting the biological father with his son, thus breaching Article 8.[82]

Both judgments in the cases of *Keegan* and *Görgülü* seem, therefore, to suggest that biology is relevant but not necessarily sufficient. While in *Keegan*, the biological link was accompanied by a sufficiently stable and lengthy interparental relationship, in *Görgülü*, biology was presented in conjunction with the applicant's caring intentions and potential. Indeed, given the lack of any previous contact between the applicant and his child, the Court could not rely on concrete instances of care.

The Court's gradual shift towards care can be discerned even before *Görgülü*. In the case of *Söderbäck v Sweden* – where the adoptive father was the mother's new partner/husband – the Court did not consider the adverse consequences of adoption on the ties existing between the applicant and his biological child disproportionate.[83] In reaching its final decision, the Court relied on a careful examination of the facts through the lens of care. In particular, it noted that the encounters that the applicant had with his daughter were 'infrequent and limited in character' and that, at the time of adoption, he had not met her for some time.[84] Despite this being partially due to the mother's opposition, the biological father had not been as prompt and proactive as possible: he had indeed waited almost three years (when the child was almost five years old) before seeking the assistance of the social welfare office to arrange contact.[85] These shortcomings were rendered even more worthy of consideration if compared to the situation of the adoptive father and his relationship with the child. As underlined by the Court, the mother's husband

---

[80] Ibid, § 46.
[81] Ibid, § 48.
[82] Ibid, § 50.
[83] *Söderbäck v Sweden*, § 32.
[84] Ibid.
[85] Ibid.

had lived with and undertaken childcare responsibilities towards the child, who regarded him as her own father, since she was eight months old.[86] The adoption order served, therefore, to merely 'consolidate and formalise' a pre-existing relationship.[87]

At least on paper, therefore, the Court seems to depart from 'conventional fatherhood': both Mr Söderbäck and the social father are, indeed, assessed on an individual basis and, therefore, fatherhood is constructed as an autonomous relationship. To the contrary, however, the indirect comparison drawn between the two competing father figures seems to suggest that fatherhood maintains its conventionally unitary nature. The Court appears concerned with keeping all parental rights and responsibilities within the same person and, to that purpose, compares the biological father's and the social father's relationship with the child against the yardstick of care. In assessing the biological father's interest and commitment, however, the Court does not seem to apply the same criteria. In particular, when the adoptive and social father is the new partner or husband of the child's mother, its evaluation of the applicant's attitude appears more rigorous thus making the threshold of legal fatherhood more difficult to reach.

While in the case of *Söderbäck* emphasis was placed on concrete instances of care, in *Görgülü*, the Court referred more generally to the father's willingness and ability to care for his child on the basis of the evaluations conducted by national authorities, thus proving to be satisfied with mere caring intentions. Likewise, in the case of *K.A.B. v Spain* – where the child was placed for adoption after the mother's deportation – what convinced the Court of the applicant's true desire to be reunited with his child were his several attempts to obtain contact arrangements, especially in light of his precarious situation, despite the limited contact between them.[88]

Similar intentions, however, did not prove sufficient in case of *Eski v Austria*,[89] where – as in *Soderbäck* – the child's adoption by the mother's husband was considered compatible with Article 8. As argued by the dissenting Judges Spielmann and Tulkens, the applicant had consistently expressed his desire to see his daughter by, inter alia, initiating legal proceedings after the child's mother refused him contact, appealing against the withdrawal of his contact rights and submitting several requests for contact rights in the subsequent months.[90] The

---

[86] Ibid, § 33.
[87] Ibid.
[88] K.A.B. v Spain, no. 59819/08, § 93, 10 April 2012.
[89] Eski v Austria, no. 21949/03, 25 January 2007.
[90] On this basis, the dissenting judges argue that *Eski* deserved to be distinguished from other cases like *Soderbäck*, in which the biological father had accepted the absence of contacts for several years.

majority, however, chose to attach relevance to different circumstances and, in particular, to the fact that – unlike the adoptive father who had been living with the child since she was six years old – the biological father had never been involved in the child's upbringing, and their contact had been 'infrequent and limited in character'.[91] The Court's increased weight attached to care is therefore evidence of an ambivalent reaction to 'conventional fatherhood'. While moving towards the paradigm of 'new fatherhood', the Court's variable standard in assessing care indirectly reveals a persisting attachment to a marital understanding of fatherhood.

Apart from having a bearing on the evaluation of care, the existence of a marital relationship between the adoptive father and the child's mother seems also to influence the extent to which positive obligations are held applicable to each case. In the cases of *Keegan* and *Görgülü*, where the adoptive father is not emotionally linked to the child's mother, the Court felt ready to interpret Article 8 as implying positive – in addition to negative – duties and, as a result, to subject the decision to place the child for adoption to a stricter scrutiny. The Court approached the applicant's complaint from the perspective of the State's positive obligations also in *K.A.B.* In this case, a violation was found on the basis that, despite their margin of appreciation, the national authorities had failed in their duty to act particularly promptly and to make appropriate or sufficient efforts to ensure respect for the applicant's right to be reunited with his son.[92] On the contrary, where the adoptive father is the new partner of the child's mother and the biological father is considered to have failed to demonstrate interest and commitment, Article 8 appears to give rise to exclusively negative duties. This would explain why, in the cases of *Söderbäck* and *Eski*, although the 'family life' limb of Article 8 was declared applicable, no reference was made to the State's positive obligations to reunite father and child or to otherwise enable their ties to develop.[93]

This trend seems therefore to confirm Kilkelly's view that Article 8's positive obligations are not uniformly applied to all family relationships by the Court.[94] In this specific context, the variable use made of the doctrine of positive obligations in each case seems to follow from the (non-)existence of a marital relationship between the child's mother and the social father and, in turn, from the applicant's adherence to the model of 'new fatherhood' as perceived by the Court. In particular, the extent to which positive obligations

---

[91] *Eski v Austria*, § 39.
[92] *K.A.B. v Spain*, § 116.
[93] See also *Chepelev v Russia*, no. 58077/00, 26 July 2007.
[94] U. Kilkelly, 'Protecting Children's Rights Under the ECHR: The Role of Positive Obligations', *Northern Ireland Legal Quarterly*, 61(3) (2010), 254.

are held applicable tends to be watered down as the biological father becomes, if compared to the social father, further detached from the construction of fatherhood supported by the Court. In this strand of case-law, the inconsistent doctrinal path undertaken by the Court appears, therefore, to be the consequence of the endorsement of a definition of fatherhood that combines 'conventional' – i.e., the attachment to a marital and unitary conception – and 'new' features – i.e., care.

2.3 Paternity Proceedings

In the case-law that follows, it is the specific function of establishing paternity – that has been traditionally performed by marriage – to be put to the test by scientific progress. The advent of DNA testing has, indeed, entailed the possibility of unmasking the artificial nature of a relationship that the law has turned into 'real' for practical purposes. It is therefore not surprising that, in recent years, the Court is being overwhelmed with applications brought by men seeking to determine the truth of biological parentage with the final aim of either establishing or disavowing their own paternity. Hence, these proceedings have more far-reaching objectives than those analysed in the previous two sections because it is the full legal status of fatherhood, as opposed to parental rights, that is at stake.

To summarise the Court's position in the domain of paternity proceedings, Article 8 tends to be interpreted as implying the State's positive obligation to 'provide an efficient system for resolving these delicate disputes'.[95] Despite recognising the State's interest in protecting the legal certainty and stability of family relationships as legitimate, the complete absence of avenues to bring one's legal position in line with biological evidence has been consistently found to be in violation of Article 8. The exact scope of the State's positive obligation to facilitate the establishment of biological filiation, however, is unclear.[96] Central to its assessment is, especially – or, at least, explicitly – in the more recent case-law, the absence of a common legal approach to paternity disputes across Europe and, as a result, the enjoyment of a wide margin of appreciation by national authorities.[97]

In addition to this doctrinal influence, however, the definition of the exact content of the positive obligation tends to vary depending on the

---

[95] A. Mowbray, *The Development of Positive Obligations under the European Convention on Human Rights by the European Court of Human Rights* (Hart, 2004), p. 148.
[96] A. Bainham, 'Truth Will Out: Paternity in Europe', *Cambridge Law Journal*, (2007), 282.
[97] *Shavdarov v Bulgaria*, no. 3465/03, § 56, 21 December 2010; *Kautzor v Germany*, no. 23338/09, § 72, 22 March 2012; *Ahrens v Germany*, no. 45071/09, § 70, 24 September 2012.

circumstances of each case. In particular, the Court is more inclined to give precedence to biological reality if no other man acts as the child's social father or, more generally, the interests of all parties involved converge.[98] Apart from paying attention to the mother's interests, the Court places emphasis on the wishes as well as on the personal circumstances – for instance, age and financial stability – of the child. In a range of cases, it even makes it clear that the father's claim could have been denied if there were evidence that allowing the paternity suit to proceed would have harmed the interests of children.[99] Even if brought by applicant fathers, therefore, paternity claims are generally approached and analysed from a relational dimension and, in particular, from the child's (as well as the mother's) point of view rather than exclusively as an aspect of the father's rights.[100]

Apart from being influenced by the existence of a conflict or concert of interests, the outcome of each case tends to be modulated by the attitude of the applicant and, more specifically, by his correspondence with a (more) engaged construction of fatherhood endorsed by the Court. Paternal involvement, however, is not assessed against the exact same yardstick. Whilst, in cases of disestablishment, the Court tends to be satisfied with the undertaking of a diligent conduct (i.e., whether the applicant had acted promptly and has availed himself of all possible routes offered by the legislative framework),[101] when the applicant is an unmarried father who aims at being recognised as the child's legal father, the Court becomes more demanding. As it will be shown, indeed, especially in its more recent case-law, the existence of a close personal tie between the child and the applicant father assumes rather decisive importance that, apart from determining the examination of the case under

---

[98] Draghici, *Legitimacy of Family Rights*, p. 109.
[99] Choudhry and Herring, *European Human Rights*, p. 182. Examples include *Rózański v Poland*; *Paulík v Slovakia*, no. 10699/05, ECHR 2006-XI (extracts); *Tavli v Turkey*, no. 11449/02, 9 November 2006.
[100] Further confirmation of the weight attached to the interests of children is to be found in the fact that complaints brought by children lamenting obstacles to establishing paternity have mostly ended with the finding of a violation of Article 8. See *Mikulić v Croatia*, no. 53176/99, ECHR 2002-I; *Jäggi v Switzerland*, no. 58757/00, ECHR 2006-X; *Phinikaradou v Cyprus*, no. 23890/02, 20 December 2007; *A.M.M. v Romania*, no. 2151/10, 14 February 2012. No violation of Article 8 was found when – as in the recent case of *Silva and Mondim Correia v Portugal*, nos. 72105/14 and 20415/15, 3 October 2017 – the child had shown lack of diligence in instituting paternity proceedings. See also D. Coester-Waltjen, 'The Impact of the European Convention on Human Rights and the European Court of Human Rights on European Family Law' in J. M. Scherpe (ed.), *European Family Law – The Impact of Institutions and Organisations on European Family Law* (vol. I), (Edward Elgar, 2016), p. 92.
[101] *Shofman v Russia*, no. 74826/01, 24 November 2005; *Mizzi v Malta*, no. 26111/02, ECHR 2006-I (extracts).

the limb of 'family life', extends to the proportionality analysis.[102] Despite the variations in the Court's appreciation of paternal care, therefore, what emerges quite clearly is the Court's move towards an understanding of fatherhood as a more autonomous relationship, contingent on the father's demonstrated interest and commitment to the child.

The case-law that follows is organised in two sections, depending on the specific scenario at stake. In the first set of cases, the legal father – identified by virtue of a legal presumption or through judicial proceedings – wishes to disavow paternity of a child born from a (broken) marriage or romantic relationship, on the basis of the results of DNA testing. In the second section, in contrast, the applicant is the (alleged) biological father who intends to contest the paternity attributed to another man and to be recognised as the legal father of his child on the strength of new biological evidence. Regardless of the aim pursued by paternity proceedings, these cases help to address the same crucial question: does biology really matter in determining who is the child's legal father? In the second stream of case-law, moreover, the Court is often faced with a tension between the value of biological truth, on the one hand, and the existence of social ties, on the other hand. Therefore, it is often called to make a choice as to what kind of ties – biological or social – should be relied on to attribute legal fatherhood. In these cases, indeed, the action initiated by the biological father might result in depriving the legal and social father of his (well-established) connection with the child. Hence, these cases offer precious opportunities to reflect upon the value attached to care and existing close personal ties vis-à-vis a different biological reality.

Fathers Contesting Paternity

In the following cases, the applicants – who had been registered as the child's legal father – were unable to challenge a legal presumption or a judicial declaration of paternity because of the expiry of the statutory time limits or other restrictions imposed by the law. In this stream of case-law, therefore, the applicant is often the former husband of the child's mother who wishes to contest the paternity of a child born in wedlock or, although less frequently, her former partner who was declared the legal father of a child born from a relationship with another man. Before turning to the analysis of the case-law, it seems worth anticipating that, different from the cases in which the applicant seeks to be recognised as the child's legal father, the Court does not pay attention to the potential existence of concrete personal ties between the child

---

[102] *Kautzor v Germany*, § 62; *Marinis v Greece*, no. 3004/10, § 57, 9 October 2014.

and the applicant. In cases of disestablishment, the Court has generally chosen – but failed to explain why – to leave the question of whether the applicant's family life is at stake open because, in any event, the determination of the father's legal relationship with his putative child concerns his identity and, therefore, his private life.[103] This, even if paternity suits are – in these cases – aimed at the dissolution in law of existing family ties and, as such, have clear consequences for family life.

Despite developing over a period of more than three decades, the approach adopted by the Court in cases of paternity disestablishment is generally consistent, from both substantive and doctrinal perspectives. Starting from the latter, any reference to the margin of appreciation tends to be rather empty.[104] In other words, with the exception of the judgment in *Rasmussen v Denmark*, the margin of appreciation tends to be mentioned as a general principle and/or in the conclusion, with no impact on the strictness of review undertaken by the Court.[105] As concerns the emerging construction of fatherhood, this stream of case-law undoubtedly suggests an increased weight attached to the legal father's interest in bringing his legal position in line with biological evidence. The importance attributed to clarifying biological parentage, however, remains conditional. In case the applicant fails to make a request at a relevant time despite having the opportunity to do so or there is a conflict of interests among the individuals concerned, the Court does not easily surrender to the rapidly declining pre-eminence of marriage in the era of biological certainty.

Before elucidating the Court's position by delving into the jurisprudence, one aspect of discontinuity deserves to be mentioned. While in its earliest judgment of *Rasmussen v Denmark* the Court found the imposition of time limits only on fathers not discriminatory, more recent case-law signals the adoption of a critical stance towards differential treatment against legal fathers. In *Rasmussen*, the Court subscribed to the stereotypical assumption underlying the law according to which 'time limits were less necessary for wives than for husbands since the mother's interests usually coincided with those of the child, she being awarded custody in most cases of divorce and separation'.[106] To support its finding of no violation of Article 14 taken in conjunction with Article 8, emphasis was placed on the wide margin of appreciation left to the

---

[103] *Rasmussen v Denmark*, 28 November 1984, § 33, Series A no. 87; *Yildirim v Austria* (Dec.), no. 34308/96, § 2, 19 October 1999; *Shofman v Russia*, § 30; *Mizzi v Malta*, § 102.
[104] Gerards, 'Margin of Appreciation and Incrementalism', p. 500.
[105] E.g., *Shofman v Russia*, § 44; *Mizzi v Malta*, §§ 113–114; *Iyilik v Turkey*, no. 2899/05, § 31, 6 December 2011.
[106] *Rasmussen v Denmark*, § 41.

State. As a justification, the Court referred to the lack of a European common approach between the laws of the Contracting States, but failed to ground its assessment on any comparative analysis.

More than two decades later, the Court had to address similar complaints in *Mizzi v Malta*[107] and *Paulík v Slovakia*.[108] In the former, the applicant was unable to contest the paternity of a child – born few months after the couple (who previously married) separated and stopped living together – because of strict time limits imposed on husbands, but not on others wishing to bring a challenge. Similarly, Mr Paulík – whose paternity was determined in a final judicial decision – complained that he had been discriminated against when compared both to fathers whose paternity had been presumed and to mothers because, unlike him, they could request the prosecutor general to challenge paternity on their behalf. In both cases, the Court adopted an anti-stereotyping attitude – that, possibly, could not be reasonably expected as early as in 1984 (when *Rasmussen* was decided) – and considered that, with respect to their interest in contesting a status relating to paternity, the applicant and the other interested parties were in analogous situations.[109] It was therefore concluded that the rigid application of time limits along with no allowance made for the specific circumstances of the applicant's case breached Article 14 taken in conjunction with Article 8.[110]

The judgments in *Mizzi* and *Paulík* are also evidence of the anticipated correlations between, on the one hand, the weight attached to the father's interest in challenging the paternity of a child who is not his own in the particular case and, on the other hand, the promptness of his reaction or the existence of convergent intentions, respectively. In *Mizzi*, the Court explicitly referred to the conduct undertaken by the applicants vis-à-vis that of Mr Rasmussen as a relevant distinguishing factor in determining the finding of a violation.[111] Although he had grounds for assuming that he was not the biological father from the first day of the child's life, the applicant in *Rasmussen* had deliberately chosen to take no action with the hope of preserving his marriage up until the separation with his former wife.[112] On the contrary, Mr Mizzi had never had the opportunity of having the results of

---

[107] *Mizzi v Malta*, no. 26111/02, ECHR2006-I (extracts).
[108] *Paulík v Slovakia*, no. 10699/05, ECHR 2006-XI (extracts).
[109] *Mizzi v Malta*, § 131; *Paulík v Slovakia*, § 54.
[110] *Mizzi v Malta*, § 134; *Paulík v Slovakia*, § 58.
[111] *Mizzi v Malta*, § 134.
[112] See also *Yildirim v Austria*. At the time of the applicant's marriage, his wife was already pregnant and the applicant knew that he was not the biological father of the future child. However, he argued that he believed the natural father was registered as the child's father on the birth certificate and he became aware he was considered the child's father only during divorce proceedings. The complaint was held inadmissible.

his daughter's blood test examined by a tribunal as, by the time the law admitted challenges on the basis of biological evidence and proof of adultery, the six-month time limit within childbirth had already expired.'[113] A similar trajectory can be discerned in the admissibility decision of *Carmel Cutajar v Malta*, where the applicant's request for a retrial alleging that a new DNA test would have allowed for more accurate results was denied.'[114] Having established that this test was already available at the time of the main paternity proceedings, the Court considered justifiable for national authorities to attach more weight to the interests of the child and the family in which she is raised than to the applicant's interest in obtaining the verification of a biological fact, 'particularly given the applicant's negligence at the time of the main proceedings'.[115]

Paulík, by way of contrast, exemplifies the impact that the existence of converging interests is likely to have on the balancing exercise and, accordingly, on the ultimate outcome of each case of disestablishment. In concluding that national authorities had failed to strike a balance between the interests involved, the Court had indeed placed emphasis on the fact that it was the child, I., – at that time almost forty years old – who had proposed to have her paternal affiliation retested and that, subsequently, all the parties – I., the applicant and the mother – accepted to undergo a genetic test to establish whether the applicant was I.'s father.[116]

The Court was even more vocal in the case of *Ostace v Romania*, where the applicant was unable to obtain the revision of a judgment establishing his paternity on the ground that the forensic examination report showing no genetic link between him and his child born out of wedlock did not exist at the time of the initial proceedings – as required by national jurisprudence.[117] Despite accepting legal certainty and stability of family relationships as a legitimate aim, the Court observed that the child – by now an adult – as

---

[113] *Mizzi v Malta*, § 134. A similar approach was taken also in *Shofman v Russia*, where the applicant had not suspected that the child was not his and reared him as his own for some two years after birth. However, the domestic law in force at the material time provided one-year limitation period to contest paternity, the starting point of which was calculated from the date the putative father was informed that he had been registered as the child's father and made no allowance for husbands in the applicant's situation. In finding a violation of Article 8, emphasis was placed inter alia on the fact that, once he became aware of a possibly divergent biological reality, the applicant had brought a legal action without delay (§ 40).
[114] *Cutajar v Malta* (Dec.), no. 55775/13, 23 June 2015.
[115] Ibid, § 'The Law', A.
[116] *Paulík v Slovakia*, § 46.
[117] *Ostace v Romania*, no. 12547/06, 25 February 2014.

well as his mother had given consent to DNA testing.[118] It was therefore concluded that, by not allowing the reopening of the paternity proceedings, 'even though all parties seemed to be in favour of determining the truth concerning the child's biological parentage',[119] national authorities had breached Article 8. National authorities were instead found to strike a fair balance between the various interests involved in the case of *Iyilik v Turkey*.[120] As emphasised by the Court itself, the latter had to be distinguished from previous jurisprudence where a violation was found because the child had refused to undergo DNA testing and, therefore, his intentions clashed with those of the father.[121]

To conclude, if it is true that a diminished concern with legal certainty has left space for the applicant's wish to bring the legal position into line with biological truth to be taken into consideration in the balancing exercise, these judgments cannot be read as supporting any absolute right to access paternity proceedings[122] and, as such, as necessarily moving towards a biological understanding of fatherhood. Rather, by attaching relevance to the existence of convergent interests among all parties concerned or placing emphasis on the diligent conduct undertaken by the applicant, the Court seems to express its willingness to preserve – as much as possible – the child's position into the marital/legal (broken) family. In cases of disestablishment, indeed, the child risks becoming fatherless due to the absence of an alternative father figure. The Court might therefore be concerned with securing the presence of a paternal figure who, although uninterested and lacking commitment towards the child, is liable for child support and, accordingly, likely to ensure

[118] Ibid, § 44.
[119] Ibid, § 45.
[120] *Iyilik v Turkey*, no. 2899/05, 6 December 2011.
[121] Ibid., § 32. Contrast with *Tavli v Turkey* (no. 11449/02, 9 November 2006), where a violation was found. In both cases, the applicant sought to reopen paternity proceedings after DNA testing had become more available and widespread but his request was denied on the ground that scientific progress was not a valid ground. According to the law applicable at the material time, a retrial was permitted in case of newly obtained evidence, that was already existent at the time of the original proceedings but inaccessible due to force majeur; and, domestic courts had decided that scientific progress did not qualify as such. On the importance attached to divergent views among the parties involved, see also *Darmon v Poland* (Dec.), no. 7802/05, 17 November 2009, held inadmissible on the ground that the daughter considered the applicant as her father and refused to undergo DNA test and the mother confirmed his paternity; *R.L. and Others v Denmark*, no. 52629/11, 7 March 2017, where the wish to reopen paternity proceedings shared by the children's mother and the legal father clashed with the alleged biological father's opposition and the children's counsel views. In light of this disagreement and the lack of conclusive biological evidence, domestic courts were considered to strike a fair balance between the interests of the applicants and other parties involved and the general interest in ensuring legal certainty of family relationships (§§ 48–51).
[122] Bainham, 'Truth Will Out', 280.

financial provision.[123] That said, the Court's unjustified decision not to delve into the complaints' potential dimension of family life and, therefore, not to investigate the concreteness of the ties (potentially) existing between the applicant fathers and their children makes the emerging construction of fatherhood automatically confined between two different – but equally 'conventional' – understandings: biological or marital/breadwinning.

Fathers Claiming Paternity

In situations in which the applicant wishes to be recognised as the child's legal father on the ground of their biological connection, the Court appears more inclined to approach the complaint through the lens of 'family life'.[124] It would therefore seem that, vis-à-vis the claim of an unmarried father who seeks to establish – as opposed to contest – his own paternity, the Court becomes concerned with elements that do not seem to be relevant when it is the disavowal of paternity that is sought and, thus, mostly divorced fathers are involved. All cases that follow, therefore, share the same starting point: the Court examines whether the bond existing between the applicant and the child amounts to 'family life' by focusing – or, at least, announcing to focus – on the type of relationship the child was born from as well as on the applicant's demonstrated interest and commitment to the child, both before and after birth. Despite this difference, the right to bring legal status into line with biological reality is, also in situations involving fathers willing to be recognised, attached weaker protection when there is a conflict of interests between the individuals involved. In particular, it would appear that, where there is a competing father figure – who tends to resonate with the husband or new partner of the mother and, apart from holding the paternal legal status, is also the child's social father – the Court assesses the applicant's claim against the (extra) requirement of care.

Although fatherhood continues therefore to be understood as a mediated relationship, the increased importance attributed to the applicant's attitude towards his biological child signals – at the same time – the Court's move towards a more engaged vision of fatherhood. As it will be shown, indeed, vis-à-vis opposite messages, the element of care tends to prevail over the inter-parental relationship and its influence might go as far as to impact the scope of the State's positive

---

[123] Ibid, 279.
[124] M. Lafferty, 'Article 8: The Right to Respect for Private and Family Life, Home, and Correspondence' in D. Harris, M. O'Boyle, E. Bates and C. Buckley (eds.), *Harris, O'Boyle, and Warbrick: Law of the European Convention on Human Rights* (Oxford University Press, 2014), p. 565.

obligation to enable existing family ties to develop. In more concrete terms, it seems that the State's action is subject to a lenient scrutiny when the applicant himself has not taken all possible routes made available to him or has otherwise failed to show serious intention to raise the child. In addition to these substantive considerations, as of the judgment in *Shavdarov v Bulgaria*,[125] the Court has begun to make the doctrinal dimension of its reasoning more tangible by spelling out the influencing factors and the role played by the margin of appreciation in the proportionality assessment. In this domain, therefore, the emerging construction of fatherhood appears to be both a matter of (predetermined) choice and the consequence of an increased doctrinal accuracy on the part of the Court.

In its very first case of this kind, *Kroon and Others v the Netherlands*, the Court was faced with a rather unusual setting: although the mother was still married when the child was born, the husband was a foreign national whose whereabouts were unknown at the time of childbirth.[126] Nonetheless, the applicants – the mother, the biological father and the child, Samir – were unable to obtain the recognition of the second applicant as the child's legal father because of the mother's impossibility of denying her (former) husband's paternity.[127] When assessing the existence of family life, the Court placed emphasis on the fact that, despite not living together, the parents had a stable and longstanding relationship from which Samir and other three children were born.[128] It followed that – in line with the principle established in *Marckx* – Samir was *ipso jure* part of that family unit from the moment of his birth and by the very fact of it.[129] It was therefore concluded that the bond existing between the biological father and Samir amounted to family life, 'whatever the contribution of the latter to his son's care and upbringing'.[130]

Having established the existence of family life, the Court went on to argue that national authorities had failed to undertake their positive obligation to 'allow complete legal family ties to be formed between Mr Zerrouk and his son Samir as expeditiously as possible'.[131] In the Court's view, the alternatives suggested by the government could not, indeed, be regarded as compatible with the notion of respect for family life. Step-parent adoption required the parents to marry one another against their will,[132] while joint custody would

---

[125] *Shavdarov v Bulgaria*, no. 3465/03, 21 December 2010.
[126] *Kroon and Others v the Netherlands*, 27 October 1994, Series A no. 297-C.
[127] Under Dutch law, only the husband could bring an action to deny his own paternity.
[128] *Kroon and Others v the Netherlands*, § 30.
[129] Ibid.
[130] Ibid.
[131] Ibid, § 36.
[132] Ibid, § 38.

have left the legal tie between Samir and his mother's former husband intact thus precluding the establishment of such tie between the applicants.[133] It was therefore concluded that, 'even having regard to the margin of appreciation left to the State', the lack of a procedure for bringing the legal position into line with the biological and social realities flew in the face of the wishes of those concerned without actually benefiting anyone and eventually breached Article 8.[134]

At first appearance, the Court's understanding of fatherhood emerging from *Kroon and Others* seems rather 'conventional': fatherhood is constructed as the product of a family project with the child's mother, rather than as a direct relationship with the child. Nonetheless, as it will be acknowledged in the subsequent case of *Nylund v Finland*,[135] the fact that the applicant was actively involved in the care of his children actually played a role in determining the outcome of the case. It is argued that, instead of reducing fatherhood to mere breadwinning, the stated irrelevance of the applicant's involvement in childcare should rather be read as indicating that the need to look for evidence of care arises only when there is an alternative father figure.

Subsequent case-law seems, moreover, to suggest that one of the factors that might have facilitated the finding of a violation in *Kroon* is the convergence of interests between the various individuals involved and the total lack of correspondence between the social and the legal realities of fatherhood. In *Nylund*, where the legal father lived with the child's mother and the couple wished to continue raising the child together, the applicant was denied the possibility to challenge the legal presumption favouring the husband's paternity on the ground that a paternity suit would have caused distress for the child and its family. To justify the inadmissibility of the complaint, the Commission relied on two distinguishing factors. First, it said that it could not disregard that the applicant had never seen or developed any emotional tie with the child who was born after the mother had married someone else.[136] Therefore, in spite of the fact that the applicant lived with the mother and was engaged to her at the time she became pregnant, no family life was found to exist between the applicant and his biological child.[137] Second, the legal father was the actual carer of the child and the mother had denied the applicant's paternity.[138] Therefore, unlike in *Kroon* where the impossibility of bringing paternity proceedings clashed with the wishes of those concerned, in this case, it

---

[133] Ibid, § 39.
[134] Ibid, § 40.
[135] *Nylund v Finland* (Dec.), no. 27110/95, § 2(a), ECHR 1999-VI.
[136] *Nylund v Finland*, p. 14.
[137] Ibid, p. 14.
[138] Ibid.

matched with the desires of the married couple in whose wedlock the child was born.[139]

In *Nylund*, therefore, the Court makes it clear that its understanding of fatherhood not only reflects continuity, but incorporates change. On the one hand, the focus on the quality of the relationship between the biological parents shows that fatherhood continues to be constructed as a mediated relationship. In other words, the fact that the marital (still intact) relationship between the child's mother and the legal father is eventually preferred over the (ended) relationship that existed between the applicant and the child's mother at the time of conception is symptomatic of the Court's persisting attachment to a marital conception. On the other hand, however, the insufficiency of biology to make someone a legal father and the fact that, vis-à-vis a competing father figure who is involved in the daily care of the child, the claim of the biological father fails reveal the Court's gradual embracement of the ideology of 'new fatherhood'.

The relevance attached to care goes as far as to penetrate the proportionality analysis in the case of *Yousef v the Netherlands*, where the applicant was unable to obtain official recognition of paternity without the consent of the child's mother.[140] Following the latter's death, the child was placed in the care of one of the mother's brothers; nonetheless, the applicant met the child once every three weeks and was granted contact rights. Despite finding the existence of family life and reiterating the ensuing positive obligation on the State,[141] the Court was satisfied with the fact that the applicant was not totally prevented from enjoying his family life with his daughter, since he continued to have contact with her.[142] *Yousef* is, therefore, confirmation of the fact that the Court can allow for a legal presumption to prevail over biological reality when it considers the matter as being one in which sufficient conflicting interests are at stake.[143] As the Court itself underlined, the applicant had sought the recognition of his paternity in order to disrupt his daughter's family unit[144] and, moreover, the mother had, before her death and in her will, opposed any involvement of the applicant in the child's life.[145]

More significantly, however, this judgment is also evidence of the increased importance attributed to care vis-à-vis diverging wishes. When assessing

---

[139] Ibid, p. 15.
[140] *Yousef v the Netherlands*, no. 33711/96, ECHR 2002-VIII.
[141] Ibid, § 67.
[142] Ibid, § 69.
[143] Choudhry and Herring, *European Human Rights*, p. 185.
[144] *Yousef v the Netherlands*, § 71.
[145] Ibid, § 15.

whether the interference was 'necessary in a democratic society', the Court underlined that the applicant had never looked after his daughter before, had never expressed his intention of doing so and had not demonstrated convincingly that he was able to do so in a responsible manner.[146] On the contrary, the family she was placed in after the mother's death had proved able to provide her with the care she needed.[147] The Court seems therefore to accept that, when the biological father has not maintained regular contact with the child, the scope of the positive obligation arising from Article 8 is narrower and, in particular, the State is justified in denying him the opportunity to recognise her.[148]

By way of contrast, when the applicant is considered to have shown 'demonstrable interest in and commitment to the child both before and after the birth',[149] the Court proves more inclined to undertake a stricter review. In the case of *Różański v Poland*, the State's positive obligation to enable the pre-existing family life to flourish is extended to a situation where the parents' wishes were not in agreement: in particular, the mother did not support the applicant's wish to be recognised as the child's legal father, as she had rather allowed her new partner to be recognised as such. The Court emphasised as relevant for the assessment of the case that the child was born out of a four-year cohabitation with the mother and the applicant had not only made several attempts to have his paternity recognised,[150] but also lived with the child for approximately two years before she was acknowledged by the mother's new partner. The lack of any procedure directly accessible to the applicant failed therefore to ensure effective respect of his family life and, 'even having regard to the margin enjoyed by the State',[151] amounted to a breach of Article 8. Both *Yousef* and *Różański* show, therefore, how substantive considerations and, in particular, the Court's understanding of how a legal father should behave can influence the extent to which positive obligations are applied to the specific case and, more generally, the intensity of review.

In more recent case-law, in addition to this correlation between substance and doctrine, the intensity of review becomes – at least, more visibly – also dependent on the width of the margin of appreciation enjoyed by the State in this field. In *Shavdarov v Bulgaria*, the children's paternity had been established in favour of their mother's husband as she was still married to him when

---

[146] Ibid, § 65.
[147] Ibid.
[148] Draghici, *Legitimacy of Family Rights*, p. 101.
[149] *Różański v Poland*, no. 55339/00, § 64, 18 May 2006.
[150] Ibid.
[151] Ibid, § 79.

she began living with the applicant. The latter had not only cohabitated with the mother for thirteen years, but had also taken care of the children after the mother left with her new partner.[152] Despite qualifying the father–child relationships as 'family life' and, as a following step, asserting the State's positive obligation to enable those ties to develop, the Court eventually focused on the absence of interference and emphasised that the existence of the de facto mono-parental family formed by the applicant and his three children had never been threatened by the authorities or the children's mother and her husband.[153] It was therefore concluded that the legal impossibility of having biological paternity established did not breach the applicant's right to respect for family life.

Two main factors were relied on to justify the lenient review undertaken by the Court, one relating to the Court's understanding of fatherhood and the other doctrinal.[154] First, emphasis was placed on the applicant's lack of diligence. In particular, the Court underlined that the applicant had not availed himself of the alternative routes to formally establish his paternal tie – such as adoption – as well as of other options – such as applying for a residence order – to alleviate the difficulties arising from the informal nature of their ties, made available by the legal framework.[155] Second – and this constitutes a novelty in this stream of case-law – the doctrine of the margin of appreciation is openly granted a decisive role in the reasoning and the award of a certain degree of discretion in the regulation of paternal affiliation appears well grounded. In particular, the Court notes that, apart from raising various moral, ethical, social and religious considerations, a comparative survey of the legislation of twenty-four Contracting States indicates the absence of a shared approach on whether a biological father should be permitted to challenge the presumption of a husband's paternity.[156]

---

[152] *Shavdarov v Bulgaria*, §§ 41 and 43.
[153] Ibid, § 56.
[154] In addition to these two factors explicitly referred to in the text of the judgment, however, also the unconventional family model provided by the applicant might have indirectly influenced the Court's approach to positive obligations and the outcome of the case. As described by the Court, the applicant and his children formed a 'de facto mono-parental family' (§ 50). Especially if compared with *Kroon and Others v the Netherlands*, this circumstance might have – in addition to the applicant's passivity – contributed to a more careful consideration of the scope of positive obligation in the present case. See Kilkelly, 'Protecting Children's Rights', 254.
[155] *Shavdarov v Bulgaria*, §§ 51–5.
[156] Ibid, § 47. While in eight States, the biological father was granted such right, the legislation of ten other States did not provide for the same right. In four countries, moreover, this right can be exercised only when the social reality does not correspond to the legal reality, while in two

This new attention directed to the margin of appreciation characterises also the judgments in *Ahrens v Germany* and *Kautzor v Germany*, where the applicants were precluded from contesting paternity because of the social relationship existing between the child and her legal father. In both cases, the Court excludes that Article 8 implies a duty to enable the biological father to challenge the legal father's status.[157] In justifying the finding of no violation, it relies on a comparative survey and observes that the majority of Contracting States allowed the presumed biological father to contest the paternity of another man established by acknowledgment even where the legal father lived with the child in a social and family relationship, while in a minority of nine States the biological father had no standing to contest the paternity of the legal father.[158] From this, the Court concluded that, despite 'a certain tendency' across Europe towards allowing the alleged biological father to contest the legal father's paternity, 'no settled consensus' – which would significantly restrict the margin – appeared to exist.[159] Apart from the wide margin enjoyed by the State in this field, the Court's decision to undertake a rather lenient review might have been influenced by the total correspondence of legal paternity and social fatherhood.[160] As such, *Ahrens* and *Kautzor* further exemplifies the precarious position reserved to biological fathers when the child is raised by his legal father[161] and the employment of care as a criterion to settle the tension between otherwise equally 'conventional', but competing father figures.

These two judgments, moreover, signal the adoption of a heightened qualitative threshold to qualify as 'family life' and, at the same time, a more decisive role attributed to paternal care. Even if placed on an equal footing as the nature of the relationship between the biological parents, in *Ahrens* and *Kautzor* as well as in later jurisprudence, paternal care tends to either be the

---

jurisdictions, it was up to the public authorities to take up a challenge on behalf of the biological father.

[157] *Ahrens v Germany*, no. 45071/09, § 74 24 September 2012.; *Kautzor v Germany*, no. 23338/09, § 77 22 March 2012.

[158] *Ahrens v Germany*, § 69; *Kautzor v Germany*, § 71.

[159] *Ahrens v Germany*, § 70; *Kautzor v Germany*, § 72. In the case of *Kautzor*, the same conclusion was reached with respect to the decision not to allow the applicant to establish his alleged paternity without changing the child's legal status (§ 79).

[160] As noted by the Court itself when differentiating between *Mizzi v Malta* and *Ahrens v Germany*: 'Mr M.'s legal paternity coincided with his factual role as the child's social father' (§ 74).

[161] Coester-Waltjen, 'The Impact of the European Convention', p. 87; E. Farnós Amorós, 'Biology-Based Systems of Parentage and Safety Valves Protecting Social Parenting' in M. González Pascual and A. Torres Pérez (eds.), *The Right to Family Life in the European Union* (Routledge, 2016), p. 122.

only factor actually taken into consideration[162] or, if pointing to different directions, to trump the inter-parental relationship in the assessment of family life. This is well exemplified by *Kautzor* where, even if the Court noted that the applicant was married to the child's mother at the time of conception, it was rather influenced by the lack of any previous contact with the child[163] and found no family life. Overall, therefore, in its more recent case-law, the Court seems to endorse a more engaged and, at the same time, realistic – as opposed to idealistic or optimistic – vision of fatherhood and, as a result, is more likely to examine the complaint as pertaining to the sphere of private life. Circumstances – such as the fact that the applicant had accompanied the mother throughout pregnancy and expressed his intention to take care of the child before birth,[164] had undergone a DNA test proving his biological paternity[165] or, more generally, had attempted to bring an action aimed at establishing his paternity[166] – are deemed insufficient signs of commitment to bring the relationship within the scope of family life.[167] What is required is actual contact and a close personal relationship between the applicant and the child and, whenever those conditions are absent, the Court does not look for the underlying causes by delving into the specific circumstances of the case.[168]

The intensified requirement of care and the more solidly grounded recognition of a wide margin of appreciation to the State go hand and hand and push in the same direction: that is expecting more from biological fathers willing to obtain the full paternal status and, at the same, loosening the State's obligation to ensure effective respect of the applicant's private and family life. Alongside these two developments, we should not lose sight of the concomitant categorisation of the more recent cases as pertaining to private life, as a further element potentially translating into a more lenient scrutiny. The finding of 'family life' brings with it the imposition of the positive obligation to enable the existing ties to develop. Regardless of the latter's variability in scope, therefore, proceeding under the limb of 'family life' is more likely to trigger the requirement for the State to take positive action to ensure effective respect of that family life. In this stream of case-law, therefore, an increased doctrinal sensitivity and a more rigorous evaluation of paternal care fruitfully intertwine

---

[162] See *Marinis v Greece*, § 55.
[163] *Kautzor v Germany*, § 62. Prior to this case, see *Nylund v Finland*, p. 14.
[164] *L.D. and P.K. v Bulgaria*, nos. 7949/11 and 45522/13, § 55, 8 December 2016.
[165] Ibid.
[166] *Ahrens v Germany*, § 59.
[167] See also *Marinis v Greece*, where no family life was found on the basis that the applicant had apparently never seen or developed emotional ties with the child, certainly not during the paternity proceedings (§ 57).
[168] Draghici, *Legitimacy of Family Rights*, p. 266.

and give shape to a construction of fatherhood that, in addition to the 'conventional' element of either biology or (pseudo-)marriage, requires some sort of paternal involvement.

3 CONCLUSIONS

In this domain, the Court has proved prepared to overcome stereotypical images of unmarried fathers by accepting that they might be genuinely interested and able to take care of their children and by promoting the idea that paternal care, in addition to financial provision, might serve the child's best interests. Against this general message, however, the meaning attached to paternal care in each case appears to vary across three distinct but sometimes overlapping criteria. First, as anticipated above, the marital status of the applicant – i.e., whether he is an unmarried or a divorced father – is likely to impact the Court's expectations towards him. Whilst in paternity proceedings brought by unmarried fathers, their interest and commitment tend to be scrutinised against their direct relationship with the child, when faced with a request for disavowal of paternity raised by a divorced father, the Court seems to be satisfied with the applicant's diligent behaviour in legal proceedings.

The second influencing factor is the legal position sought by the applicant. In particular, when the latter applies for parental rights, the Court seems to be satisfied with assessing the potential of the father–child relationship – rather than its reality – and, therefore, gives due regard to the fact that its development might be obstructed by external parties. The same readiness and – to a certain extent – blind trust towards the claims of unmarried fathers, however, does not shine through the jurisprudence on establishment of paternity. In those cases where the applicant seeks to be recognised as the child's legal father – especially in more recent ones – the Court in fact requires evidence of concrete ties and, therefore, grounds its assessment of family life and its proportionality analysis on a (more) realistic – as opposed to aspirational – vision of fatherhood. The third and final factor influencing the evaluation of paternal care is the position of the competing father figure vis-à-vis the child's mother. More specifically, in situations where the adoptive or otherwise social father is married to the child's mother, the biological unmarried father willing to oppose non-consensual adoption or to establish his own paternity is required to demonstrate a higher threshold of paternal care.

Interestingly, therefore, the increased attention devoted to the 'new' element of paternal care reveals the persisting force of a marital understanding of fatherhood. All three variables eventually indicate the Court's willingness to keep the marital family intact and, as a consequence, to facilitate the preservation of the father–child tie through marriage or, at least, to keep the inter-parental relationship as a criterion for testing the true commitment of unmarried fathers towards their children. Therefore, although separation and even extra-marital childbirth suggest cracks in the conventional family model, the Court's approach can be seen as part of a broader legal tendency to extend the rights and responsibilities of marriage to those relationships that most closely reproduce the marital family.[169] In fatherhood terms, the allocation of the full paternal status as well as of parental rights is extended beyond the marital family, but it benefits primarily those who most closely resemble some features of the 'conventional' father figure. Moreover, in cases where there are two competing father figures, the focus on paternal care uncovers another trait of continuity in as much as it is used as a parameter against which the Court indirectly identifies the more meritorious one. Although possibly influenced by the antagonistic nature of the disputes at stake, therefore, the Court does not display any effort in accommodating the practical dimension of 'fragmenting fatherhood' into the legal domain.

If it is true that fatherhood continues to be constructed as mediated and unitary, at the same time, the Court takes distance from 'conventional fatherhood' by reducing the role traditionally attributed to biology. Apart from being insufficient – as the Court made explicit in *Lebbink v the Netherlands* – the existence of a biological link has, throughout time, possibly become even irrelevant in granting parental rights or the full status of legal father. When faced with two conflicting father figures, the rule followed by the Court seems to be that, if there is a more caring father, his claim should prevail over that of the biological father.[170] In a similar vein, by taking into consideration the applicant's diligence when dealing with cases of disestablishment, the Court tends to maintain the child's legal position anchored to the marital family as much as possible, even if there is a divergent biological reality. Therefore, not only has biology failed to replace marriage in grounding legal fatherhood, but it has progressively lost ground to a more engaged, but yet marriage-related conception of fatherhood.[171]

---

[169] Collier and Sheldon, *Fragmenting Fatherhood*, p. 203.
[170] Farnós Amorós, 'Biology-Based Systems', p. 121.
[171] See also *Nazarenko v Russia*, no. 39438/13, ECHR 2015 (Extracts), where the complete and automatic exclusion of the applicant (a divorced father) from the child's life after it was established he was not his biological father was found in violation of Article 8. The Court held that Article 8 can be interpreted 'as imposing on Member States an obligation to examine on a case-by-case basis whether it is in the child's best interests to maintain contact with a person, whether biologically related or not, who has taken care of him or her for a sufficiently long period of time' (§ 66).

Finally, rather than stemming from consistent and methodologically sound doctrinal paths, the above understanding of fatherhood appears to be mainly the consequence of a predetermined moral position. In other words, it is the applicant's resemblance to fatherhood – as constructed by the Court – that contributes to moulding the ways in which doctrines, in particular positive obligations, are applied in each case, and not vice versa. The jurisprudence on non-consensual adoption and paternity establishment, in particular, shows that the influence of a marital construction of fatherhood and the relevance attributed to paternal care, respectively, might go as far as to penetrate the proportionality analysis and to impact the extent to which positive obligations are held applicable. The doctrine of positive obligations has therefore, in this context, served as an expedient to facilitate the Court's achievement of a moral agenda that could not otherwise be easily sustained by consistent doctrinal choices.

5

Fatherhood and Family–Work Reconciliation

1 WOMEN IN THE WORKPLACE AND CONVENTIONAL FATHERHOOD

This chapter tracks the Court's attachment to and/or departure from 'conventional fatherhood' in the context of family–work reconciliation.[1] Historically, fatherhood has been understood as profoundly tied to employment. In as much as it enables a father to secure adequate housing and financial support for his family,[2] employment represents, in fact, the 'way of meeting the expectations of the providing facet of fatherhood'.[3] Although constructed as a sign of commitment and, thus, as an expression of paternal love, however, employment is also likely to alienate fathers from the realm of family life and, therefore, to hinder the development of emotional ties with their children.[4] These dynamics are, at the same time, the cause and the effect of a gendered division of labour that considers breadwinning as the essence of the paternal role and childcare as the primary responsibility of mothers.[5]

In recent decades, however, all major industrialised societies have witnessed an increased participation of women in the labour market. This phenomenon

---

[1] This chapter develops an earlier contribution to *Revaluing Care in Theory, Law and Policy: Cycles and Connections (ed. Harding, Fletcher & Beasley, Routledge: 2017)*.

[2] N. Townsend, *The Package Deal: Marriage, Work, and Fatherhood in Men's Lives* (Temple University Press, 2004), p. 78.

[3] Ibid, p. 130.

[4] A. C. Crouter, M. F. Bumpus, M. R. Head, S. M. McHale, 'Implications of Overwork and Overload for the Quality of Men's Family Relationships', *Journal of Marriage and Family*, 63 (2001), 404–16.

[5] Williams explains that such division of labour rests on the 'ideology of domesticity', according to which 'men "naturally" belong in the market because they are competitive and aggressive; women belong in the home because of their "natural" focus on relationships, children, and an ethic of care'. See J. Williams, *Unbending Gender: Why Family and Work Conflict and What to Do about It* (Oxford University Press, 2000), p. 1.

has marked the decline of the male breadwinner/female carer model[6] and, therefore, given rise to family dynamics that break from 'conventional fatherhood' in two significant and interrelated ways. First, breadwinning ceases to be a paternal prerogative and, in line with a broader climate of change around fatherhood, the image of the father as a mere breadwinner is increasingly juxtaposed and confronted with that of the father as an active participant in the everyday family life.[7] Second, women's changed employment patterns are therefore also responsible for a particular dimension of 'fragmenting fatherhood' that results in the split of the conventional paternal feature of breadwinning – not between two or more men, as in the other domains – but rather between men and women. In this context, therefore, the fragmentation of fatherhood consists in the practical disaggregation of a gendered division of labour: economic provision and childcare stop being two separate roles performed by people of different sex, but rather become – albeit to a varying extent – shared responsibilities between men and women.

If it is true that the male breadwinner model has been mainly supplanted by a dual-earner model in the public sphere, gender imbalances have remained almost untouched in the private sphere: indeed, even if men's engagement in unpaid care work has slightly increased, women's time remains more tied up in domestic and childcare activities than does men's.[8] Therefore, what has been mainly altered by the decline of the breadwinner model is women's working behaviour, as they tend to face a double burden of domestic and market work.[9] This 'incomplete revolution'[10] is attributable, inter alia, to a widespread understanding of family–work reconciliation as a 'women- only

[6] J. Lewis, 'The Decline of the Male Breadwinner Model: Implications for Work and Care', *Social Politics*, 8(2) (2001), pp. 152–69; S. Harkness, 'The Household Division of Labour: Changes in Families' Allocation of Paid and Unpaid Work' in J. Scott, S. Dex and J. Wadsworth (eds.), *Women and Employment: Changing Lives and New Challenges* (Edward Elgar, 2008), pp. 234–67.
[7] T. Johansson and J. Andreasson, *Fatherhood in Transition: Masculinity, Identity and Everyday Life* (Palgrave Macmillan, 2017), p. 4.
[8] See, inter alia, G. Ellison, A. Barker and T. Kulasuriya, *Work and Care: A Study of Modern Parents* (Equality and Human Rights Commission, 2009), online at https://dera.ioe.ac.uk/11 030/1/15._work_and_care_modern_parents_15_report.pdf (last access on 15 February 2019).
[9] A. R. Hochschild, *The Second Shift* (Penguin Group, 2003).
[10] G. Esping-Andersen, *Incomplete Revolution: Adapting Welfare States to Women's New Roles* (Polity Press, 2009). See also A. Hochschild and A. Machung, *The Second Shift: Working Parents and the Revolution at Home* (Viking Penguin, 1989), p. 11; J. Scott and E. Clery, 'Gender Roles: An Incomplete Revolution?' in A. Park, C. Bryson, E. Clery, J. Curtice and M. Phillips (eds.), *British Social Attitudes: The 30th Report*, online at http://www.bsa.natcen.ac.uk/media/38723/bsa30_full_report_final.pdf (last access on 15 February 2019); N. Fraser, *Fortunes of Feminism: From State-Managed Capitalism to Neo-Liberal Crisis* (Verso Books, 2013).

issue"[11] and, therefore, as mainly directed to ameliorating the working conditions of women employees with scant regard given to the private sphere of parenthood and, more specifically, of fatherhood.[12]

The law has certainly played a role in bringing about and perpetuating such asymmetry.[13] The attempt to secure maternity rights has been at the heart of decades of struggles for women's equality. Despite supporting women in the experience of maternity and childbirth thus taking their gendered lives into account, the specific-rights approach has also been considered to produce negative effects. By treating pregnancy and maternity as a continuum,[14] it might result in reinforcing and entrenching – rather than dislodging – women's responsibility for childcare.[15] This objection has been raised especially with respect to the European approach to family–work reconciliation. Although the making of some portion of maternity leave compulsory[16] has served to regulate the employee–employer relationship by protecting workers from downward pressure to keep their leave as short as possible,[17] special entitlements for maternity have inevitably improved the competitive advantage of those who are not eligible, *in primis* fathers.

This is especially so given that – to date – there is no sister directive on paternity leave at the European Union level[18] and, in all European States, the

---

[11] E. Caracciolo di Torella and A. Masselot, *Reconciling Work and Family Life in EU Law and Policy* (New York: Palgrave Macmillan, 2010), p. 53.

[12] C. McGlynn, *Families and the European Union: Law, Policy and Pluralism* (Cambridge University Press, 2006), p. 87; S. Fredman, 'Reversing Roles: Bringing Men into the Frame', *International Journal of Law in Context*, 10(4) (2014), 443; E. Ruspini and I. Crespi, 'Editors' Introduction: Men, Fathers, and Work-Family Balance – An Exploration across Continents' in E. Ruspini and I. Crespi (eds.), *Balancing Work and Family in a Changing Society: The Fathers' Perspective* (Palgrave, 2016), p. 3. The intersections between fatherhood, work–life balance and gender are a subject that is underexplored in academic scholarship. Apart from Ruspini and Crespi's edited collection, another significant exception is provided by R. Collier's recent work on fatherhood in the legal profession: R. Collier, 'Fatherhood, Gender and the Making of Professional Identity in Large Law Firms: Bringing Men into the Frame', *International Journal of Law in Context*, 15(1) (2019), 1–20.

[13] See K. O'Donovan, *Sexual Divisions in Law* (Weidenfeld & Nicolson, 1985), Chapter 1.

[14] Fredman, 'Reversing Roles', 449.

[15] Fredman, *Women and the Law* (Clarendon Press, 1997), 192; J. Suk, 'From Antidiscrimination to Equality: Stereotypes and the Life Cycle in the United States and Europe', *American Journal of Comparative Law*, 75 (2012), 79.

[16] At the EU level, the Directive 92/85/EEC of 19 October 1992 ('On the Introduction of Measures to Encouraging Improvements in the Safety and Health at Work of Pregnant Workers and Workers Who Have Recently Given Birth or Are Breastfeeding') requires all States to provide for at least fourteen weeks of paid maternity leave, two of which are compulsory.

[17] J. Suk, 'Are Gender Stereotypes Bad for Women? Rethinking Antidiscrimination Law and Work–Family Reconciliation', *Columbia Law Review*, 110(1) (2010), 53.

[18] See, however, European Commission, *Proposal for a Directive of the European Parliament and of the Council on Work–Life Balance for Parents and Carers and Repealing Council Directive*

duration of maternity leave is significantly longer than paternity leave.[19] The assumption that the mother, rather than the father, is the primary caregiver to a newborn child is also reflected in some parental leave schemes. As it will be shown by the case-law analysed, until not long ago, some legal systems provided for parental leave allowances to be paid only to mothers – thus excluding fathers – on the ground that a similar distinction mirrored the outlook of society and, therefore, the distribution of roles at the time. Even today, in those jurisdictions in which parental leave is not framed as an individual entitlement, fathers' actual opportunity to take it might be contingent upon, for instance, the mother's position in paid work.[20] The risk of 'crystallising historically embedded gender norms',[21] thus precluding fathers from the possibility of being either entitled or required to undertake equal caretaking responsibilities, lies therefore also with respect to policies framed in gender-neutral terms.

Some European countries have distinguished themselves for their proactive policies to enhance fathers' nurturing role and, more generally, for their particularly strong capacity for adapting to the weakening of the male breadwinner norm.[22] In Sweden, which possibly remains the most well-known example of this approach, the law offers 480 days of parental leave per child that can be shared between the parents according to their individual preferences, with the exception of at least three 'use-it-or-lose-it' months that are reserved to each parent. Despite achieving its short-term goal of increasing fathers' take-up rates, the discrepancy in leave between mothers and fathers remains wide.[23] Most importantly, there seems to be no evidence that fathers who claim more parental leave actually engage more in

2010/18/EU (COM/2017/253), 26 April 2017, online at https://eur-lex.europa.eu/legal-content/EN/TXT/?uri=CELEX%3A52017PC0253 (last access on 14 February 2019).

[19] For detailed information about maternity leave and paternity leave currently available in EU States, see U. Jurviste, M. Prpic and G. Sabbati, 'Maternity and Paternity Leave in the EU', *European Parliamentary Research Service Infographic*, December 2016, online at http://www.europarl.europa.eu/RegData/etudes/ATAG/2016/593543/EPRS_ATA%282016%29593543_EN.pdf (last access on 14 February 2019).

[20] Eurofound, *Parental and Paternity Leave – Uptake by Fathers* (Publications Office of the European Union, 2019), online at https://euagenda.eu/upload/publications/untitled-199581-ea.pdf (last access on 15 February 2019), pp. 20–21. In the UK, for instance, fathers are entitled to shared parental leave only if the mother of their child is entitled to maternity leave.

[21] R. de Silva de Alwis, 'Examining Gender Stereotyping in New Work/Family Reconciliation Policies: The Creation of a New Paradigm for Egalitarian Legislation', *Duke Journal of Law and Policy*, (2010–2011), 306.

[22] B. Hobson and D. Morgan, 'Introduction' in B. Hobson (ed.), *Making Men into Fathers – Men, Masculinities and the Social Politics of Fatherhood* (Cambridge University Press, 2002), p. 3.

[23] Swedish Social Insurance Agency, *Social Security in Figures 2017*, online at https://www.forsakringskassan.se/wps/wcm/connect/6fa0e434-a212-4e6b-8c8d-5d7a498a253d/socialforsakringen-i-siffror-2017-engelsk.pdf?MOD=AJPERES&CVID= (last access on 15 February 2019).

childcare.[24] Therefore, although the image of the father as caregiver has certainly become hegemonic in Swedish society and even before in the law, not even 'compulsory fatherhood' by granting fathers an exclusive right to a portion of parental leave has proved sufficient to produce more engaged fathering practices.[25]

Although statistics support the notion that, even when at their disposal, parental leave is not yet fully exploited by fathers,[26] existing case-law displays also another dimension of contemporary fatherhood: that of men who would like to take time off work to care for their children in their first years of life or even to be their primary caretakers, yet they might have to face legal obstacles due to deeply ingrained gender stereotypes underlying the formulation of the law. Similar stories have crossed national borders and reached Strasbourg, thus providing the Court with the chance to rethink fatherhood beyond economic provision and, accordingly, to reconceptualise care as not necessarily maternal. Particularly emblematic of the Court's (re-)positioning in the debate around paternal involvement in childcare is the case-law stemming from the exclusion of fathers from social security schemes aimed at supporting newborn children and those responsible for raising them. As it will be shown, such exclusion is based on provisions that are clearly informed by 'sex-role stereotypes' – namely, those stereotypes that describe the 'proper roles of men and women not by reference to individuals' personality traits, but by the type of conduct desirable for each sex'.[27] It follows that, in this context – perhaps more than in others – the Court's departure from a conventional understanding of

---

[24] J. Ekberg, R. Eriksson and G. Friebel, 'Parental Leave – A Policy Evaluation of the Swedish "Daddy-Month" Reform', *Journal of Public Economics*, 97 (2013), 142. Statistical data suggest that fathers tend to avail of parental leave mostly during summer months and around Christmas. In such context, parental leave risks not supporting the underlying ideology of participatory fathering, and is instead used as a means of prolonging a vacation with the child's mother. Moreover, mothers predominantly take the transferrable portion of leave. See The Tavistock Institute, *Shared Parental Leave to Have Minimum Impact on Gender Equality*, May 2014, online at http://www.tavinstitute.org/news/shared-parental-leave-minimal-impact-gender-equality/ (last access on 13 May 2015).

[25] H. Bergman and B. Hobson, 'Compulsory Fatherhood: The Coding of Fatherhood in the Swedish Welfare State', in B. Hobson (ed.), *Making Men into Fathers – Men, Masculinities and the Social Politics of Fatherhood* (Cambridge University Press, 2002), p. 93.

[26] Eurofound, *Parental and Paternity Leave*, p. 23. Three main obstacles have been identified: first, the design and feature of the leave (especially, the compensation rate and flexibility); second, the perceived scant support of the employer; third, fathers' lack of eligibility to take the leave and receive compensation (p. 19).

[27] D. Gans, 'Stereotyping and Difference: Planned Parenthood v Casey and the Future of Sex Discrimination Law', *Yale Law Journal*, 104 (1994–1995), 1877. See also R. Ashmore and F. Del Boca, 'Conceptual Approaches to Stereotypes and Stereotyping' in D. Hamilton (ed.), *Cognitive Processes in Stereotyping and Intergroup Behaviour* (Erlbaum Associates, 1995), p. 21.

fatherhood depends considerably on its anti-stereotyping efforts and, in particular, on its ability to uncover and contest the generalised view that men should be the primary breadwinners, whilst women should be mothers and homemakers.

2 CHILDCARE-RELATED ENTITLEMENTS FOR FATHERS AND THE ECTHR: ONE STEP AT A TIME

Family–work reconciliation and, more specifically, the grant of childcare-related entitlements is a relatively recent area of intervention of the Court. After the earliest case of *Petrovic v Austria*, which was settled in 1998,[28] this issue was brought to the attention of the Court again in 2009 and, since then, only two judgments have contributed to discussing and, to some degree, to advancing the roles of fathers in the early stages of a child's life: *Weller v Hungary*[29] and *Konstantin Markin v Russia*.[30] All three cases originate from the application of an 'unconventional' father who is denied a leave or an allowance that would enable him to take time off work to look after his newborn child, as a consequence of legal provisions that reserve the sought measure to mothers and/or other categories of caretakers. The legal question that runs through this jurisprudence is, therefore, whether the exclusion of fathers from social security schemes directed to support all those responsible for raising newborns amounts to a violation of Article 14 taken in conjunction with Article 8. Although Article 8 does not guarantee a right to parental leave or related benefits, these measures are considered to fall within its scope because, by allowing one of the parents to stay home and take care of the child, they promote family life and influence the way it is organised.[31]

As early as 1998, the Court was of the opinion that, 'whilst being aware of the differences which may exist between mother and father in their relationship with the child', mothers and fathers are 'similarly placed' as far as the role of looking after a child is concerned.[32] Despite sharing the same starting point

---

[28] *Petrovic v Austria*, 27 March 1998, Reports of Judgments and Decisions 1998-II.
[29] *Weller v Hungary*, no. 44399/05, 31 March 2009.
[30] *Konstantin Markin v Russia* [GC], no. 30078/06, ECHR 2012 (Extracts). On the different – but related – issue of child benefits, see *Okpisz v Germany*, no. 59140/00, 25 October 2005 and *Niedzwiecki v Germany*, no. 58453/00, 25 October 2005. In these cases, the Court found the exclusion of the applicant fathers from child benefits because not in possession of a stable residence permit in breach of Article 14 taken in conjunction with Article 8.
[31] *Petrovic v Austria*, § 29; *Okpisz v Germany*, § 32; *Niedzwiecki v Germany*, § 31; *Weller v Hungary*, § 29; *Markin v Russia* [GC], § 102.
[32] *Petrovic v Austria*, § 36; *Weller v Hungary*, § 33; *Markin v Russia* [GC], § 132. Contrast with *Alexandru Enache v Romania*, no. 16986/12, 3 October 2017, where the Court considers the

and developing along similar doctrinal lines, the three judgments eventually reach opposite outcomes and, therefore, support different constructions of fatherhood. Over a period of fifteen years, the Court's understanding has – indeed – shifted from the conventional image of the father as a mere breadwinner to the model of 'new fatherhood', according to which a father combines his breadwinning functions – rather than abandoning them once for all – with childcare responsibilities through the take-up of parental leave.[33] This evolution has, however, occurred gradually and gone through an intermediate stage in which the Court begins to contemplate, but does not feel prepared yet to openly endorse a more engaged vision of fatherhood.

The reconstruction of fatherhood has therefore gone through three main phases, each of which corresponds to a specific judgment and has clear doctrinal underpinnings. The first coincides with the judgment in *Petrovic*, where the Court shows itself satisfied with mere breadwinning on the ground that, at that time, the majority of Contracting States did not provide for parental leave allowances to be paid to fathers.[34] The second phase is represented by the judgment in the case of *Weller*: here, the Court takes advantage of the 'magnifying effects'[35] of Article 14 to extend the prohibition of discrimination to cover also those rights that are voluntarily provided for by the State, and eventually holds the exclusion of fathers from childcare-related benefits incompatible with the Convention. The explicit overcoming of a gendered division of labour and the endorsement of the complex image of the 'new father', however, is accomplished only when a wide international consensus on granting parental leave and related entitlements to fathers could be established. In the landmark case of *Markin v Russia*, which occupies the third and final phase, the Court contests the man-breadwinner/woman-homemaker stereotype as an insufficient ground for justifying a difference in treatment

---

special nature of maternity and the special bond that exists between the mother and a child in its first year of life sufficient to justify differential treatment between male and female offenders with respect to the possibility of deferring the starting date for serving the sentence until the child's first birthday.

[33] A similar turn has also occurred in the jurisprudence of the Court of Justice of the European Union. See Fredman, 'Reversing Roles', p. 453; E. Caracciolo di Torella, 'Brave New Fathers for a Brave New World? Fathers as Caregivers in an Evolving European Union', *European Law Journal*, 20(1) (2014), 102–104.

[34] *Petrovic v Austria*, para 39.

[35] O. M. Arnardóttir, 'Discrimination as a Magnifying Lens – Scope and Ambit under Article 14 and Protocol No. 12' in E. Brems and J. Gerards (eds.), *Shaping Rights in the ECHR – The Role of the European Court of Human Rights in Determining the Scope of Human Rights* (Cambridge University Press, 2013), pp. 337–8.

between men and women,[36] and openly advocates for the participation of fathers in childcare through the use of parental leave. In this jurisprudential domain, therefore, the relationship between the construction of fatherhood and doctrines is exceptionally straightforward: the doctrinal path undertaken by the Court is 'determinative of'[37] its revised understanding of what it means to be a father. The following sections are devoted to analyse each of the abovementioned three phases in detail.

2.1 Restating Conventional Fatherhood

In the earliest case of *Petrovic v Austria*, the applicant – a student, working part time – took parental leave to look after his newborn child, while his wife – already employed full time – carried on working. At the core of his application is the denial of parental leave allowance on the ground that, under the Unemployment Benefit Act 1977, only mothers could benefit from it.[38] Before the Strasbourg organs, therefore, he alleged to be the victim of discrimination on the grounds of sex in breach of Article 14 taken in conjunction with Article 8. Despite acknowledging the similar position of mothers and fathers vis-à-vis the need to take care of a child in the period of parental leave, this judgment eventually accepts a gendered division of labour and, in so doing, reduces fatherhood to just breadwinning. The failed departure from 'conventional fatherhood' is, at it will be shown, the consequence of two interrelated doctrinal dynamics: the prevalence of the alleged – although not grounded on comparative materials – lack of a European consensus over the 'suspect' ground of discrimination as a determinant of the intensity of scrutiny[39] and the absence of an anti-stereotyping approach or, at least, mentality on the part of the Court.

---

[36] *Markin v Russia* [GC], § 43. It should be noted that, despite the trend in fighting stereotypes observed in Chapter 4, the Court never used the word 'stereotype' with respect to the claims of unmarried fathers. Rather, it preferred to talk about 'general considerations' (*Sahin v Germany*, no. 30943/96, §§ 58–59, 11 October 2001), 'general feature' (*Zaunegger v Germany*, no. 22028/04, § 56, 3 December 2009), and 'general legal assumption' (*Schneider v Germany*, no. 17080/07, § 100, 15 September 2011).

[37] P. Johnson, *Homosexuality and the European Court of Human Rights* (Routledge, 2013), p. 82.

[38] The law was subsequently amended. As of 1 January 1990, a father is entitled to a parental leave allowance on condition that he is employed, he is the primary caretaker and the child lives under the same roof. Moreover, the mother must either be entitled to parental leave and have waived that right in whole or in part or, if not entitled, to be unable to look after her child as a result of employment.

[39] S. Haverkort-Speekenbrink, *European Non-Discrimination Law – A Comparison of EU Law and the ECHR in the Field of Non-Discrimination and Freedom of Religion in Public Employment with an Emphasis on the Islamic Headscarf Issue* (Intersentia, 2012), p. 169.

Having established the applicability of Article 14 taken in conjunction with Article 8, the Court begun by carefully differentiating between maternity leave and parental leave: while the former was defined as primarily designed 'to enable the mother to recover from the fatigue of childbirth and to breastfeed her baby if she so wishes', parental leave was understood to cover the subsequent period and 'to enable the beneficiary to stay home to look after the infant personally'.[40] Although mothers and fathers were therefore 'similarly placed' with respect to the latter, the decision to reserve parental leave allowance to mothers was considered not to exceed the State's margin of appreciation. In determining the strictness of review, the Court had to take two influencing factors – pointing to opposite conclusions – into account: on the one hand, the 'suspect' nature of sex as a ground of discrimination that demands 'very weighty reasons' for a differential treatment to be held compatible with the Convention;[41] on the other hand, the lack of a common standard in the field of parental leave that, on the contrary, requires a wide margin of appreciation to be left to the State.[42] Although mentioned, the 'very weighty reasons' test was, in fact, never applied. The Court acknowledged the advancement of gender equality as a major goal in the Contracting States, but nevertheless proceeded to place greater emphasis on those circumstances justifying a rather lenient scrutiny.[43]

In particular, it noted that, at the end of the 1980s, there was no shared approach in this area, as most jurisdictions reserved a right to parental leave allowance only to mothers.[44] The extension of similar allowances to fathers – the Court added – occurred gradually, in conjunction with an increasingly equal sharing of childcare responsibilities between men and women.[45] This evolution had also taken place within the Austrian legal system, where fathers were recognised the right to parental leave in 1989 and became eligible for the associated allowance in 1990.[46] The Court found it difficult, therefore, to condemn the Austrian government for having extended parental leave measures to fathers in a progressive manner, especially given that the amended legislation was very forward thinking in Europe.[47] Indeed, in the Court's view, even at the time of the Strasbourg proceedings, there remained a great

---

[40] *Petrovic v Austria*, § 36.
[41] Ibid, § 37.
[42] Ibid, § 42.
[43] O. M. Arnardóttir, *Equality and Non-Discrimination under the European Convention on Human Rights* (Martinus Nijhoff, 2003), p. 119.
[44] *Petrovic v Austria*, § 39.
[45] Ibid.
[46] Ibid, § 41.
[47] Ibid.

disparity between the laws of the Contracting States: while parental leave had been made increasingly available to fathers, the latter had access to the related allowances only in a few States.[48] Hence, the exclusion of the applicant father from the sought allowance was considered not to breach Article 14 taken in combination with Article 8.

Apart from impacting the strictness of review, the absence of a uniform approach seems to have dissuaded the Court from assuming an anti-stereotyping attitude. Although not acknowledged, it is clear that the Austrian legislation was grounded on the implicit sex-role stereotype of women as mothers and homemakers and men as primary breadwinners. Indeed, the extent to which the reality of parenthood is actually gendered and, accordingly, gender-neutral parenting reflects only an aspirational view of fatherhood are irrelevant considerations to determine whether a generalised view can be classified as a stereotype.[49] As long as one's needs, wishes, abilities and circumstances are not attached any weight, any generalisation applied to him/her will eventually reach the threshold of stereotyping, even if it describes the actual position of the individual concerned.[50] Nonetheless, in the Court's mind, the legal realities of the Contracting States were not yet sufficiently convergent to question the environment of legitimacy and normalcy around legislation excluding fathers from parental leave allowances.[51] As a result, the Court ended up perpetuating the man-breadwinner/woman-homemaker stereotype implicit in the Unemployment Benefit Act 1977 with the de facto result of supporting a 'conventional' construction of fatherhood.

This judgment seems, indeed, to convey the message that a father cannot afford to stay at home and receive no remuneration because he is expected to financially provide for his family. If, on the one hand, this cautious attitude might express the legitimate concern not to push the interpretation of the Convention too far beyond national choices, on the other hand, what makes it potentially problematic is the absence of any comparative analysis of domestic laws that substantiates their claimed divergence. This inaccurate approach to the identification of European consensus, coupled with the latter's clear prevalence over the 'suspect' ground, might trigger doubts as to the potentially

---

[48] Ibid, § 42.
[49] R. Cook and S. Cusack, *Gender Stereotyping – Transnational Legal Perspectives* (University of Pennsylvania Press, 2010), p. 11.
[50] Ibid.
[51] On the role played by the (non-)existence of a common ground in the development of the case-law on suspect discrimination ground, see O. M. Arnardóttir, 'The Differences That Make a Difference: Recent Developments on the Discrimination Grounds and the Margin of Appreciation under Article 14 of the European Convention', *Human Rights Law Review*, 14 (2014), 649–52.

selective use of doctrines to support a predetermined moral position on fatherhood. However, if regard is given to the development of the case-law in this field, the failure to quote comparative data is more likely to be just an instance of doctrinal inaccuracy – quite common in the Court's early case-law[52] – with no strategic purpose.

Yet, the judgment in *Petrovic* remains a milestone in the Court's path towards 'new fatherhood' because of the dissenting opinion of the Judges Bernhardt and Spielmann. Different from the majority, they adopted a critical attitude towards the justifications submitted by the State and made two rather succinct but meaningful points that constitute the crux of the reasoning guiding the following two judgments. First, they expressly acknowledged that discriminating against fathers reproduces a traditional distribution of family responsibilities and, in so doing, it eventually has negative effects also on the mother: indeed, if parents choose an 'unconventional' arrangement whereby the mother continues her professional career and the father stays at home, the family loses ipso facto the allowance to which it would be entitled if the mother took time off from work.[53] Second, despite accepting the lack of a uniform practice in Europe, the dissenting judges expressed the view that, when choosing to grant additional rights, States are not permitted to do so in a discriminatory manner and, taken to a further extent, 'traditional practices and roles in family life alone' may not be invoked to justify differential treatment between mothers and fathers.[54] Their opinion will eventually prove prophetic and the judgment in *Weller* acted as a bridge in its final journey to the stage of majority.

2.2 Contemplating 'New Fatherhood'

In the case of *Weller v Hungary*, the first applicant, a Hungarian national, married a Romanian citizen, who gave birth to their twin sons, the second and third applicants. The first applicant applied for maternity allowance in his own name and on behalf of his children. His request was rejected as, according to the Family Support Act, only mothers with Hungarian citizenship, adoptive parents and guardians were entitled to the benefit in question and a natural father could only request such an allowance if the mother died. To justify its refusal, the Regional Court explained, inter alia, that 'the purpose of

---

[52] K. Dzehtsiarou, *European Consensus and the Legitimacy of the European Court of Human Rights* (Cambridge University Press, 2015), pp. 40–41.
[53] *Petrovic v Austria*, Joint Dissenting Opinion of Judges Bernhardt and Spielmann.
[54] Ibid.

maternity benefit was to support the mother and not the entire family or the children'.[55]

On the contrary, the applicants – and, more importantly, the Court – were of the opinion that, given the wide range of potential beneficiaries, the nature of the allowance was primarily financial and, rather than aiming only at 'reducing the hardship of giving birth sustained by the mother', it was more generally directed to support newborn children and the whole family raising them.[56] Therefore, just as in *Petrovic*, the Court was called upon to decide whether excluding fathers from benefits connected to childcare – in relation to which, both parents are similarly placed – constituted a discrimination contrary to Article 14, taken in conjunction with Article 8.[57] However, given that adoptive parents and guardians – regardless of their sex – were not excluded from the maternity benefits in question, the Court stated that the differential treatment suffered by the applicant father was more connected to his parental status, than to his sex.[58]

Apart from approaching the discrimination claim under a different ground, in *Weller*, the Court reached the opposite outcome: it refused – even if only implicitly – to accept a justification that is informed by a stereotyped perception of the group to which the applicant father belongs. What led to the finding of a violation appears to be the Court's willingness to extend the scope of its review to cover the right to maternity benefits, although not guaranteed by Article 8. Through *Weller*, indeed, part of the dissenting opinion expressed by Judges Bernhardt and Spielmann in *Petrovic* became majoritarian: despite acknowledging that Contracting States continued to enjoy a certain margin of appreciation in shaping their social security systems, the Court held that the absence of a common European approach did not free them from the responsibility to grant these allowances without discrimination.[59] In this specific case, given that the Hungarian government had spontaneously gone beyond its obligations by creating a right to maternity benefits, the latter fell within the wider ambit of Article 8 with the effect that its provision must be grounded on eligibility criteria compatible with Article 14. Since no reasonable and objective justification could be found, the Court

---

[55] *Weller v Hungary*, § 12.
[56] Ibid, § 30.
[57] The applicants contended also that the refusal to grant the benefit to the children as a result of their mother's nationality, even if they were Hungarian nationals by birth, amounted to a difference in treatment compared with other Hungarian children. The Court agreed and found a breach of Article 14 taken in conjunction with Article 8.
[58] *Weller v Hungary*, § 33.
[59] Ibid, § 34.

concluded that excluding natural fathers from a scheme aimed at supporting all those taking care of newborns breached Article 14, in conjunction with Article 8.[60]

The ultimate outcome of *Weller* is, therefore, that of refusing the misconception that fathers are unwilling and unable to take care of their children, thus implicitly challenging a gendered division of labour. Despite reaching the 'right' conclusion, however, the Court missed the opportunity to unpack the meaning of the legal provision in question, to dig more deeply into the reasons behind the exclusion of natural fathers from such benefit and, as a further step, to spell out the potential adverse consequences of undue (since not related to either pregnancy or childbirth) specific rights. By failing to undertake an explicit anti-stereotyping analysis, the Court delivers an outcome that departs from 'conventional fatherhood' only indirectly and whose effect is therefore limited to contemplating – rather than pushing for – a more equal sharing of childcare responsibilities between men and women.

Whilst breaking – although not yet vocally – from *Petrovic* in a substantive sense, however, this ruling shows consistency from a doctrinal perspective. It confirms, indeed, the existence of a certain correlation between the Court's understanding of fatherhood and doctrines, in particular the role played by the latter in reshaping the former in this strand of case-law. The 'magnifying effects' of Article 14 seem indeed to have empowered the Strasbourg judges to undertake a strict(er) review, despite the persisting (alleged) absence of a uniform approach in the field of family allowance schemes. The employment of Article 14 to cover also additional rights has therefore spared the Court from having to uphold conservative national legislation in the name of the States' margin of appreciation, thus smoothing its path towards 'new fatherhood'.

2.3 Pushing for 'New Fatherhood'

The implicit *ratio decidendi* behind the finding of a violation in the case of *Weller* became an integral part of the reasoning in the judgment of *Konstantin Markin v Russia*. In this case, the applicant was a military serviceman and father of three children. Following his divorce with the mother, the couple agreed that the three children would live with their father, while the mother would pay child support. His children being very young at that time, Mr Markin applied for three years' parental leave but his request was denied because, according to the provisions of the Military Service Act, a leave of

---

[60] Ibid, § 35.

such duration could only be granted to military servicewomen. When rejecting the applicant's claim that this amounted to sex discrimination, the Russian Constitutional Court explained that: '[B]y granting, on an exceptional basis, the right to parental leave to servicewomen only, the legislature took into account, firstly, the limited participation of women in military service and, secondly, the special role of women associated with motherhood.'[61]

The Grand Chamber concluded that a distinction on the basis of sex with respect to parental leave entitlements amounts to a violation of Article 14, taken in combination with Article 8. This judgment represents the logical continuation of the case-law thus far analysed from both substantive and doctrinal viewpoints. On the wake of *Weller*, indeed, the Court refuses the conventional image of the father as a breadwinner with no engagement in the upbringing of children, but this time explicitly. The adoption of a revised definition of fatherhood that openly contests a gendered division of labour is, in turn, presented as the consequence of two distinct, but interrelated doctrinal developments. First, in line with *Petrovic*, the Court's reasoning attests to the decisive weight attached to the existence of a shared common ground towards extending parental leave to fathers as a factor influencing the width of the margin of appreciation and, consequently, the intensity of review. Different from the previous cases, however, in *Markin*, European consensus is accurately identified on the basis of a comparative and international law survey undertaken by the Court.

Second, vis-à-vis changed social and legal realities, the Court feels ready to undertake an anti-stereotyping analysis. The perception – acquired through European consensus – that the man-breadwinner/woman-homemaker stereotype has become acknowledged as particularly harmful, across Europe and internationally, empowers the Court to tackle it and to be vocal about the negative consequences of stereotyping, thus making the normative content of Article 14 more explicit than in *Weller*.[62] Apart from evolving at the same pace as European consensus, therefore, the Court's (re-) definition of fatherhood goes hand in hand with increased doctrinal accuracy in identifying consensus and, more generally, with greater clarity in illustrating the need for applying strict scrutiny.

When examining the government's argument relating to the special role of women in the upbringing of children, the Court considered it impossible not to take note of the evolution that society had undergone since its judgment in

---

[61] *Markin v Russia* [GC], § 34. Although the argument pertaining to the limited participation of women in the armed forces is imbued with gender stereotyping as much as the first, the present analysis engages only with the 'motherhood' argument, as it is more relevant to decipher the Court's understanding of fatherhood.

[62] Arnardóttir, 'Differences That Make a Difference',654.

Petrovic.⁶³ Special emphasis was placed on an increased convergence between domestic legislation: in the majority of Contracting States, including Russia, parental leave entitlements had been made available to both mothers and fathers (in twenty-eight out of the thirty-three States considered) and, more importantly, to both servicemen and servicewomen (in twenty-three out of thirty-three States considered).⁶⁴ In the Court's view, this was an unequivocal sign that contemporary European societies had gradually moved towards a more equal sharing of childcare responsibilities between men and women and that, most importantly, men's caring role had gained recognition.⁶⁵ As a result, the position upheld in *Petrovic* was considered no longer tenable as its basic underlying argument reflected a vision of the roles of men and women that, although held true for several years and decades, had become obsolete.

In addition to invoking the existence of a widespread consensus in the field of parental leave, the reasoning insists on gender stereotyping as both the cause and the effect of discrimination against fathers. Indeed, through *Markin*, also the second part of the dissenting opinion raised by Judges Bernhardt and Spielmann in the case of *Petrovic* reaches the stage of majority. This judgment displays what Arnardóttir calls a 'social-contextual approach' to Article 14.⁶⁶ In other words, in addressing the applicant's discrimination claim, the Court adds an express reference to social context, thus connecting the individual case to the wider implications that the provisions of the Military Service Act have for 'women's career and men's family life'.⁶⁷ Differently from the case-law involving unmarried fathers and possibly due to the ambiguity surrounding the applicant's family situation,⁶⁸ however, the Court does not attempt to prove the untenability of sex-role generalisations through references to the specific circumstances of the applicant – for instance, by emphasising his engagement in childcare as a single father after his divorce with the children's mother. Rather, it develops an abstract anti-stereotyping reasoning that might give the impression to support the award of parental leave

---

63   *Markin v Russia* [GC], § 140.
64   Ibid.
65   Ibid.
66   Arnardóttir, 'Differences That Make a Difference', 663.
67   *Markin v Russia* [GC], § 141.
68   After the Chamber's judgment, new relevant circumstances emerged that casted doubt over the accuracy of the factual account initially provided: as submitted by the government, Markin had remarried his former wife in April 2008, they had a fourth child together in August 2010 and, apparently, they had never ceased living together. *Markin v Russia* [GC], § 41.

to fathers on the grounds of an aspirational – as opposed to realistic – vision of fatherhood.[69]

As a first step, the Grand Chamber clarified that, rather than qualifying as a measure of positive discrimination (as argued by the government), the effect of excluding military servicemen from parental leave was that of perpetuating the generalised view of men as primary breadwinners and women as primary childcarers.[70] Second, the Grand Chamber acknowledged the double harm of gender stereotyping.[71] In other words, rather than stopping – as the Chamber did – at exposing how servicemen are affected by stereotypes in this case, it sheds light on the other side of the coin: that is, how stereotypes place the burden of childcare on women and, therefore, restrict women's access to professional careers and their quality.[72] Third, and most importantly, the Court is explicit in contesting the man-breadwinner/woman-homemaker stereotype as insufficient justification for differential treatment[73] and, accordingly, concludes that a violation of Article 14, taken in conjunction with Article 8, had occurred. Through these steps, therefore, the Court clarifies the significance of sex as a 'suspect' ground of discrimination as a further – in addition to European consensus – influencing factor of the width of the margin of appreciation and, more generally, contributes to making the rationale for undertaking a strict review more explicit than before.[74]

Although the majority does not go as far as to envisage States' positive obligations in the field of parental leave,[75] this judgment remains ground breaking as it attempts to 'challenge the deeply ingrained gender roles and gendered ideology on which society is based'.[76] It does so by piercing through

---

[69] J. Wallbank, '(En)Gendering the Fusion of Rights and Responsibilities in the Law of Contact' in J. Wallbank, S. Choudhry and J. Herring (eds.), *Rights, Gender and Family Law* (Routledge, 2009), pp. 116–17.

[70] *Markin v Russia*, para 141.

[71] J. Williams and N. Segal, 'Beyond the Maternal Wall: Relief for Family Caregivers Who Are Discriminated against on the Job', *Harvard Women's Law Journal*, 26 (2003), 79.

[72] Ibid.

[73] Ibid, para 143.

[74] Arnardóttir, 'Differences That Make a Difference', 652.

[75] This is, however, suggested by Judge Pinto De Albuquerque, in his partly concurring opinion. In his view, the establishment of a wide international consensus should be further interpreted as signaling a new understanding of the right to parental leave as an integral component of the right to respect for family life and, therefore, as a Convention right itself. As a result, States are – according to Pinto De Albuquerque – under the obligation to provide for parental leave policies. See A. Mowbray, *The Development of Positive Obligations under the European Convention on Human Rights by the European Court of Human Rights* (Hart, 2004), pp. 180–1.

[76] A. Timmer, 'Toward an Anti-Stereotyping Approach for the European Court of Human Rights', *Human Rights Law Review*, 11(4) (2011), 712.

the gender stereotype that men are not caring and their role is only in the market.[77] By refusing that references to traditional division of roles between men and women can form justification to exclude fathers from the right to parental leave, it promotes the idea that fathers are able to nurture children as much as mothers. In so doing, the Court embraces the ideology of 'new fatherhood', which presupposes an overlap of the traditionally gendered roles – care and breadwinning – and is achievable through effective work–family balance.

Essentially, what determined the overruling of *Petrovic* and, therefore, the Court's departure from 'conventional fatherhood' is a changed significance of the suspect ground of discrimination for the intensity of scrutiny that, in turn, is contingent on the complete formation of a European common ground in the field of parental leave. While in *Petrovic*, the Court watered down the 'very weighty reasons' test by granting a wide margin of appreciation to the State on the ground of the absence of a shared approach, in *Markin*, the existence of a European consensus enabled the 'suspect' ground of discrimination to effectively play a role in determining the width of the margin, and resulted in the undertaking of a more rigorous scrutiny. Hence, whilst taking the opposite direction from a substantive perspective, *Markin* shows doctrinal consistency and, more specifically, confirms the Court's reliance on European consensus as 'productive of'[78] a revised understanding of fatherhood in the field of childcare-related entitlements.

3 CONCLUSIONS

In the face of women's enhanced participation in paid employment, the Court has fully seized the opportunity to promote a concomitant increased involvement of men in childcare. In the case-law concerning the exclusion of fathers from childcare-related entitlements, the image of the 'new father', who combines economic provision with caring responsibilities through the take-up of parental leave, has indeed gradually supplanted the 'conventional' image of the father as a mere breadwinner. In so doing, the Court contests a gendered division of labour and, even further, calls for the extension of parental leave to fathers as a means of enhancing a more equal distribution of childcare and breadwinning responsibilities between mothers and fathers. Its departure from

---

[77] A. Timmer, 'From Inclusion to Transformation: Rewriting *Konstantin Markin v Russia*' in E. Brems (ed.), *Diversity and European Human Rights: Rewriting Judgments of the ECHR* (Cambridge University Press, 2012), p. 157.
[78] Johnson, *Homosexuality and the ECtHR*, p. 88

'conventional fatherhood' is therefore twofold: apart from (and by) including care in its redesigned construction, it accepts a particular dimension of the fragmentation of fatherhood.

This transformation at the substantive level has been accompanied and, even, facilitated by a symmetrical shift at the doctrinal level. The driving force behind the Court's redefinition of fatherhood lies, indeed, in the progressive establishment of a widespread consensus towards the extension of childcare-related entitlements to fathers. More specifically, the (non-)existence of consensus worked as an empowering tool in the Court's jurisprudence in two distinct, but connected ways. First, by influencing the width of the margin of appreciation enjoyed by the State and, consequently, the standard of review undertaken by the Court. This first effect of consensus becomes particularly visible if we compare the decisions in *Petrovic* and *Markin*. While the absence of a shared approach on the issue under scrutiny led to a lenient assessment in *Petrovic*, in the case of *Markin*, the government no longer enjoyed a wide margin of appreciation and, therefore, the Court felt justified to undertake a stricter scrutiny because the disputed distinction had by then become generally disapproved of.

Second, apart from increasing the likelihood of finding a violation, the existence of a common ground has also impacted the type of reasoning used by the Court to substantiate such conclusion. In other words, it has enabled the Court to rely on changed social and legal realities in order to use the Convention as a means of combating gender stereotypes and, therefore, of asserting a new definition of fatherhood untied from the man-breadwinner/woman-homemaker stereotype. This second type of influence exercised by consensus emerges from the transition from *Weller* to *Markin*. In the latter, as a by-product of the existence of a European consensus, the Court felt prepared to take an openly critical attitude towards the justifications put forward by the State, thus making the anti-stereotyping reasoning implicitly underlying the finding of a violation in the case of *Weller* explicit.

The exceptional synchrony between the Court's (re-)construction of fatherhood and doctrines that characterises this strand of case-law can be observed also in the evolution from *Petrovic* to *Weller*. In the latter, indeed, the Court fills the gap between the lack of a common ground in the 1980s and the establishment of a wide international consensus in 2012 by extending the prohibition of non-discrimination to the maternity benefits sought by the applicant. The employment of Article 14 as a 'magnifying lens' has therefore allowed the Court to silently depart from a 'conventional' definition of fatherhood as mere breadwinning, even if no common ground could already be found. In so doing, the Court alleviates one of the dangers inherent in (over-)reliance on European consensus: that lies in, as exhibited by *Petrovic*, blindly accepting the currently dominant legal approach even if that means marginalising the most problematic human rights issues.[79] In this jurisprudential domain, therefore, the Court chooses to ground each of the three steps that mark its shift from 'conventional fatherhood' to 'new fatherhood' on a consistent use of its doctrines of interpretation, to avoid being perceived as 'going too far too fast'. While the reliance on consensus has served to prove respectful of national choices, Article 14 in its reinterpreted scope has assisted the Court in making an otherwise radical redefinition smoother and, therefore, easier to receive by national authorities.[80]

---

[79] Arnardóttir, 'Differences That Make a Difference', 652.
[80] P. Mahoney, 'Judicial Activism and Judicial Self-Restraint in the European Court of Human Rights: Two Sides of the Same Coin', *Human Rights Law Journal*, 11(1–2) (1990), 86; J. Fraser, 'Conclusion: The European Convention on Human Rights as a common European endeavour' in S. Flogaitis, T. Zwart and J. Fraser (eds.), *The European Court of Human Rights and Its Discontents – Turning Criticism into Strength* (Edward Elgar, 2013), p. 198.

6

Fatherhood and Homosexuality

1 HOMOSEXUAL FAMILIES AND CONVENTIONAL PARENTHOOD: POINTS OF DISJUNCTURE

In this last jurisprudential chapter, the Court's understanding of fatherhood is tested in what is possibly the most challenging domain: that of homosexuality. Historically, fatherhood and, more generally, parenthood have been inextricably linked to heterosexuality and heteronormativity.[1] Apart from constituting a conventional feature of fatherhood itself, heterosexuality often represents a prerequisite for the existence of other conventional characteristics. As such, the image of homosexual men becoming fathers calls into question basic traditional assumptions about family life, gender and sexuality[2] and, more specifically, departs from the conventional paradigm of fatherhood at multiple levels. First, despite the trend of providing some form of legal recognition to same-sex relationships mainly through civil partnership, the institution of marriage and, most importantly, the rights and benefits associated to it – for instance, adoption rights or access to ARTs – remain mostly reserved for heterosexual couples.[3]

Second, given the 'social infertility'[4] of homosexual couples, also the biological tie between the father and the child characterising 'conventional fatherhood' is likely to be missing. Homosexuals individuals or couples willing

---

[1] E. Lewin, 'Family Values: Gay Men and Adoption in America' in K. Wegar (ed.), *Adoptive Families in a Diverse Society* (Rutgers University Press, 2006), p. 130; D. Berkowitz and W. Marsiglio, 'Gay Men: Negotiating Procreative, Father, and Family Identities', *Journal of Marriage and Family*, 69(2) (2007), 367.

[2] A. I. Lev, 'Gay Dads. Choosing Surrogacy', *Gay and Lesbian Psychology Review*, 7(1) (2006), 726.

[3] For an updated picture of partnership and parental rights of LGBTI individuals and couples in Europe, see ILGA-Europe, https://rainbow-europe.org/#0/8682/0 (last access on 15 February 2019).

[4] 'Social infertility' or 'relational infertility' is linked to relationship status, as opposed to 'clinical infertility' which is due to a medical condition. See W. Lo and L. Campo-Engelstein, 'Expanding the Clinical Definition of Infertility to Include Socially Infertile Individuals and

to become parents can – at least, in principle – choose between two main alternatives, both of which prescind from the biological contribution of either one or both intended parents and therefore lead to scenarios involving more than two individuals fulfilling complementary parental functions. The first parenthood route available to homosexuals is adoption, which – as already ascertained in relation to heterosexual couples – departs from the conventional rule of biology and challenges the bi-parental structure of the conventional family. Apart from cases of single-parent adoption, this becomes particularly evident in cases of second-parent adoption, namely where one's homosexual partner wishes to adopt the former's child born out of his previous heterosexual relationship or via ARTs. In such a scenario, the child will be predictably exposed to a multi-parental environment: two biological and, possibly, legal parents, one of which is also acting as a social parent and an additional social parent – namely the homosexual partner of the resident biological parent who, de jure, might struggle for recognition and remain a legal stranger to the child.

In the ARTs domain, available parenthood routes are unquestionably more limited for gay men, compared to those for lesbians. Whilst lesbians can resort to the relatively uncomplicated and affordable option of donor insemination, the option of resorting to surrogacy in the transition to fatherhood poses great economic barriers and often exposes aspiring fathers to complex interpersonal dynamics and, more generally, to societal views that conceive parenting in heteronormative terms.[5] Similarly, co-parenting arrangements – in which, for instance, a lesbian conceives and gives birth to a child genetically related to a gay man, under the agreement that the child will be raised jointly and, possibly, together with their respective partners – have proved a difficult choice, in light of the emotional challenges they trigger.[6] The prospects of either surrogacy or a co-parenting arrangement remain limited also from a legal perspective, due to all the restrictions surrounding access to ARTs by homosexuals and the uncertain legal consequences they produce whenever

---

Couples' in L. Campo-Engelstein and P. Burcher (eds.), *Reproductive Ethics II – New Ideas and Innovations* (Springer, 2018), pp. 71–83.

[5] On the issues faced by gay men seeking to have children through surrogacy, see A. May and K. Tenzek, '"A Gift We Are Unable to Create Ourselves": Uncertainty Reduction in Online Classified Ads Posted by Gay Men Pursuing Surrogacy', *Journal of GLBT Family Studies*, 12(5) (2016), 430–50; W. Norton, N. Hudson and L. Culley, 'Gay Men Seeking Surrogacy to Achieve Parenthood', *Reproductive BioMedicine Online*, 27 (2013), 271–9.

[6] S. Jennings, L. Mellish, P. Casey, F. Tasker, M. Lamb and S. Golombok, 'Why Adoption? Gay, Lesbian and Heterosexual Adoptive Parents' Reasons for Adoptive Parenthood', *Adoption Quarterly*, 17(3) (2014), 221.

these procreative paths are undertaken abroad. As a result, adoption tends to be a particularly common parenting choice for gay men.

Gay fatherhood breaks from the conventional paradigm in a third way. Men – regardless of their sexual orientation – continue to encounter obstacles in proving their ability to parent as much as childcare continues to be perceived and conceptualised as the domain of women. Gay men's ambition to achieve fatherhood brings such gender scripts into question, in a particularly stark way.[7] It is therefore not surprising that fathers are more likely to be affected by harmful stereotypes about homosexuality and parenting.[8] In addition to arguments challenging the aptitude of gays and lesbians to childrearing, gay fathers have to face the notion that women have stronger caring and parenting abilities than men and, therefore, only the former should be engaged in childcare. Gay fathers are therefore potential victims of 'compounded stereotypes', namely those gender stereotypes that result from the ascription of traits and/or roles based on more grounds and have a disproportionate negative impact on a specific subgroup of men or women.[9]

Due to the above, gay fatherhood and, more generally, homo-parenthood[10] might trigger a fundamental turn in the Court's understanding of what it means to be a parent and on what basis legal parenthood is attributed. This chapter aims therefore to investigate the extent to which heterosexuality continues to shape the Court's jurisprudence involving (prospective) homosexual parents and, more specifically, fathers. Given that the traditional connectors of fathers to children are likely to be missing, the Court is likely to be left with care or caring intentions as the only elements against which assessing the applicants' claim for parenthood. Therefore, in addition to disclosing the Court's attachment or departure from heteronormativity, the case-law on homo-parenthood constitutes a unique opportunity for testing the sufficiency of care and caring intentions in the absence of conventional paternal features.

---

[7] T. Johansson and J. Andreasson, *Fatherhood in Transition: Masculinity, Identity and Everyday Life* (Palgrave Macmillan, 2017), p. 139.
[8] E. Ruspini, *Diversity in family life – Gender, Relationships and Social Change* (Policy Press, 2013), p. 122.
[9] R. Cook and S. Cusack, *Gender Stereotyping – Transnational Legal Perspectives* (University of Pennsylvania Press, 2010), p. 29.
[10] Ruspini defines 'homo-parenthood' as 'denoting a situation in which at least one adult refers to him or herself as homosexual who is or wishes to be a father or mother of at least one child'. See Ruspini, *Diversity in Family Life*, p. 144.

2 THE ECTHR AND HOMOSEXUAL RELATIONSHIPS: A TWO-STAGE DEVELOPMENT

The above points of disjuncture between 'conventional fatherhood' (and, more generally, parenthood) and homosexual families explain why, even in the most broad-minded societies, the inclusion of same-sex couples within a legal framework of the family has only taken place progressively and in a fragmented fashion.[11] A general trend reveals that legal recognition of same-sex couples has gone through – or, is about to go through – two stages of development, in most jurisdictions. The first phase is characterised by the recognition of same-sex couples as couples[12] and implies therefore the extension of partnership rights traditionally conferred on heterosexual couples to their homosexual counterparts. At this stage, the most visible demand for recognition relates to access to the institution of marriage or to a formal marriage-like relationship status, such as civil partnership.[13] The second phase, which is more relevant for current purposes, focuses on the legal recognition of homosexual individuals and couples as parents and, as such, consists in the extension of parental status and parental rights to them.[14] In most European countries, this second dimension of development is still 'on the way'. In spite of a rapid and heightened legal recognition of same-sex relationships, the main differences between marriage and registered partnership laws are likely to concern children-related matters.[15]

The ECtHR jurisprudence on homosexuality displays a similar pattern, at least from a chronological perspective: initially concerned with defining the partnership rights of the applicants, the Court entered the domain of homo-parenthood only in 1999. A similar two-step evolution has concerned also substantive dimensions of the Court's approach to homosexuality. The initial

---

[11] M. Jänterä-Jareborg, 'Parenthood for Same-Sex Couples – Scandinavian Developments' in K. Boele-Woelki and A. Fuchs (eds.), *Legal Recognition of Same-Sex Relationships in Europe – National, Cross-Border and European Perspectives* (Intersentia, 2012), p. 91.

[12] Ibid, 92.

[13] On the formalisation and legal consequences of same-sex marriages and partnerships in European countries, see Part I of K. Boele-Woelki and A. Fuchs (eds.), *Legal Recognition of Same-Sex Relationships in Europe – National, Cross-Border and European Perspectives* (Intersentia, 2012); otherwise, for a less recent but world-wide perspective, see R. Wintemute and M. Andenaes (eds.), *Legal Recognition of Same-Sex Partnerships – A Study of National, European and International Law* (Hart, 2001).

[14] Jänterä-Jareborg, 'Parenthood for Same-Sex Couples', p. 92.

[15] N. Polikoff, 'Recognising Partners but Not Parents/Recognising Parents but Not Partners: Gay and Lesbian Family Law in Europe and the United States', *New York Law School Journal of Human Rights*, 17 (2000–2001), 712.

'privatisation of homosexuality'[16] has made room for the subsequent development of the 'family life' limb of Article 8 in the terrain of homosexuality. The Court has for a long time understood homosexuality as an essentially private manifestation of human personality and, therefore, has failed to analyse a wide array of matters relating to same-sex relationships through the lens of family life.[17] Up until 2010, the Court – and before the Commission – had repeatedly excluded that the emotional and sexual relationship of a same-sex couple constituted family life – even in cases of long-term cohabitation – in contrast to its own jurisprudence involving unmarried families.[18] Furthermore, it had even declared discrimination on grounds of sexual orientation compatible with Article 14, in light of 'the special protection to be afforded to the traditional family'.[19]

The Court's heteronormative definition of family life was left unquestioned for almost three decades, until when the Court accepted that a same-sex couple is capable of establishing family life for the purposes of Article 8 in the landmark decision of *Schalk and Kopf v Austria*.[20] Taking account of the 'rapid evolution of social attitudes towards same-sex couples' that had occurred in many Member States over the previous decade, the Court considered it 'artificial' to confirm the position that, different from a heterosexual couple, a homosexual couple cannot enjoy 'family life' for the purposes of Article 8.[21] Having regard to this very specific point, this judgment was therefore perceived as a milestone in the process of ensuring equal enjoyment of family rights to homosexual couples by signalling the adoption of a more consistent approach to non-traditional families and alleviating the pre-existing hierarchy between unmarried heterosexual couples and their homosexual counterparts.[22] *Schalk and Kopf* marked therefore the beginning of a second phase in the Court's approach to homosexual families that, in more recent years, has gone even further by extending the definition of 'family life' under

---

[16] P. Johnson, *Homosexuality and the European Court of Human Rights* (Routledge, 2013), p. 120.
[17] See P. Johnson, '"An Essentially Private Manifestation of Human Personality": Constructions of Homosexuality in the European Court of Human Rights', *Human Rights Law Review*, 10 (2010), 67–97.
[18] *X. and Y. v the United Kingdom*, no. 9369/81, Commission Decision of 3 May 1983, p. 221; *C. and L.M. v the United Kingdom*, no. 14753/89, Commission Decision of 9 October 1989, 'The Law', § 1; *Mata Estevez v Spain* (Dec.), no. 56501/00, 'The Law', ECHR 2001-VI.
[19] *C. and L.M v the United Kingdom*, § 2.
[20] *Schalk and Kopf v Austria*, no. 30141/04, ECHR 2010.
[21] Ibid, §§ 93–94.
[22] L. Hodson, 'A Marriage by Any Other Name? *Schalk and Kopf v Austria*', *Human Rights Law Review*, 11(1) (2011), 174–5; N. Bamforth, 'Families but Not (Yet) Marriages? Same-Sex Partners and the Developing European Convention "Margin of Appreciation"', *Child and Family Law Quarterly*, 23 (2011), 137.

Article 8 to include parent–child relationships developed in a homosexual household.[23] However, the revolutionary potential of *Shalk and Kopf* was dramatically reduced, not only by the lack of any definition of the elements that entailed the finding of 'family life' in the case under scrutiny,[24] but especially by the 'untouchable, almost sacred'[25] qualities attributed to marriage. As to the issue of whether access to marriage was a prerequisite to the applicants' effective enjoyment of their family life, the Court affirmed that the Convention could not be interpreted as imposing an obligation on Contracting States to grant same-sex couples access to marriage.[26]

The legacy of *Schalk and Kopf* is particularly visible in the following jurisprudence, including that on homo-parenthood. The Court has taken a rather (internally) consistent, albeit ambivalent, approach to the discrimination experienced by same-sex aspiring parents. On the one hand, it has proved reluctant to consider the situation of a homosexual couple comparable to that of a married heterosexual couple for the purposes of considering alleged discrimination under Article 14. Where rights are reserved to married couples, and homosexual couples have no right to contract marriage, it has been made clear that differences in treatment between married heterosexual couples and unmarried homosexual couples – for instance, in respect of the adoption of a child or the registration of the birth of a child – do not amount to discrimination under Article 14 taken in conjunction with Article 8.[27] On the other hand, when the rights in question are available to unmarried heterosexual couples, complaints about alleged discrimination on the grounds of sexual orientation are likely to succeed. This represents therefore a third dimension of the two-stage development characterising the Strasbourg case-law in this domain. Differently from the two forms previously identified, however, the Court is still very much stuck at the first phase: aspiring homosexual parents are protected against discrimination on the grounds of sexual orientation only in as far as they are denied rights granted to unmarried heterosexual couples.

The Court's jurisprudence on homo-parenthood herein analysed can be divided in three periods, which reflect also the arrival of three different issues

---

[23] *Gas and Dubois v France*, no. 25951/07, § 37, ECHR 2012; *X and Others v Austria* [GC], no. 19010/07, § 96, ECHR 2013; *Boeckel and Gessner-Boeckel v Germany* (Dec.), no. 8017/11, § 27, 7 May 2013.
[24] Bamforth, 'Families but Not (Yet) Marriages?', 137.
[25] Hodson, 'A Marriage by Any Other Name?', 177.
[26] *Shalk and Kopf v Austria*, § 63; *Hämäläinen v Finland* [GC], no. 37359/09, § 71, ECHR 2014; *Oliari and Others v Italy*, nos. 18766/11 and 36030/11, § 192, 25 July 2015.
[27] *Gas and Dubois v France*, § 68; *X and Others v Austria*, § 108; *Boeckel and Gessner-Boeckel v Germany*, § 31.

at the Court's premises.[28] In *Salgueiro da Silva Mouta v Portugal*, the Court had to deal with the refusal of parental responsibility to a homosexual man living with another man.[29] Up until that case, the Court had refused to investigate the discrimination complaint brought by homosexual applicants, arguing that the issues raised under Article 14 had already been considered by finding a violation of Article 8.[30] The judgment in *Salgueiro da Silva Mouta v Portugal* signalled, therefore, a change in the Court's attitude by formally adding sexual orientation to the list of grounds protected by Article 14[31] and, according to some,[32] by further asserting homosexuality as a 'suspect' classification that requires 'very weighty reasons' before a distinction can be justified.

In the following two cases, *Fretté v France*[33] and *E.B. v France*[34], the issue at stake was the exclusion of single homosexuals from the right to seek authorisation to adopt. Given their similar factual accounts, the contrast between the two opposite findings reached by the Court – coupled with the reasoning employed – offers the chance to compare the legal treatment accorded to lesbian and gay single prospective adoptive parents, respectively, and therefore sheds light on the persistence of a gendered division of labour in the Court's construction of fatherhood. Finally, the third issue that has come to the Court's attention is access to second-parent adoption by homosexual couples.

---

[28] In recent years, three additional issues related to homo-parenthood reached the Court's premises: the refusal to include a woman registered as the mother's civil partner on the birth certificate of a child born through sperm donation and co-raised since his birth (*Boeckel and Gessner-Boeckel v Germany*); the refusal to allow a same-sex couple to have a child through artificial insemination (*Charron and Merle-Montet v France* (Dec.), no. 22612/15, 8 February 2018); and, the refusal to grant joint exercise of parental responsibility to two women, living as a couple, each of whom had a child born as a result of ARTs (*Bonnaud and Lecoq v France* (Dec.), no. 6190/11, 1 March 2018). All applications were declared inadmissible. In the first case, the Court considered that the applicants were not in a relevantly similar situation to a married husband and wife in respect of the entries made in the birth certificate at the time of childbirth. While the application of Ms Charron and Ms Merle-Montet failed for non-exhaustion of national remedies, in *Bonnaud and Lecoq v France*, the Court held that the assessment made by domestic courts did not disclose any differential treatment on the ground of sexual orientation. See also *R.F. and Others v Germany* (no. 46808/16, Pending) concerning the refusal to acknowledge a genetic mother's legal motherhood with respect to a child born to her same-sex civil partner through sperm donation.

[29] *Salgueiro da Silva Mouta v Portugal*, no. 33290/96, ECHR 1999-IX.

[30] C. Nikolaidis, *The Right to Equality in European Human Rights Law – The Quest for Substance in the Jurisprudence of the European Courts* (Routledge, 2015), pp. 58–9.

[31] *Salgueiro da Silva Mouta v Portugal*, § 28.

[32] O. M. Arnardóttir, *Equality and Non-Discrimination under the European Convention on Human Rights* (Martinus Nijhoff, 2003), pp. 153–4; J. Gerards, *Judicial Review in Equal Treatment Cases* (Martinus Nijhoff, 2005), p. 207.

[33] *Fretté v France*, no. 36515/97, ECHR 2002-I.

[34] *E.B. v France* [GC], no. 43546/02, 22 January 2008.

Although both stemming from the application of a lesbian couple, the judgments in *Gas and Dubois v France*[35] and *X and Others v Austria*[36] contribute to providing the bigger picture regarding the tenacity of heterosexuality as an essential parameter of legal parenthood, and offer interesting insights as to the persistence of a heteronormative understanding of marriage within the Court's jurisprudence.[37]

While the relationships of homosexual fathers with their biological children find unquestionable support in the Strasbourg jurisprudence, sexual orientation remains a potential barrier for prospective parents wishing to adopt a child or to formalise their social ties with the biological child of their homosexual partner. In fact, despite the expansion of the scope of 'family life' to incorporate homosexual relationships, the case-law that follows does not generally advance the position of homosexual (aspiring) parents – as well as of the children potentially involved – to any considerable extent. Marriage continues to be an insurmountable obstacle to fighting discrimination on the grounds of sexual orientation.[38] Intentions and care are valued only to the extent that they are provided by an otherwise conventional father, homosexuality aside. Rather than having solid doctrinal underpinnings, the preservation of such conventional understanding appears mostly a matter of choice. This is not to say that the doctrines of interpretation relied on by the Court have not played any role in hindering a departure from 'conventional fatherhood'; but, rather, that they seem to have been deliberately used in a variable manner to advance the Court's moral positions on gay fatherhood.

2.1 Homosexual Fathers and Their Biological Children

The Court entered the delicate terrain of homo-parenthood only in 1999 and, due to the particular circumstances of the case, it was rather a smooth/progressive entrance. In the case of *Salgueiro da Silva Mouta v Portugal*, the applicant is a man who became a father in the context of a heterosexual marriage and began living in a homosexual relationship only after divorce. Despite admitting that 'no doubt is being cast on the father's love for his daughter and ability to look after her', the Lisbon Court of Appeal concluded that 'a young child needs the care which only the mother's love can provide'

---

[35] *Gas and Dubois v France*, no. 25951/07, ECHR 2012.
[36] *X and Others v Austria* [GC], no. 19010/07, ECHR 2013.
[37] Prior to these two decisions, see *Kerkhoven, Hinke and Hinke v the Netherlands*, no. 15666/89, Commission Decision of 19 May 1992. The Commission declared this application inadmissible by arguing that, for the purposes of Article 14, 'as regards parental authority over a child, a homosexual couple cannot be equated to a man and a woman living together' ('The Law', § 2).
[38] P. Johnson, 'Marriage, Heteronormativity, and the European Court of Human Rights: A Reappraisal', *International Journal of Law, Policy and the Family*, 29 (2015), 57.

and therefore awarded parental responsibility to his former wife.[39] It also referred to his homosexual orientation as 'abnormal'[40] and emphasised that, even if society were becoming increasingly tolerant of homosexuality:

> It cannot be argued that an environment of this kind is the healthiest and best suited to a child's psychological, social and mental development, especially given the dominant model in our society. (...) The child should live in a family environment, a traditional Portuguese family, which is certainly not the set-up her father has decided to enter into, since he is living with another man as if they were man and wife.[41]

The applicant alleged that his request for parental responsibility had been denied exclusively on the ground of his sexual orientation. The ECtHR ruled in his favour, arguing that the different treatment afforded to the applicant amounted to discrimination contrary to Article 14 in conjunction with his right to respect for family life.

In reaching its decision, the homophobic tone of the justifications adduced by the Lisbon Court of Appeal played a crucial role in convincing the Court of the discriminatory nature of the difference in treatment complained of.[42] By referring to the above excerpts of the contested decision, it observed that these were not 'merely clumsy or unfortunate' statements or mere obiter dicta, as suggested by the government, but rather indicated the decisive role attached to the applicant's homosexuality in the final decision.[43] This conclusion was – as the Court itself recognises – further substantiated by the fact that, when ruling on his right to contact, the Lisbon Court of Appeal had advised the applicant not to assume conduct that would make the child, M., understand that he was living with another man in a stable relationship.[44] Therefore, despite being justified by the need to protect the health and rights of the child, the contested decision made a distinction that was not acceptable under the Convention and, therefore, breached Article 8 taken in conjunction with Article 14.

This outcome is – at least prima facie – the expression of the Court's departure from a heterosexual construction of fatherhood. One of the clear messages conveyed is, indeed, that being non-heterosexual per se is not seen as amounting to a lack of fitness for fatherhood. It is argued that both the finding of a violation and the updated construction of fatherhood that derives from it

---

[39] *Salgueiro da Silva Mouta v Portugal*, § 14.
[40] Ibid.
[41] Ibid.
[42] Johnson, *Homosexuality and the ECtHR*, p. 131.
[43] *Salgueiro da Silva Mouta v Portugal*, § 35.
[44] Ibid.

are the consequences of two specific doctrinal moves on the side of the Court: first, its decision to examine the case under Article 14, taken in conjunction with Article 8; second, its (implicit) anti-stereotyping approach.

Starting from the former, this judgment constitutes evidence of one kind of 'magnifying effects' of Article 14.[45] As its very first step, the Court examined the applicability of Article 8 and established that the Lisbon Court of Appeal's decision – just like any decision awarding custody to one or other parent after divorce – amounted to an interference of the applicant's right to respect for family life.[46] Yet, it preferred not to address the complaint under Article 8 in isolation, but to focus on the discriminatory element of the case and, as such, to deal with the subject matter exclusively under Article 14 in conjunction with Article 8. In this case, therefore, the dimension of discrimination operated as an aggravating factor[47] and, therefore, the Court's choice to examine the application under Article 14 in conjunction with Article 8 led to facilitating the finding of a violation and, as a result, the departure from a heterosexual understanding of fatherhood.

Second, what further contributed to (re-)constructing fatherhood is also the Court's willingness to contest the stereotypical perception of fathers and, more specifically, of gay fathers underlying the domestic court's decision. Gender stereotypes undoubtedly formed the cornerstone of the Lisbon Court of Appeal's judgment. As emerging from the above quotes, the refusal of custody to the applicant was heavily informed by two stereotypical notions: the man-breadwinner/woman-homemaker stereotype and the assumption that homo-parenting is not in the child's best interests. Whilst the first falls within the subcategory of sex-role stereotypes, the second embodies a 'compounded stereotype'.[48] In this specific instance, the traits of the applicant as a homosexual man and, therefore, his gender and sexual orientation were compounded in a way that denied him parental responsibility in respect of his daughter.

Despite not talking explicitly of 'stereotypes', the reasoning of the Court clearly reveals its refusal to accept general considerations as a means of adjudicating the allocation of parental rights to homosexuals. And, by denying

---

[45] O. M. Arnardóttir, 'Discrimination as a Magnifying Lens – Scope and Ambit under Article 14 and Protocol No. 12' in E. Brems and J. Gerards (eds.), *Shaping Rights in the ECHR – The Role of the European Court of Human Rights in Determining the Scope of Human Rights* (Cambridge University Press, 2013), p. 336.
[46] *Salgueiro da Silva Mouta v Portugal*, § 22.
[47] Arnardóttir, 'Discrimination as a Magnifying Lens', 336.
[48] R. Cook and S. Cusack, *Gender Stereotyping – Transnational Legal Perspectives* (University of Pennsylvania Press, 2010), p. 29.

any legitimate connection between one's sexual orientation and his/her ability to raise a child, it contributes to challenging the persistence of heterosexuality as a conventional ground for attributing parental rights to biological fathers. This judgment is therefore undoubtedly progressive not only for its outcome, but also for the underlying anti-stereotyping mentality.

At the same time, however, Hodson warns us of its 'limited relevance for children of LGBT families'[49] and, I would add, for gay non-biological fathers. The extent to which the final decision is disconnected from heterosexuality remains indeed to be ascertained. With the exception of his sexual orientation, the applicant embodied the image of the 'conventional father': first, he was the biological father of the child, with respect to whom he applied for parental responsibility; second, he was the ex-husband of the child's mother and M. was born within wedlock; third, as emerging from the Lisbon Court of Appeal's judgment, he could allegedly financially provide for his child.[50] Therefore, although his homosexuality became a barrier to the attribution of parental responsibility, the father–child relationship at stake concerned a child born within wedlock and his biological father and, in light of this, 'the law could not depart too flagrantly from reality'.[51] Hence, the suspicion that, rather than approaching the case as one of homo-parenthood, Mr Salgueiro's complaint was framed as the refusal of parental responsibility to a biological and divorced father.

As reported in the factual account relied on by the Lisbon Court of Appeal,[52] prior to divorce, the applicant had cohabitated with his former wife and M. for almost three years. Moreover, following the lower court's conferral of parental responsibility on the applicant, he had lived with and took care of M. for an additional period of nine months. Furthermore, his caring and parenting abilities had been documented by psychological evidence collected during the proceedings before the lower court and, more importantly, relied on by the same court to rule on the transfer of the parental responsibility of M. from her mother to the applicant. Therefore, although not spelled out by the Court, one could argue that – in the wake of its own jurisprudence pertaining to post-separation parenting – the applicant's demonstrated interest in maintaining contact with his child as well as the

---

[49] L. Hodson, 'Ties That Bind: Towards a Child-Centred Approach to Lesbian, Gay, Bisexual and Transgender Families under the ECHR', *International Journal of Children's Rights*, 20 (2012), 511.
[50] *Salgueiro da Silva Mouta v Portugal*, § 14.
[51] B. Perreau, *The Politics of Adoption – Gender and the Making of French Citizenship* (MIT Press, 2014), p. 68.
[52] *Salgueiro da Silva Mouta v Portugal*, § 14.

existence of close personal ties between them – coupled with his other conventional features – might have played a role in shaping the Court's decision. In such case, the judgment in *Salgueiro* would still depart from 'conventional fatherhood', but in a more limited fashion: heterosexuality is no longer a requirement for someone to be granted parental rights, provided that he is otherwise 'conventional'.

2.2 Single-Parent Adoption: Gays versus Lesbians

In its second jurisprudential period, the Court was called to decide on the issue of suitability of non-heterosexual individuals to obtain an authorisation to adopt children as single applicants. In the case of *Fretté v France*, the applicant was a single homosexual man who, 'despite his clear personal qualities and aptitude for bringing up children' was denied access to adoption on the ground that, due to his 'lifestyle', he was unable to provide the child with a suitable environment from an educational, psychological and family perspective.[53] In the case of *E.B. v France*, which was decided six years later, the same elements crop up: E.B. was refused authorisation to seek adoption in spite of 'her undoubted personal qualities and aptitude for bringing up children'[54] and, therefore, despite being described as possessing all types of capacity needed in an adoptive parent. Different from Mr Fretté, however, the applicant in E.B. was a woman in a stable relationship with a long-term female partner. The justifications adduced by the French authorities were the lack of a paternal role model or referent and the ambiguous attitude of E.B.'s partner, who did not support the adoption plan.

In both cases, the Court acknowledged that the applicant's sexual orientation was consistently at the centre of deliberations and had played a decisive role in determining his/her rejection from the adoption process.[55] Nonetheless, while dismissing Mr Fretté's complaint, it concluded that Ms E.B. had suffered a difference in treatment contrary to Article 14 in conjunction with Article 8. It is argued that, despite appearing the mere consequence of the different doctrinal paths undertaken by the Court in *Fretté* and *E.B.* respectively, these opposite outcomes are also the expression of the Court's own moral position on the issue of adoption by single homosexuals and, in particular, of its understanding of fatherhood that ultimately sustains a gendered division of labour. Hence, just as in the domain of ARTs, this case-law shows that doctrines – and, more specifically, their selective use – are at

---

[53] *Fretté v France*, §16.
[54] *E.B. v France* [GC], § 24.
[55] *Fretté v France*, § 32; *E.B. v France* [GC], § 89.

the same time 'determined by'[56] and 'determinative of'[57] the construction of fatherhood endorsed by the Court.

Whilst differing in its core, the reasoning developed in the two judgments takes its cue from a shared doctrinal starting point: the Court's reliance on Article 14 to magnify the scope of Article 8 and, ultimately, to review a decision that was largely based on stereotyping.[58] It was indeed clarified that Article 8 does not guarantee the 'right to adopt as such' or protect the 'mere desire to found a family' and, therefore, there was no interference with Article 8 taken in isolation.[59] Yet, considering that French law authorised single persons to apply for adoption but disallowed the applicant from doing so on the basis of his sexual orientation, the Court concluded that the facts of the case inevitably fell within the ambit of Article 8.[60] Like explained by the Court itself in *E.B.*, therefore, the majority found Article 8, in conjunction with Article 14, applicable in so far as, by providing the additional right to apply for authorisation to adopt, France had gone beyond its obligations under Article 8 and, as a result, had a duty to implement the single-parent adoption system in a non-discriminatory manner.[61]

After this common premise, the Court's assessment whether the difference in treatment suffered by the applicant was discriminatory took rather opposite directions and the underlying reason lies, most likely, in the Court's inconsistent approach to consensus analysis. While present and at the core of the reasoning in *Fretté*, the (non-) existence of European consensus was never considered in *E.B.* Rather, in the latter, the Court relied on the 'living instrument' doctrine to conclude that the differential treatment of individuals seeking authorisation for adoption on the basis of their sexual orientation amounted to discrimination under the Convention. This poorly justified departure from precedent has given rise to diversified reactions in scholarship: while some commentators have stressed the Court's failure to provide supporting arguments for such radical change of policy,[62] others have found the irrelevance of European consensus justified by the Court's engagement in the moral reading of Convention rights.[63] To be sure, what the comparison

---

[56] Johnson, *Homosexuality and the ECtHR*, p. 82.
[57] Ibid.
[58] Nikolaidis, *The Right to Equality*, p. 61.
[59] *Fretté v France*, § 32; *E.B. v France* [GC], § 41.
[60] *Fretté v France*, § 32; *E.B. v France* [GC], § 49.
[61] *E.B. v France* [GC], § 49. The same point is made by the Joint Partly Dissenting Opinion of Judges Bratza, Fuhrmann and Tulkens in *Fretté v France*, § 1.
[62] I. Curry-Sumner, 'E.B. v France: A Missed Opportunity?', *Child and Family Law Quarterly*, 21 (3) (2009), 363.
[63] G. Letsas, 'The ECHR as a Living Instrument: Its Meaning and Legitimacy' in A. Føllesdal, B. Peters and G. Ulfstein (eds.), *Constituting Europe – The European Court of Human Rights*

between *Fretté* and *E.B.* seems to indirectly reveal is the Court's adherence to a gendered division of labour, and perhaps the potential role of doctrines as 'subservient to'[64] support a conventional understanding of fatherhood in the context of single-parent adoption.

In *Fretté*, the Court considered it 'quite natural' that 'the national authorities ... should enjoy a wide margin of appreciation' when they are asked to make rulings about the suitability of a single gay man, as opposed to a single heterosexual, to adopt a child.[65] To support the latter, it invoked the 'better placed' argument – according to which, given their direct and constant connection with local realities, national authorities are better placed than an international court to assess local needs and conditions[66] – and relied on a mixed form of consensus analysis. Apart from finding little common ground between the laws of the Contracting States,[67] the Court considered expert opinion and, in particular, the division within the scientific community over the possible consequences of a child being adopted by one or more homosexual parents.[68] As a result, it was held that national authorities were legitimately and reasonably allowed to consider that the right to be able to adopt was restricted by the interests of the children eligible for adoption. Given the wide margin of appreciation and the need to protect children's best interests, therefore, the difference in treatment suffered by Mr Fretté was considered not discriminatory within the meaning of Article 14.

The text of the judgment seems therefore to depict the conclusion reached in *Fretté* as the outcome of a consistent application of the doctrine of the margin of appreciation: the lack of consensus resulted in the award of broad parameters of discretion and, as a further consequence, in a lenient – or rather, in this case, almost absent – review. On the one hand, therefore, the emerging attachment to a heterosexual understanding of fatherhood can certainly be viewed as the 'product' of the doctrinal path followed by the Court. In particular, deference led to a problematic outcome because, as noted by the Judges Bratza, Fuhrmann and Tulkens in their Partly Dissenting Opinion, the *Conseil d'Etat*'s refusal was absolute and precluded any real consideration of the situation of the applicant and of the interests at stake.[69] On the other hand,

---

in a National, European and Global Context (Cambridge University Press, 2013), p. 124; Johnson, *Homosexuality and the ECtHR*, p. 87.
[64] Johnson, *Homosexuality and the ECtHR*, p. 88.
[65] *Fretté v France*, § 41.
[66] Ibid.
[67] Ibid.
[68] Ibid, § 42.
[69] Partly Dissenting Opinion of Judges Bratza, Fuhrmann and Tulkens, § 2(c).

however, as it will become clearer from a comparison with the later judgment in E.B., the Court's failure to back up its conclusions as to the lack of a common approach with accurate comparative research,[70] coupled with the missed application of the 'very weighty reasons' test despite the suspect ground of sexual orientation, seem to suggest a rather instrumental recourse to consensus directed to legitimise the endorsement of a 'conventional' construction of fatherhood: that of an heterosexual man, breadwinner, who is unable or unwilling to provide childcare, in a couple.

In the following judgment, *E.B. v France*, the doctrinal path undertaken by the Grand Chamber differs from the reasoning developed in *Fretté* in three distinct ways. First, as one would have expected also in the previous case (on the wake of *Salgueiro*), the Grand Chamber argued that, whenever sexual orientation is in question, there is a need for particularly convincing and weighty reasons to justify a difference in treatment that affects Article 8 rights.[71] Second, it stated that the Convention is a 'living instrument' and, therefore, it has to be interpreted in light of present-day conditions.[72] However, and third, the existence of a presumed consensus across Contracting States on the issue of adoption by homosexual applicants is not discussed at all in the judgment and, therefore, the Court fails to explain the alleged changed conditions underlying the need for dynamic interpretation. In light of the above and given that French law allows for single-parent adoption, the Court concluded that the reasons advanced by the government could not be considered as sufficiently convincing and weighty to justify the refusal to grant authorisation to adopt to Ms E.B. and, therefore, found a violation of Article 14 taken in conjunction with Article 8.[73]

E.B. marked a rapid shift in the case-law that, if considered only in its outcome, might be welcomed as a challenge to the heteronormative structure of kinship[74] and, more generally, to heteronormativity as an organising principle of contemporary social relations and a determinant of social inequalities.[75] At the same time, however, especially because of the abovementioned unjustified

---

[70] To support the alleged disparity of legal approaches, the Court did not more than observing that: 'Although most of the Contracting States do not expressly prohibit homosexuals from adopting where single persons may adopt, it is not possible to find in the legal and social orders of the Contracting States uniform principles on these social issues on which opinions within a democratic society may reasonably differ widely' (§ 41).

[71] *E.B. v France* [GC], § 91.

[72] Ibid, § 92.

[73] Ibid, § 93.

[74] L. Hart, 'Individual Adoption by Non-Heterosexuals and the Order of Family Life in the European Court of Human Rights', *Journal of Law and Society*, 36(4) (2009), 551.

[75] P. Johnson, 'Heteronormativity and the European Court of Human Rights', *Law and Critique*, 23 (2012), 44.

doctrinal inconsistencies, these two judgments – if read in conjunction – seem to understand the role of fathers as limited to breadwinning. Indeed, while in *Fretté*, the Court implicitly accepted the view that to be raised by a single homosexual father would be harmful to the child under any circumstances, in *E.B.* it clarified that a woman seeking to adopt a child cannot be prevented from doing so merely on the basis of her sexual orientation. Even before this, Mr Fretté's qualities and conduct were not at the core of the analysis, either of the French authorities or, more problematically, of the Court. Rather, what was questioned and eventually rejected was the general idea of a single homosexual man raising a child to whom he has no biological or legal connection.[76] In contrast, *in E.B.*, the Grand Chamber chose to refuse the stereotypical notions underlying the *Conseil d'Etat*'s refusal and, just before finding a violation of Article 14 in conjunction with Article 8, it stressed that the applicant possessed 'undoubted qualities and an aptitude for bringing up children', which were certainly compatible with the child's best interests.[77]

Despite the anti-stereotyping attitude characterising *E.B.*, the Court appears to eventually engage in stereotyping itself. In particular, one could argue that sex-role stereotypes, according to which women have stronger nurturing and parenting abilities than men, might have contributed to the success of Ms E.B.'s complaint and, at the same time, to precluding the same positive outcome for a gay single man, like Mr Fretté. In so doing, the Court seems to support a 'conventional' understanding of fatherhood at, at least, two levels. First, it confirms the indispensability of heterosexuality to make someone a potential adoptive father. Second, it replicates a traditional division of labour that, by relying on the image of the male breadwinner, excludes fathers from the domain of childcare.

Apart from being the consequence of divergent doctrinal approaches, therefore, the opposite outcomes in *Fretté* and *E.B.* might also be read as the manifestation of the Court's willingness to restate a 'conventional' construction of fatherhood, where heterosexuality and breadwinning are restated as essential requirements to make someone a potential adoptive father. In light of this, consensus and, as a result, the doctrine of the margin in *Fretté* and the 'living instrument' doctrine in *E.B.* might be better understood as 'a framework through which the Court legitimises'[78] its (moral) understanding of fatherhood. In *Fretté*, the Court insisted on the absence of consensus to withhold Convention rights from a homosexual prospective adopter – more explicitly,

---

[76] Hart, 'Individual Adoption', 549.
[77] *E.B. v France* [GC], para 95.
[78] Johnson, *Homosexuality and the ECtHR*, p. 89.

to deny access to legal fatherhood to a potential 'unconventional' father. Conversely, in *E.B.*, the Court did not consider the issue of consensus at all but nonetheless advanced a dynamic interpretation of Article 8 in order to uphold the complaint of a female applicant who had been refused authorisation to adopt. The different approaches adopted in these two cases eventually show that the extent to which the Court proves ready to trigger rather than to wait for change at the national level and, more specifically, to contest a heteronormative consensus tends to fluctuate also depending on the adherence of the applicant to the paradigm of 'conventional fatherhood'.

2.3 Second-Parent Adoption and the 'Special Status' of Marriage

In its third jurisprudential period on homo-parenthood, the Court was faced with two cases stemming from the refusal to allow a woman living in a stable relationship with a same-sex partner to have her social tie with the latter's biological child recognised through second-parent adoption, without severing the existing mother–child legal relationship. In *Gas and Dubois v France*, the child – who had been conceived through anonymous sperm donation – had lived all her life in the shared home of the applicant civil partners, had been jointly raised by them and had no relationship with the biological father. In *X and Others v Austria*, the applicants had co-parented the child – born out of wedlock from a heterosexual relationship – since he was five years old, but the father maintained regular contact with his son, paid alimony and refused to grant his consent to second-parent adoption.

Despite the partner's demonstrated active involvement in ensuring the child's emotional and material wellbeing and the undisputed existence of concrete family ties among the applicants, both requests for adoption were rejected by domestic courts. The ground given for refusal was that the legal implications of the sought adoption order would not be in the child's best interests because it would entail the transfer of parental responsibility to the adoptive parent while depriving the biological mother of her own parental rights, despite her willingness to continue raising the child. The applicants alleged they had been subject to discriminatory treatment based on their sexual orientation, vis-à-vis both married couples and heterosexual unmarried couples. Ms Gas and Ms Dubois were unable to adopt jointly as a result of an indirect prohibition: in France, the law provides for the sharing of parental responsibility only in cases where the adoptive parent is the spouse of the biological parent and, at the material time, only heterosexual couples were allowed to marry. Austrian law, differently, did extend second-parent adoption to heterosexual unmarried couples, but not to homosexual couples.

This factual difference led to two apparently opposite – but substantially consistent – rulings: while the Court found no violation in *Gas and Dubois*, in the following case, the Grand Chamber concluded that Austrian law gave rise to a difference in treatment based on sexual orientation that was contrary to Article 14 taken in conjunction with Article 8, but only in as far as the rights in question were available to unmarried heterosexual couples. Although both complaints were brought by lesbian couples, this case-law contributes to clarifying the extent to which heterosexuality remains at the core of the Court's wider construction of parenthood. The message conveyed is, although consistent with the Court's practice, rather ambiguous: while a situation where a child can have two legal parents of the same sex is ultimately endorsed in *X and Others*, marriage – in its heteronormative meaning – is supported as the ideal locus for parenthood to the detriment of homosexual couples. Homosexuality per se, therefore, is no longer an obstacle to creating parent–child relationships worthy of Article 8's protection, even less a legitimate justification for differential treatment. Yet, it continues to hinder the legal recognition of these ties as a consequence of the privileged position reserved for married couples, and of the Court's inconsistent approach in cases where restrictive second-parent adoption laws are challenged by heterosexual unmarried couples and homosexual couples.

Both *Gas and Dubois* and *X and Others* confirm the now established trend according to which sexual orientation is considered a 'suspect ground' and, therefore, when a differential treatment is based on such considerations, the State's margin of appreciation is narrow.[79] This further entails that – as the Grand Chamber recalls – differences in treatment based on sexual orientation are subject to a strict scrutiny: in *X and Others*, the government was asked to demonstrate that the exclusion of homosexuals from second-parent adoption was not merely suitable, but 'necessary' for achieving the legitimate aim of protecting the traditional family.[80] Despite such a robust proportionality analysis, the privileged status reserved to marriage was eventually accepted as a justification for differential treatment. In *Gas and Dubois*, when assessing the situation of the applicants – who, as mentioned above, were in a civil partnership – vis-à-vis that of a married heterosexual couple, the Court reiterated its ruling in *Schalk and Kopf*, according to which Article 12 does not impose an obligation to allow same-sex couples access to marriage.[81] It further stated that, when a State provides homosexual couples with an alternative

---

[79] *Gas and Dubois v France*, § 59; *X and Others v Austria* [GC], § 140.
[80] *X and Others v Austria* [GC], § 140.
[81] *Gas and Dubois v France*, § 66.

means of recognition, it enjoys a certain margin of appreciation in relation to the exact status conferred.[82] Given the 'special status' that marriage confers on those who enter it, therefore, the applicants could not be considered in a comparable position to married heterosexual couples and, therefore, no discrimination was found.[83] The same conclusion was reached vis-à-vis heterosexual unmarried couples on the ground that, under French law, they were also excluded from second-parent adoption.[84]

Taking a different stance, in *X and Others*, the Grand Chamber upheld the applicants' complaint under Article 14 taken in conjunction with Article 8, but only in as far as they were denied rights that were available to unmarried heterosexual couples.[85] Having established that the applicants had been discriminated against on the basis of sexual orientation, the Court accepted that the protection of the family in the traditional sense – as argued by the Austrian courts and government – was, in principle, a weighty and legitimate reason that could justify a difference in treatment.[86] That being said, however, when designing measures to protect the family, States were also required to take into consideration recent developments in society and changed perceptions of social and intimate relations, 'including the fact that there is not just one way or one choice when it comes to leading one's family or private life'.[87]

It was found that, in the present case, the government had failed to adduce any evidence to show that it would be detrimental to the child to be brought up by a homosexual couple or to have two mothers and two fathers for legal purposes. On the contrary, by allowing single individuals – regardless of their sexual orientation – to adopt, the legislature had actually accepted that a child might grow up in a homosexual household without any adverse consequences on her wellbeing.[88] The Grand Chamber further noted that, different from cases of individual adoption, second-parent adoption cases involve existing family ties with the child and, in line with its previous jurisprudence, could not but recall the importance of providing legal recognition to de facto family life.[89] In light of the above, the Court concluded that considerable doubts on the proportionality of the absolute exclusion of homosexual couples

---

[82] Ibid.
[83] Ibid, § 68.
[84] Ibid, § 69.
[85] When the applicants' situation was compared to that of married couple, in contrast, the Court confirmed its ruling in *Gas and Dubois* and, therefore, found no violation of Article 14 taken in conjunction with Article 8. See §§ 105–10.
[86] *X and Others v Austria* [GC], § 138.
[87] Ibid, § 139.
[88] Ibid, § 142.
[89] Ibid, § 145.

from second-parent adoption existed and declared the distinction complained of by the applicants in violation of Article 8 taken in conjunction with Article 14.

X and Others makes an important contribution, therefore, to eradicating differences based on sexual orientation between unmarried couples. Yet, this positive outcome bears the burden of a continuing preference for marriage and, therefore, leaves the heteronormativity of legal regimes that seek to deny rights and benefits to homosexual couples unchallenged. In fact, when analysing the situation of the applicants vis-à-vis that of a married couple, the Grand Chamber confirmed that being denied legal rights reserved for married couples does not amount to discrimination. This finding confirms the relevance of heterosexuality as a parameter of parenthood, especially if it is read against the background of the Court's previous judgment in *Emonet and Others v Switzerland*, where the severing of the mother–child tie following the adoption by the mother's long-term (heterosexual) partner was considered in violation of Article 8.[90] Mr Emonet had already adopted the disabled adult daughter of his partner when the parties learnt that, according to Swiss law, previously existing parental ties were extinguished on adoption except in respect of the spouse of the adoptive parent. The mother and the daughter opposed the effects of the adoption process and attempted to restore their legal relationship, but national authorities refused to do so.

Even if not called to examine whether the applicants – an unmarried heterosexual couple – were subject to discrimination compared with a married couple, the Court expressed the view that 'the Government's argument that the institution of marriage guaranteed the adopted person greater stability than adoption by an unmarried couple who lived together is not necessarily relevant nowadays'.[91] It would therefore seem that marriage becomes 'special' when the Court is faced with the claims of homosexual civil or cohabiting partners, but not also when the prospective adopter is a heterosexual unmarried person.[92] Another crucial difference between *Emonet* and the cases involving homosexuals concerns the weight attached to the pre-existing family ties and, therefore, to the interests of the child involved. In *Emonet*, the Court stated that 'respect for the applicants' family life required that biological and social reality be taken into account to avoid the blind, mechanical operation of the provisions of the law to this very

---

[90] *Emonet and Others v Switzerland*, no. 39051/03, 13 December 2007.
[91] Ibid, § 81.
[92] B. Tobin, 'The European Court of Human Rights' Inconsistent and Incoherent Approach to Second-Parent Adoption', *European Human Rights Law Review*, (2017), 65.

particular situation for which they were clearly not intended'.[93] While accepting that limiting the number of parent–child relationships was – in principle – in the interest of the adoptee, the Court contested the applicability of this reasoning to the specific circumstances of the case: the adoptee was an adult with a serious disability, to whose adoption all the interested parties had given free and full consent.

In the cases involving homosexual couples, by way of contrast, although family life was found to exist between the applicants, no regard was given to the 'social reality' of their family[94] and, consequently, the child-centric perspective characterising *Emonet* is missing.[95] As argued by Judge Villiger in its dissenting opinion to the majority's decision in *Gas and Dubois*, 'the judgment focuses on the adults, but not on the children who are nevertheless an integral part of the applicants' complaints'.[96] Although the finding of a violation can be read as calling for a case-by-case decision to allow the child's best interests to be taken into account, child-related concerns were at the core of the Grand Chamber's reasoning not even in *X and Others*. In the latter, the Court insisted on the limited scope of its own task, which was not deciding whether or not the applicants' adoption request should have been granted in the circumstances of the case, but on the narrow (and abstract) issue of alleged discrimination between unmarried heterosexual and homosexual couples in respect of second-parent adoption.[97] It is exactly by framing the applications as discrimination cases that the Court shifted the attention from the welfare of the child to the interests of the adults.[98]

This comparison brings to light the variability – in terms of arguments used – of the Court's approach to second-parent adoption.[99] In particular, it would seem that pre-existing de facto ties – and, as a consequence, the best interests of the child involved – are taken into consideration only if they have developed within a union that reflects, to some extent, the conventional family

---

[93] *Emonet and Others v Switzerland*, § 86.
[94] D. Coester-Waltjen, 'The Impact of the European Convention on Human Rights and the European Court of Human Rights on European Family Law' in J. M. Scherpe (ed.), *European Family Law – The Impact of Institutions and Organisations on European Family Law*, vol. I (Edward Elgar, 2016), p. 79.
[95] L. Bracken, 'Strasbourg's Response to Gay and Lesbian Parenting: Progress, then Plateau?', *International Journal of Children's Rights*, 24 (2016), 374; P. Johnson, 'Adoption, Homosexuality and the European Convention on Human Rights: *Gas and Dubois v France*', *Modern Law Review*, 75(6) (2012), 1146.
[96] *Gas and Dubois v France*, Dissenting Opinion of Judge Villiger.
[97] *X and Others v Austria* [GC], § 132.
[98] C. Draghici, *Legitimacy of Family Rights in Strasbourg Case Law: Living Instrument or Extinguished Sovereignty?* (Hart, 2017), p. 153.
[99] Tobin, 'The ECtHR' Inconsistent Approach', 59.

model. It follows that, similar to the judgment in *Fretté*, 'social reality' and, consequently, care are valued only if the family is – in one aspect or another – somehow 'conventional' – i.e., marital or, at least, heterosexual. At the same time, however, in *X and Others*, the Court ultimately accepts a situation where a child can have two legal parents of the same sex. These two dimensions of the same case-law coexist as a result of the Court's inconsistent use of doctrines. In particular, while European consensus and the doctrine of evolutive interpretation were used in their activist dimensions to prohibit discrimination vis-à-vis heterosexual unmarried couples, the reinterpreted scope of Article 14 was used in a restrained version to protect the 'special status' of marriage.

From a doctrinal viewpoint, what attracted particular criticism is the majority's narrow approach to European consensus in *X and Others*.[100] The Grand Chamber specified that the issue at stake was the difference in treatment between heterosexual unmarried couples and homosexual couples with respect to second-parent adoption, not the general question of access to this type of adoption by homosexual couples.[101] As a consequence, despite having information at its disposal on thirty-nine Contracting States, the majority grounded the analysis of consensus only on those ten States that permitted second-parent adoption by unmarried couples and came to the rather unusual conclusion that, due to the narrowness of the sample employed, no conclusion could be drawn as to the existence of a possible consensus.[102] As the dissenters rightly point out, this deduction is, 'to say the least, curious'.[103] Given that six of these ten countries treated heterosexual couples and homosexual couples in the same manner while the remaining four adopted the same position as Austria, the more straightforward reaction would have been to acknowledge a diversity of approaches and, therefore, the absence of European consensus.[104]

[100] S. Smet, 'X and Others v Austria (Part II): A Narrow Ruling on a Narrow Issue', *Strasbourg Observers*, 6 March 2013, online at https://strasbourgobservers.com/2013/03/06/x-and-others-v-austria-part-ii-a-narrow-ruling-on-a-narrow-issue/ (last access on 15 February 2019); P. Johnson, 'X and Others v Austria', *ECHR Blog*, 21 February 2013, online at http://echrblog.blogspot.com/2013/02/x-v-austria-judgment.html (last access on 15 February 2019); L. Wildhaber, A. Hjartarson and S. Donnelly, 'No Consensus on Consensus? The Practice of the European Court of Human Rights', *Human Rights Law Journal*, 33 (7–12) (2013), 261; J. Nozawa, 'Drawing the Line: Same-Sex Adoption and the Jurisprudence of the ECtHR on the Application of the "European Consensus" Standard under Article 14', *Merkourios – Utrecht Journal of International and European Law*, 29/77 (2013), 73.
[101] X and Others v Austria [GC], § 149.
[102] Ibid.
[103] X and Others v Austria, Joint Partly Dissenting Opinion of Judges Casadevall, Ziemele, Kovler, Jočienė, Sikuta, De Gaetano and Sicilianos, § 14.
[104] Ibid.

The majority's attitude shows that consensus analysis is sometimes used as a 'device through which "reality" is selectively represented in order to add weight to its moral reasoning'.[105] Looking at a broader sample would have indeed made the lack of European consensus an even more inescapable conclusion. And, establishing and attaching weight to the lack of a common ground would have meant granting a wide margin of appreciation to States, thus potentially alleviating the strictness of review demanded by the suspect ground and, ultimately, compromising the finding of violation. *X and Others* offers therefore a further illustration of how European consensus does not always work as an argument that leads the ECtHR towards a specific result, but rather as a posteriori rationalisation and justification for a result that the Court has already reached.[106] Despite discarding the consensus argument entirely, moreover, the majority relies on the 'living instrument' doctrine as one of the factors whereby assessing the compatibility of the discrimination between the applicants and unmarried heterosexual couples with the Convention. As argued by the dissenters, therefore, 'the majority went beyond the usual limits of the evolutive method of interpretation' by anticipating social change rather than recognising it.[107] Similarly to *E.B.*, therefore, in *X and Others*, the Court shows its 'activist and voluntaristic face'[108] and, in particular, makes an instrumental – and methodologically unsound – use of the consensus analysis to advance its own moral views.

In this specific case, the outcome the Court has in mind is the preservation of the 'sacred' nature of marriage and, as a consequence, of a marital understanding of parenthood to the detriment of homosexual parents. The same predetermined choice seems to have equally influenced the selective use of another doctrinal tool, namely the reinterpreted scope of Article 14. Like in the cases on single-parent adoption, *in X and Others*, one of the doctrinal premises upon which the proportionality test is undertaken is that, although Article 8 does not protect a right to adopt, once this additional right is provided, the State cannot ensure its recognition in a discriminatory manner. While being critical in the assessment of the applicants' situation vis-à-vis heterosexual unmarried couples, the Court has not yet proved prepared to take advantage of a reinterpreted scope of Article 14 to contest the 'special status' of marriage, thus reducing the gap between the parental rights of married heterosexual couples and homosexual couples.

[105] Johnson, 'X and Others v Austria'.
[106] Smet, 'X and Others v Austria'.
[107] X and Others v Austria, Joint Partly Dissenting Opinion of Judges Casadevall, Ziemele, Kovler, Jočienė, Sikuta, De Gaetano and Sicilianos, § 23.
[108] Wildhaber et al., 'No Consensus on Consensus?', 261.

To conclude, despite originating from lesbian couples, the judgments in *Gas and Dubois* and *X and Others* make a significant contribution to clarifying the Court's approach to fatherhood in as much as they further exemplify the Court's ambivalent approach to homo-parenthood. On the one hand, the Court seems to contest the relevance of heterosexuality as a determining factor for granting parental and adoption rights, thus requiring particularly convincing and weighty reasons to justify a difference on the grounds of sexual orientation. On the other hand, however, heterosexuality is kept alive as a relevant feature through the Court's persisting attachment to a heteronormative view of marriage and, therefore, the restatement of marriage as premise and guarantee for a positive development of children. This ambivalence is also mirrored in the way doctrinal tools – in particular, European consensus, Article 14 and the 'living instrument' – are employed by the Court. While in relation to unmarried heterosexual couples, the Court feels ready to deploy its doctrines to their most activist degree possible, in relation to married couples, doctrines are used in their restrained version. Hence, also in this context, the emerging construction of fatherhood and, more generally, parenthood is, at the same time, the product of and the reason for the doctrinal choices made by the Court.

3 CONCLUSIONS

While unmarried families deviate from the conventional model of partnership and parenting due to their non-marital nature, the biological link – regardless of its sufficiency or not – served as a trait d'union between the ideal and the alternative. Similarly, when discussing the employment of ARTs by heterosexual couples, despite the partial/full departure from biology, their adherence to a different-sex, bi-parental family model has been relied on for inclusive purposes. Differently, within the domain of homosexuality, the chances to mimic the traditional family are significantly lower. The typical 'as if' attitude of the law has a limited, if any, margin of operation in the terrain of homosexual families. Biology as well as marriage can be rarely relied on as grounds to allocate parental status and parental rights to homosexual fathers and parents, more generally. With the exception of *Salgueiro*, what is sought by the applicants is the establishment or, in the case-law on second-parent adoption, the recognition of mere social relationships with neither legal nor biological basis. Hence, this is a particularly fruitful context where to assess the relevance – if any – attributed to care and caring intentions.

As it so often is, the construction of fatherhood emerging from the Court's jurisprudence is not clear cut. On the one hand, the Court seems to value care and caring intentions only if they are complemented by conventional features, such as biology, marriage and heterosexuality. At the same time, however, the (partial) finding of a violation in *X and Others v Austria* opens the way for the legal recognition of two parents of the same sex and, as such, represents an exception to the predominantly heteronormative understanding of parenthood endorsed by the Court.

Despite not explicitly, the judgment in *Salgueiro* conveys the important message that there can be no legal presumption that the heterosexual parent is, a priori, the preferred one who is granted custody rights.[109] Nonetheless, especially in light of *Fretté*, its precedential value for advancing the legal position of gay prospective fathers is rather questionable. Mr Salgueiro's complaint was arguably framed as the refusal of parental responsibility to a biological and divorced father, rather than to a homosexual man living with another man. The finding of a violation, therefore, even more so if read in light of the following decisions, suggests that biology and marriage make a difference in the legal treatment of homosexual fathers. In other words, it is by virtue of his adherence to the 'conventional' image of the father – apart from his sexual orientation – that the applicant's relationship with his (biological and born in wedlock) son finds support against discrimination. *Salgueiro*, therefore, does not establish a new right.[110] It is rather the mere extension of the principle – well established in the Court's case-law on post-separation parenting – according to which any relationship between a biological father and his child deserves to be protected and preserved also after the end of the relationship between the parents.

While the relationship of homosexual fathers with their biological children is afforded protection against discrimination, the Court has proved much less supportive of complaints brought by homosexuals in relation to non-biological parent–child relationships.[111] The most blatant example is provided by *Fretté*, where it implicitly accepted the view that sexual orientation can be a bar to eligibility to adoption. In this judgment, the Court seems to suggest that, when prospective gay fathers are in question, their demonstrated aptitude for raising a child needs to be supplemented with other, conventional features. In fact, Mr Fretté's caregiving and emotional abilities were undisputed; nonetheless, he was found to have 'difficulties in envisaging the practical consequences of the upheaval occasioned by the arrival of a child',[112] possibly because of the

---

[109] Draghici, *Legitimacy of Family Rights*, p. 215.
[110] M. Levinet, 'Couple et vie familiale' in F. Sudre (ed.), *Le droit au respect de la vie familiale dans la Convention européenne des droits de l'homme* (Nemesis-Bruylant, 2002), p. 142.
[111] Johnson, *Homosexuality and the ECtHR*, p. 131.
[112] Decision of the Paris Social Services Department, referred to in *Fretté v France*, § 10.

sole fact that he was a single man. Mr Fretté would have indeed become an 'unconventional' father in all respects.

Similarly, in the case-law on second-parent adoption, 'social reality' and, in particular, the existence of concrete ties between the child and the biological mother's partner are taken into account only if the family at stake displays conventional traits. In the case of *Emonet and Others v Switzerland*, where severing the mother–child tie was considered a violation of Article 8, the applicants were an unmarried, but heterosexual couple. Differently, in both *Gas and Dubois v France* and *X and Others v Austria*, the applicants were homosexual partners and, as such, were considered not comparable to a married heterosexual couple, to whom the institute of second-parent adoption was reserved. In these cases, therefore, although sexual orientation per se is ruled out as a legitimate justification for more restrictive legislation on second-parent adoption, heterosexuality is implicitly restated as a conventional feature of parenthood[113] and, therefore, as a determinant for the allocation of adoption rights by leaving the 'special status' of marriage untouched. By finding the differential treatment suffered by the applicants vis-à-vis married couples not discriminatory, therefore, the Court seems to suggest that the existence of a marital union between the biological parent of the child and the prospective adopter makes the concrete ties developed among them worthy of consideration.

One situation in which caring intentions and abilities per se were considered relevant is that of *E.B.*, which, however, concerned a lesbian woman seeking authorisation to adopt. Despite displaying a distinctive critical approach to the privilege of heterosexuality,[114] this judgment – especially in light of the poorly justified departure from *Fretté* – ultimately reinforces a 'conventional' understanding of fatherhood that regards women as better equipped to take care of children and reduces men's role to economic provision. Therefore, if regard is given to the wider construction of parenthood emerging from this case-law, *X and Others v Austria* constitutes the only real exception to the above trend. By holding the inaccessibility of second-parent adoption by homosexual couples, while available to heterosexual unmarried couples, contrary to Article 14 in conjunction with Article 8, the Court accepts the idea of a child having two legal parents of the same sex. As such, it clearly departs from a heterosexual and heteronormative understanding of parenthood.

[113] D. A. Gonzalez-Salzberg, *Sexuality and Transsexuality under the European Convention on Human Rights: A Queer Reading of Human Rights Law* (Hart, 2019), p. 106.
[114] Johnson, 'Heteronormativity and the ECtHR', 47; Johnson, 'Adoption, Homosexuality', 1146.

Overall, therefore, despite being given the possibility and, to some extent, even forced to go beyond the conventional paradigm, the Court has ruled out heterosexuality as a relevant ground for allocating parental and adoption rights only partially. This incomplete departure, in turn, is attributable to the Court's specific – erratic and methodologically unsound – employment of its doctrines of interpretation. While Article 14 was employed in its reinterpreted scope to fight discrimination vis-à-vis heterosexual unmarried couples, it was not considered 'magnificent' enough to overcome a heteronormative conception of marriage and, therefore, to contest legal regimes favouring marriage-based parenthood. European consensus has been subject to a similarly instrumental use. In *X and Others*, the majority's decision to focus on a narrow sample and the conclusion of no relevance reflect and, eventually, lend support to the Court's willingness to subject differential treatment among unmarried couples based on sexual orientation to a strict scrutiny. Apart from preventing the grant of a wide margin of appreciation in *X and Others*, the inconsistent reliance on consensus analysis appears also one of the main factors underlying the opposite outcomes in *Fretté* and *E.B.* and, therefore, the ultimate support for a definition of fatherhood based on a gendered division of labour.

Rather than being arguments that accompany the Court towards a specific outcome, therefore, doctrines have often been used to justify the Court's moral preferences: in this context, the tenacity of marriage as a conventional feature of parenthood, as much as of biology and breadwinning as conventional traits of fatherhood. It follows that the construction of fatherhood and, more generally, of parenthood emerging from this case-law is mostly a matter of choice that the Court itself legitimises by pulling its doctrinal tools in the most convenient way.

7

Fatherhood at the ECtHR

INTRODUCTION

This book has explored how the ECtHR has reacted to evolving family and fatherhood realities and, more particularly, to what extent it has contributed to challenge and/or to reproduce 'conventional fatherhood' by relying in particular on Article 8, taken alone or in conjunction with Article 14. The preceding chapters have explored how fatherhood has been understood and regulated in different areas of case-law, accurately chosen as particularly emblematic of the fragmentary impact of social change on notions and practices of fatherhood. The following sections now aim to bring the various lines of thought together to provide a more comprehensive picture of the emerging understanding of fatherhood as well as of the roles played by doctrines in this process of (re-)construction. As it will be shown, the definition of fatherhood endorsed by the Court is far from clear cut in two respects. First, although increasingly valuing a father's interest and commitment to his child, the Court does not abandon 'conventional fatherhood'. The rights of fathers continue therefore to be adjudicated on the ground of their adherence to the model of 'conventional fatherhood', to which – however – the 'new' requirement of care is added. Second, although the emerging construction of fatherhood appears to be mostly a matter of choice, doctrines have – depending on the case at hand and to varying extents – also retained their role as 'productive of'[1] decision making. Hence, it is not rare that doctrinal and moral forces interact in bringing the Court more closely to the ideology of 'new fatherhood'.

---

[1] P. Johnson, *Homosexuality and the European Court of Human Rights* (Routledge, 2013), p. 88.

1 THE CONSTRUCTION OF FATHERHOOD IN THE ECTHR JURISPRUDENCE

Towards 'New Fatherhood'

The construction of fatherhood endorsed by the Court reflects – to a large extent – the ideology of 'new fatherhood', as it combines conventional features and roles with an increased importance attached to the 'new' element of care. Rather than departing from a conventional understanding of fatherhood, the Court tends to 'simply' add a new layer to it: paternal care in its various manifestations, which range from the expression of nurturing intentions to the establishment of close personal ties with the child. Fatherhood – as understood by the Court – simultaneously incorporates therefore both change and continuity.

The importance of biology to make someone a legal father – although jeopardised in practice by the advent of ARTs – is confirmed by the Court's reaction to the claims brought by fathers of children born from these techniques. Biology proved indispensable for securing the allocation of the legal status of fatherhood to the advantage of a transsexual father, despite his active involvement as the child's social father since birth.[2] In the field of surrogacy, the opposite outcomes reached in *Mennesson v France*[3] and *Paradiso and Campanelli v Italy*[4] are primarily dependent on the nature – biological or merely social – of the father–child tie at stake.[5] While in the former biological relatedness played a decisive role in finding a violation of the children's right to respect for private life, in the more recent case, the absence of any biological link contributed to finding no family life and, eventually, to holding the child's removal from the intended parents compatible with Article 8.

Fatherhood, moreover, maintains a predominantly mediated nature. More concretely, father–child relationships continue – to a varying extent – to be assessed and thus regulated as a derivative of the relationship between the child's biological parents. The father's non-formalised relationship with the child's mother is rejected as a priori justification for the more precarious position of separated unmarried fathers – if compared to divorced fathers – with respect to their biological children. Yet, the nature of the relationship from which the child was born and the intentions surrounding conception

---

[2] *X, Y and Z v the United Kingdom*, 22 April 1997, *Reports of Judgments and Decisions* 1997-II.
[3] *Mennesson v France*, no. 65192/11, ECHR 2014 (extracts).
[4] *Paradiso and Campanelli v Italy* [GC], no. 25358/12, 24 January 2017.
[5] L. Bracken, 'Assessing the Best Interests of the Child in Cases of Cross-Border Surrogacy: Inconsistency in the Strasbourg Approach?', *Journal of Social Welfare and Family Law*, 39(3) (2017), 373.

continue to be relevant in establishing whether the father–child tie at stake qualifies as 'family life', as well as in determining the criteria against which paternal care is assessed. 'Marital fatherhood', therefore, holds out against the phenomenon of extra-marital childbearing, but in a revisited form: it is replaced by alternative organising concepts, such as cohabitation, length and stability.[6]

The relevance of marriage also survives the era of biological certainty. Vis-à-vis requests of paternity disestablishment, the Court does not seem satisfied with DNA evidence indicating a divergent biological reality. Rather, it shows its efforts to keep the paternal status attached to marriage by imposing the extra burden of acting promptly and diligently on the applicant legal fathers.[7] The Court's privileging of 'marital fatherhood' influences also its approach to the issue of becoming genetic parents via ARTs. In particular, it contributes to explain why the parental project of a married couple[8] – but not that of a single mother against the wishes of the biological father[9] – was considered worthy of realisation through the use of ARTs.

Continuity can also be traced in relation to breadwinning. In spite of supporting a more engaged vision of fatherhood, the Court does not free fathers from their traditional role of providers. In fact, it is exactly through their participation in paid employment that they are granted time off work to take care of their children through parental leave entitlements. Breadwinning is restated as a conventional feature of fatherhood even more firmly in the case-law on single-parent adoption by homosexuals. Whilst expressing the Court's willingness to contest heteronormativity, the Court's position in *E.B v France*[10] – especially in light of its poorly justified departure from *Fretté v France*[11] – seems to implicitly support a gendered division of labour that justifies valuing caring intentions and abilities differently, depending on whether the applicant is a man or a woman.

Also the privilege of heterosexuality remains largely uncontested in the Court's jurisprudence. One of the clear messages conveyed by the judgment in *Salgueiro da Silva Mouta v Portugal*[12] is that being non-heterosexual is not seen as amounting to a lack of fitness for fatherhood. Still, given that the child was born from a previous marriage, the extent to which the finding of violation signals a true departure from a heterosexual conception of fatherhood – or, rather, merely confirms biology and marriage as grounds for attributing custody rights – is disputable. Surely, heterosexuality is kept alive as a relevant feature through the

---

[6] R. Collier, *Masculinity, Law and the Family* (Routledge, 1995), p. 205.
[7] See Chapter 4, section 2.3.
[8] *Dickson v UK* [GC], no. 44362/04, ECHR 2007-V.
[9] *Evans v UK* [GC], no. 6339/05, ECHR 2007-I.
[10] *E.B. v France* [GC], no. 43546/02, 22 January 2008.
[11] *Fretté v France*, no. 36515/97, ECHR2002-I.
[12] *Salgueiro da Silva Mouta v Portugal*, no. 33290/96, ECHR 1999-IX.

Court's attachment to a heteronormative definition of marriage. By maintaining the view that marriage confers a 'special status' upon those who enter it,[13] the Court perpetuates the exclusion of same-sex couples from parental rights that, in the current legal context of Europe, remain mostly attached to marriage.[14]

While restating the relevance of all those conventional features, the Court has also clarified their limits and expressed the need for some instances of care – manifested in various forms – in order to make someone a legal father.[15] In the assessment of family life between an unmarried father and his biological child, the conventional focus on the relationship between the biological parents shares the stage with the father's interest and commitment to the child both before and after birth. Care, however, is also a feature of the model of fatherhood that is *definitely* accorded protection under the Convention. The relevance attached to the attitude of the applicant and, more precisely, the extent to which the Court perceives him as interested and committed to his child penetrates also the proportionality assessment and, ultimately, has a bearing on the outcome of the case. In the context of paternity proceedings, for instance, care is employed as the parameter against which the tension that can potentially arise between the child's legal father and the applicant biological father is solved. These developments show that the Court has gradually begun to examine the claims of fathers through the additional lens of care and, in spite of the persisting function of marriage as a connector, to understand father–child ties as more autonomous.

It can therefore be argued that – just as in national legal contexts – the Court's focus has moved from a predominant concentration on horizontal relationships towards an increasing attention towards vertical relationships, as a response to social change and the ensuing subdivision of fatherhood as a practice.[16] Otherwise, the Court's reaction to 'fragmenting fatherhood' has been mostly unreceptive and limited to one specific dimension: that is, the disaggregation of a gendered division of labour in heterosexual families. In encouraging the combination of parenting and breadwinning tasks within fatherhood as essential in ensuring a similar arrangement for mothers,[17] the Court proves itself aware that breadwinning is no longer a paternal prerogative, but rather a shared role with mothers.

---

[13] *Gas and Dubois v France*, no. 25951/07, ECHR 2012, § 68.
[14] P. Johnson, 'Marriage, Heteronormativity, and the European Court of Human Rights: A Reappraisal', *International Journal of Law, Policy and the Family*, 29 (2015), 57.
[15] On the insufficiency of biology, see *J.R.M. v the Netherlands*, no. 16944/90, Commission decision of 8 February 1993, 'The Law', § 1; *Lebbink v the Netherlands*, no. 45582/99, § 37, ECHR 2004-IV.
[16] R. Collier and S. Sheldon, *Fragmenting Fatherhood: A Socio-Legal Study* (Hart, 2008), p. 306.
[17] See Chapter 5.

This exception aside, its overall reluctance to accept the reality of 'fragmenting fatherhood' has become particularly visible in the context of post-separation and unmarried fatherhood. Therein, the Court appears driven by an 'assumption of exclusivity',[18] according to which each child can have only one 'real'[19] father. Hence, it does not seem to contemplate the coexistence of two men – who tend to resonate with the biological father and the mother's new partner who act as the child's social father – and, accordingly, does not provide any hint on how legally recognising the contribution of each of them in the child's life. Fatherhood continues therefore to be largely conceptualised as a bundle of rights and responsibilities that, in spite of being split up and shared between different men in society, are kept together in the law.

The Relationship between Change and Continuity

Apart from coexisting, change and continuity mutually reinforce each other in the Court's understanding of fatherhood. Indeed, care is taken into consideration only if expressed in an otherwise 'conventional' context and, as a consequence, the conditional importance attached to care inevitably reveals the Court's persisting attachment to the conventional paradigm. Interdependence is self-explaining in the context of family–work reconciliation, where – as mentioned above – the undertaking of 'new' caring responsibilities through parental leave entitlements is premised on the father's continued role as a breadwinner. A similar dynamic is visible also in the context of unmarried and post-separation fatherhood. In the presence of two competing father figures, the care provided by the biological father is subject to a more rigorous evaluation if the social father is married to the child's mother.[20] The Court's appreciation of paternal care seems to vary also according to the marital status of the applicant father: when an unmarried father seeks to have his paternity established, attention is brought to the actual bonds existing between the unmarried father and his child; when faced with a divorced father's request for disavowal, instead, the Court seems satisfied

---

[18] S. Sheldon, 'Fragmenting Fatherhood: The Regulation of Reproductive Technologies', *Modern Law Review*, 68(4) (2005), 550.

[19] The Court speaks about 'real' paternal filiation in the case of *Mandet v France*, no. 30955/12, 14 January 2016. The applicants – the mother, her husband and the child – complained about the quashing of the recognition of paternity and about the annulation of the child's legitimation. In finding no violation of Article 8, the Court argues that, in considering the child's best interests as resonating less with the preservation of his concrete relationships with the other applicants than in establishing his 'real' paternal filiation, domestic courts had acted within their margin of appreciation (§ 59).

[20] See Chapter 4, sections 2.2 and 2.3.

with the applicant's diligent conduct in legal proceedings.[21] This variability in the assessment of paternal care is, therefore, the consequence and, at the same time, the manifestation of the Court's endorsement of a marital understanding of fatherhood.

Other examples can be found in the ARTs domain: therein, care is attached relevance or, at least, more relevance when it takes place within a reality of 'conventional fatherhood' or when, in cases of unconceived children, it is aimed at creating such a reality. Since its earliest intervention in *X, Y and Z v UK*, the dismissal of X's complaint reveals the insufficiency of care and, at the same time, confirms heteronormativity and biology as grounds for allocating the paternal status. Care and conventional features mutually reinforce each other also in the case-law on surrogacy. The different weight attributed to the couple's parental project and the quality of their ties with the surrogacy-born children in *Mennesson* and *Paradiso and Campanelli* uncovers, indeed, the enduring importance of biological relatedness in reaching the threshold of legal fatherhood. The divergent outcomes reached in *Evans v UK* and *Dickson v UK* further suggest that care – here, in the form of intentionality – is more likely to be taken seriously when it is provided by a conventional-to-become father, thus confirming the endurance of 'conventional fatherhood' in its unitary and pseudo-marital dimensions.

Finally, homo-parenthood represents the field where the interdependent relationship between care and 'conventional fatherhood' comes to light most clearly. With one exception,[22] the family relationships at stake or sought by the applicants have neither a marital nor a biological basis and are therefore made exclusively of care. This is the outcome of the particularly problematic coexistence of homosexuality and 'conventional fatherhood'. Homo-parenthood, if compared to the other sociological developments outlined in Chapter 1, has indeed the potential to challenge the conventional paradigm almost in its entirety: apart from departing from the norm of heterosexuality, it implies biological unrelatedness and, most likely, also the absence of a marital relationship between the parents. Vis-à-vis complaints brought by homosexuals, therefore, the Court is left with few chances to make appeal to some conventional features and, as a consequence, also the possibility of endorsing a mixed definition – that incorporates both change and continuity – is limited to exceptional situations. The case of *Salgueiro* is one of those: the finding of a violation reveals the importance of marriage and biology as preconditions for

---

[21] See Chapter 4, section 2.3.
[22] *Salgueiro da Silva Mouta v Portugal*.

valuing care as well as relevant factors in the allocation of parental responsibility to fathers.

2 THE ROLE(S) OF DOCTRINES

The relationship between doctrines and the construction of fatherhood emerging from the ECtHR jurisprudence has assumed various forms, depending on the case under scrutiny as well as on the specific doctrinal tool at issue. In some cases, the Court has shown genuine concern for methodological consistency. In such circumstances, the construction of fatherhood endorsed by the Court is – apart from being presented as such in the text of the judgment – the outcome of the consistent and 'mechanical' deployment of its interpretative repertoire. The context where the role of doctrines as 'productive of' the Court's approach to fatherhood is most evident is that of family–work reconciliation. Therein, the Court's understanding of fatherhood has – over a period of fifteen years – shifted from restating the conventional image of the father as a mere breadwinner to promoting the model of 'new fatherhood'. As shown in Chapter 5, this reconstruction has been the product of the gradual establishment of a European consensus that, apart from narrowing the margin of appreciation left to the State, has empowered the Court to undertake an anti-stereotyping analysis.

This case-law domain aside, however, the often variable use of doctrines seems to suggest that the Court's moral standpoint on fatherhood is one of the factors and, sometimes, the main factor that influences the doctrinal path undertaken by the Court. In other words, doctrines appear to be often employed to provide support and even to legitimise what being a father means, according to a predetermined moral position already adopted by the Court. This 'agenda-driven recourse'[23] to doctrines becomes particularly visible if attention is paid to the Court's approach to positive obligations as well as to its reliance on European consensus – with its obvious spillovers on dynamic interpretation and the margin of appreciation. Before delving into those, however, it is important to stress that the employment of doctrines as 'subservient to' the Court's moral views on fatherhood does not necessarily exclude, but rather often coexist with their more ordinary use as 'productive of' legal fatherhood.

The case-law on second-parent adoption as well as the most recent judgments concerning paternity establishment are clear examples of how doctrinal

---

[23] C. Draghici, *Legitimacy of Family Rights in Strasbourg Case Law: Living Instrument or Extinguished Sovereignty?* (Hart, 2017), p. 402.

and moral considerations might join forces in shaping the definition of fatherhood endorsed by the Court. *X and Others v Austria*[24], for instance, illustrates not only the impact of the suspect ground on the intensity of review (through the application of the 'very weighty reasons' test), but additionally reveals the selective use of European consensus and dynamic interpretation as factors that led to strict scrutiny, but only of the differential treatment between unmarried couples. This doctrinal inaccuracy, if read together with the Court's reluctance to directly compare the applicants with married heterosexual couples, seems to have been determined by the Court's choice to perpetuate the heteronormativity of marriage and the exclusion of same-sex couples from second-parent adoption. In recent times, the Court's reaction to the claims of unmarried fathers seeking paternity establishment displays a similar pattern: the emerging construction of fatherhood is attributable to both the role of the non-existent European consensus in widening the margin enjoyed by States and the variable application of positive obligations informed by the Court's heightened importance attributed to paternal care.

Interestingly, the interaction between doctrines and moral views can go as far as to render the latter an integral part of the consistent application of the former. This dynamic finds expression in the case-law on surrogacy, where the absence or presence of biological parentage has been the reason for widening the margin in *Mennesson* whilst restricting it in *Paradiso and Campanelli*, and, as such, had a bearing on their opposite outcomes. Even before these cases, a biological understanding of fatherhood seems to have also been incorporated in the development of positive obligations arising from Article 8. By arguing that the tie between a natural father and his child should be protected against irreversible processes, such as those triggered by adoption, and holding that States have the positive obligation to facilitate their reunion, the Court inevitably identifies biology as a relevant ground for the allocation of parental rights to fathers. In such cases, therefore, distinguishing between moral and doctrinal forces is hardly possible.

European Consensus

The Court has never provided a definition of 'European consensus' in its judgments. Although this might reflect a deliberate intention to keep the concept 'fuzzy enough to avoid the consequences of adopting one particular theory out of the many held by judges and academics',[25] the lack of clear

---

[24] *X and Others v Austria* [GC], no. 19010/07, ECHR 2013.
[25] L. Wildhaber, A. Hjartarson and S. Donnelly, 'No Consensus on Consensus? The Practice of the European Court of Human Rights', *Human Rights Law Journal*, 33 (7–12) (2013), 249.

parameters makes consensus analysis particularly malleable and, thus, open to variable use. In relation to fatherhood, European consensus is referred to in most of the analysed jurisprudence and remains a frequent basis for advancing a dynamic interpretation or granting a margin of appreciation. Yet, the way it is employed varies to such an extent that it cannot be considered a determinant of the width of the margin of appreciation, or the 'tipping point necessary for evolution',[26] in any straightforward manner. Rather, it serves more as a 'process through which reality is constructed'[27] in order to support the Court's predetermined moral position on what makes someone a legal father and, overall, to facilitate its move towards 'new fatherhood'.

In the jurisprudence herein analysed, European consensus has been employed to achieve two main purposes: to legitimise a dynamic interpretation of Article 8 or as a mechanism to limit the positive obligations of Contracting States. Starting from the latter, the judgment in X, Y and Z illustrates the potential use of European consensus to withhold Convention rights from 'unconventional' fathers and, therefore, to endorse judicial conservatism. The Court argued that no European shared approach could be found with respect to the conferral of parental rights on transsexuals, but it failed to include the comparative data relied on in the text of the judgment. In this case, therefore, the unsubstantiated finding of no consensus has contributed to justify the Court's decision not to extend the positive obligation to grant legal recognition to the social tie existing between a transsexual father and his child and, ultimately, to legitimise its persisting attachment to 'conventional fatherhood'.

The reasoning in X and Others and Zaunegger v Germany[28] exemplifies, by way of contrast, the employment of consensus to endorse judicial activism. In both cases, the Court advances a controversial interpretation of evidence in order to 'construct a view of consensus'[29] that is conducive to supporting its moral agenda. In X and Others, the majority decided to focus on a small sample and concluded that consensus was not helpful in settling the matter at stake; yet, it then relied on the doctrine of 'living instrument' to assess the compatibility of the discrimination at hand with Article 14. In this case, therefore, European consensus is likely to have been used by the Court as a device to legitimise its own moral reasoning about the need to extend second-parent adoption to same-sex couples, when available to unmarried heterosexual couples. With similar

---

[26] I borrow this expression from Dzehtsiarou, *European Consensus and the Legitimacy of the European Court of Human Rights* (Cambridge University Press, 2015), p. 142.
[27] Johnson, *Homosexuality and the ECtHR*, p. 83.
[28] *Zaunegger v Germany*, no. 22028/04, 3 December 2009.
[29] Johnson, *Homosexuality and the ECtHR*, p. 81.

implications, in *Zaunegger*, the Court proved satisfied with consensus at the level of principles – in spite of clear divergences in national legislation – to ground the interpretation of the Convention as a 'living instrument'. This particular approach to consensus identification – together with the application of the 'very weighty reasons' test – led to strict scrutiny as well as to the adoption of an anti-stereotyping analysis, thus legitimising the Court's choice to incorporate care into its construction of fatherhood.

Positive Obligations

In spite of its widespread resort to positive obligations, the Court never felt the need to articulate a general theory.[30] Rather, it has preferred to adopt a case-by-case approach, thus leaving the ratio and the principles that guide a correct application of positive obligations obscure.[31] Moreover, due to their open-ended scope, positive obligations can – at least, in principle – be claimed everywhere – a fact that can trigger both problems and opportunities.[32] What appears clear, however, is that resorting to the doctrine of positive obligations in the context of Article 8 has supported the Court in advancing its moral views on fatherhood. The case-law analysed seems to indicate that it is often the applicant's profile that influences the variable application of both positive obligations to facilitate the reunification of a biological father with his child and to grant legal recognition to existing family ties. In their application, the Court seems to be driven by a selective logic that brings advantage to those relationships that display both change and continuity. The trend identified by Kilkelly[33] – according to which positive obligations do not apply equally to all family relationships – finds therefore multiple confirmations in the case-law pertaining to fatherhood.

The earliest judgment displaying such pattern is that of X, Y and Z. This judgment clarifies that, even though a relationship might be considered to qualify as 'family life', Article 8's positive obligation to respect that family life applies only to those enjoying ties that, apart from being social, have a biological basis. In its reasoning, the Court explicitly grounds its departure

---

[30] L. Lavrysen, 'The Scope of Rights and the Scope of Obligations – Positive Obligations' in E. Brems and J. Gerards (eds.), *Shaping Rights in the ECHR – The Role of the European Court of Human Rights in Determining the Scope of Human Rights* (Cambridge University Press, 2013), p. 163.

[31] Ibid.

[32] D. Xenos, *The Positive Obligations of the State under the European Convention on Human Rights* (Routledge, 2012), p. 4.

[33] U. Kilkelly, 'Protecting Children's Rights under the ECHR: The Role of Positive Obligations', *Northern Ireland Legal Quarterly*, 61(3) (2010), 245–61.

from *Marckx* on the 'unconventional' nature of the relationship between the applicants: as explained by the Court, the child was not biologically related to his social father, who is a transsexual. Although the Court attempted to draw support for its finding from the lack of a European consensus, as mentioned above, the lack of clarity as to the comparative materials relied on ends up confirming the use of doctrines to arrive at a predetermined conclusion. *X, Y and Z* illustrates, therefore, the 'subservient' role played by the doctrine of positive obligations – together with European consensus – to legitimise the Court's choice to restate biology and heteronormativity as grounds for attributing the status of legal father.

In the case-law on non-consensual adoption, rather, it seems to be the Court's attachment to a marital conception of fatherhood that underlies the inconsistent application of positive obligations.[34] In particular, the extent to which States are called to take positive action tends to vary depending on the relationship between the adoptive father and the child's mother. In cases where the child had been placed in a foster family, the Court feels prepared to interpret Article 8 as giving rise to positive obligations and to subject the contested measure to strict scrutiny. Conversely, in cases where the adoptive father is the mother's new partner and the biological father is considered not to have demonstrated sufficient commitment to his child, the Court proves reluctant to approach the analysis from the perspective of the State's positive obligations. Hence, the application of positive obligations waters down as the biological father becomes, if compared to the adoptive father, further detached from the construction of fatherhood endorsed by the Court.

Finally, moving to the context of paternity proceedings, the variable use of the doctrine of positive obligations seems to have been 'determined by' the Court's choice to include care in its definition of fatherhood.[35] In cases where the biological father seeks to be recognised as the child's legal father, in particular, there seems to exist a correlation between the Court's perception of the applicant's caring intentions – as perceived by the Court – and the extent to which Article 8's positive obligations are held applicable. If the applicant father has not taken all possible routes made available to him or has otherwise failed to demonstrate his interest in raising the child, the Court's jurisprudence seems to suggest that the State is justified to deny the applicant the opportunity to be legally recognised as the child's legal father. On the contrary, when the biological father is considered to have shown sufficient

---

[34] See Chapter 4, section 2.2.
[35] See Chapter 4, section 3.3.

interest in the child's life, the Court proves more inclined to expect the State to take positive action to enable their father-child tie to develop.

3 FINAL THOUGHTS

Wildhaber has argued that 'it is not ... the Court's role to engineer changes in society or to impose moral choices'.[36] The limits of its own task have sometimes been recognised by the Court itself. In the context of homo-parenthood, for instance, some of the judges sitting on the Court have expressed the view that it is not the Court's role to 'pass moral judgments' on issues as controversial as adoption by homosexuals, neither to support a family model more than others.[37] Yet, the case-law analysed in this book has shown a partially different reality. The Court has, in fact, attempted to establish its moral views on how a father should behave and what features he should possess and, more generally, on what family context is more appropriate for a child to be raised in. Whilst, in some cases, the expression of such views has followed from the consistent application of doctrines, in other cases, it has been enabled – or at least facilitated – by the use of doctrines beyond their usual limits and/or according to variable standards.

European consensus has often been deployed more as a 'transformative', rather than a 'reflective' tool. Therefore, despite giving the impression to take a rather cautious approach, the Court's recourse to the 'living instrument' doctrine has often ended up imposing new social and legal standards, rather than reflecting present-day conditions. The Court's erratic approach to positive obligations has displayed the doctrine's potential to ensure (or to deny) active respect to the family life of a wide range of 'unconventional' fathers. At the same time, however, it has supported the impression that the Court engages in moral reasoning to redefine the rights of fathers. Apart from adding evidence to the idea that doctrines might serve simply as 'a cover for subjective *ad-hockery*',[38] these doctrinal inaccuracies have also resulted in questioning the legitimacy of the Court's interpretative role. The Court has often been considered to go 'too fast too soon', especially in an area such as family law where – in spite of the emergence of common patterns – domestic legislations remain quite State specific or are in the process of adjusting to social change.

---

[36] L. Wildhaber, 'The European Court of Human Rights in Action', *Ritsumeikan Law Review*, 21 (2004), 86.

[37] *Fretté v France*, Joint Partly Dissenting Opinion of Judge Bratza, Judge Fuhrmann and Judge Tulkens, § 2(c).

[38] A. Mowbray, The Creativity of the European Court of Human Rights, *Human Rights Law Review*, 5(1) (2005), 71.

Without discrediting these understandable concerns, this book has also been driven by a different intent: to acknowledge the 'expressive powers' of the Court and to focus on the messages it actually radiates. Apart from producing new ideas about responsibility on the part of both parents, social change has also suggested a new role for the law in 'setting out normative expectations', conveying messages about fathers' desirable attitude towards their children and, even, attempting to modify their behaviour.[39] This applies also to the European Court of Human Rights. As effectively argued by Lõhmus: 'Convention rights can be seen as particularly important institutional and rhetorical means of expressing, contesting and enhancing values that European society sees as being essential to humanity and to the good life of its members.'[40]

If the Court's persisting attachment to 'conventional fatherhood' can be seen as a partially missed opportunity, at the same time, the inclusion of care as a relevant parameter for granting legal fatherhood certainly represents a first promising step. Thanks to its creativity in the interpretation and application of the Convention, the Court has come to embrace the different nature of notions and practices of fatherhood in contemporary European societies from those existing at the time when the Convention was drafted.[41] In so doing, the Court has become an important actor in the social and legal processes through which the meaning of fatherhood is being reconsidered, renegotiated and reconstructed. In more concrete terms, although leaving the claims of some 'unconventional' fathers out in the cold, the Strasbourg jurisprudence has certainly brought genuine advantages to an increasing number of fathers by virtue of their interest and commitment to their children.

What remains to be ascertained, however, is the extent to which the Court has taken the interconnectedness of relationships between men, women and children into account when developing its construction of fatherhood.[42] An important task for future research is, therefore, to focus on the implications of

---

[39] Collier and Sheldon, *Fragmenting Fatherhood*, p. 206.
[40] K. Lõhmus, *Caring Autonomy: European Human Rights Law and the Challenge of Individualism* (Cambridge University Press, 2015), p. 5.
[41] Mowbray, 'The Creativity of the ECtHR', 79.
[42] On the dangers of redefining fatherhood in isolation (although in other contexts), see N. E. Dowd, 'From Genes, Marriage and Money to Nurture: Redefining Fatherhood', *Cardozo Women's Law Journal*, 10 (2003–2004), 144; N. E. Dowd, *Redefining Fatherhood* (New York University Press, 2000), p. 182; B. Featherstone and L. Trinder, 'New Labour, Families and Fathers', *Critical Social Policy*, 21(4) (2001), 534–6; B. Featherstone and S. Peckover, '"Letting Them Get Away with It": Fathers, Domestic Violence and Child Protection', *Critical Social Policy*, 27(2) (2007), 181–203; D. Callahan, 'Bioethics and Fatherhood', *Utah Law Review*, (1992), 736.

the Court's reframing of legal fatherhood for the positions of other potentially affected parties, primarily mothers and children. Has the Court's move towards 'new fatherhood' resulted in marginalising the views and experiences of women and, more generally, in ignoring the existence of potential tensions between the interests of the various individual involved? Have children been made participants in this process of reconstruction or, rather, been treated as mere recipients of an adult-centric vision of family life? These are just some of the crucial questions that remain to be addressed.

Bibliography

Alexy, R., *A Theory of Constitutional Rights* (Oxford University Press, 2002)

Amato, P. and Gilbreth, J., 'Non-Resident Fathers and Children's Well-Being: A Meta-Analysis', *Journal of Marriage and the Family*, 61(3) (1999), 557–73

Ambrus, M., 'The European Court of Human Rights and the Standards of Proof – An Evidentiary Approach towards the Margin of Appreciation' in L. Gruszczynski and W. Werner (eds.), *Deference in International Courts and Tribunals – Standard of Review and Margin of Appreciation* (Oxford University Press, 2014), pp. 235–53

Arnardóttir, O. M., 'The Differences That Make a Difference: Recent Developments on the Discrimination Grounds and the Margin of Appreciation under Article 14 of the European Convention on Human Rights', *Human Rights Law Review*, 14 (2014), 647–70

Arnardóttir, O. M., 'Discrimination as a Magnifying Lens – Scope and Ambit under Article 14 and Protocol No. 12' in E. Brems and J. Gerards (eds.), *Shaping Rights in the ECHR – The Role of the European Court of Human Rights in Determining the Scope of Human Rights* (Cambridge University Press, 2013), pp. 330–49

Arnardóttir, O. M., *Equality and Non-Discrimination under the European Convention on Human Rights* (Martinus Nijhoff, 2003)

Arnardóttir, O. M., 'Rethinking the Two Margins of Appreciation', *European Constitutional Law Review*, 12(1) (2016), 27–53

Andenas, M. and Bjorge, E., 'National implementation of ECHR rights' in A. Føllesdal, B. Peters and G. Ulfstein (eds.), *Constituting Europe – The European Court of Human Rights in a National, European and Global Context* (Cambridge University Press, 2013), pp. 181–262

Arai-Takahashi, Y., *The Margin of Appreciation Doctrine and the Principle of Proportionality in the Jurisprudence of the ECHR* (Intersentia, 2002)

Arai-Takahashi, Y., 'The Margin of Appreciation Doctrine: A Theoretical Analysis of Strasbourg's Variable Geometry' in A. Føllesdal, B. Peters and G. Ulfstein (eds.), *Constituting Europe – The European Court of Human Rights in a National, European and Global Context* (Cambridge University Press, 2013), pp. 62–105

Arold Lorenz, N., Groussot, X. and Petursson, G., *The European Human Rights Culture – A Paradox of Human Rights Protection in Europe?* (Martinus Nijhoff, 2013)

Ashmore, R. and Del Boca, F., 'Conceptual Approaches to Stereotypes Sex Stereotypes and Stereotyping' in D. Hamilton (ed.), *Cognitive Processes in Stereotyping and Intergroup Behaviour* (Erlbaum Associates, 1981), pp. 1–35

Ashmore, R. and Del Boca, F., 'Sex Stereotypes and Implicit Personal Theory: Towards a Cognitive-Social Psychological Conceptualization', *Sex Roles*, 5(2) (1979), 219–48

Bainham, A., 'Contact as a Right and Obligation' in A. Bainham, B. Lindley, M. Richards and L. Trinder (eds.), *Children and Their Families: Contact, Rights and Welfare* (Hart, 2003), pp. 61–88

Bainham, A., 'Homosexual Adoption', *Cambridge Law Journal*, 67(3) (2008), 479–81

Bainham, A., 'Parentage, Parenthood and Parental Responsibility': Subtle, Elusive Yet Important Distinctions' in A. Bainham, S. Day Sclater and M. Richards (eds.), *What Is a Parent? A Socio-Legal Analysis* (Hart, 1999), pp. 25–46

Bainham, A., 'Sex, Gender and Fatherhood: Does Biology Really Matter?', *Cambridge Law Journal*, 56 (1997), 512–15

Bainham, A., '"Truth Will Out": Paternity in Europe', *Cambridge Law Journal*, (2007), 278–82

Bamforth, N., 'Families but Not (Yet) Marriages? Same-Sex Partners and the Developing European Convention "Margin of Appreciation"', *Child and Family Law Quarterly*, 23 (2011), 128–43

Bamforth, N., Malik, M. and O'Cinneide, C., *Discrimination Law: Theory and Context, Text and Materials* (Sweet & Maxwell, 2008)

Barnett, R., Marshall, N. and Pleck, J., 'Men's Multiple Roles and Their Relationship to Men's Psychological Distress', *Journal of Marriage and the Family*, 54(3) (1992), 358–67

Bates, E., *The Evolution of the European Convention on Human Rights: From Its Inception to the Creation of a Permanent Court of Human Rights* (Oxford University Press, 2010)

Bending, B., 'Images of Men in Feminist Legal Theory', *Pepperdine Law Review*, 20 (1993), 991–1052

Benvenisti, E., 'Margin of Appreciation, Consensus and Universal Standards', *New York University Journal of International Law and Politics*, 31(4) (1999), 843–54

Bergman, H. and Hobson, B., 'Compulsory Fatherhood: The Coding of Fatherhood in the Swedish Welfare State' in B. Hobson (ed.), *Making Men into Fathers – Men, Masculinities and the Social Politics of Fatherhood* (Cambridge University Press, 2002), pp. 92–124

Berkowitz, D. and Marsiglio, W., 'Gay Men: Negotiating Procreative, Father, and Family Identities', *Journal of Marriage and Family*, 69(2) (2007), 366–81

Berlant, L. and Warner, M., 'Sex in Public', *Critical Inquiry*, 24(2) (1998), 547–66

Beynon, J., *Masculinities and Culture* (Open University Press, 2002)

Boele-Woelki, K., Ferrand, F., González-Beilfuss, C. Jäntera-Jareborg, M., Lowe, N., Martiny, D. and Pintens, W. (eds.), *Principles of European Family Law Regarding Parental Responsibilities* (Intersentia, 2007)

Boyd, S., 'Backlash against Feminism: Canadian Custody and Access Reform Debates of the Late Twentieth Century', *Canadian Journal of Women and the Law*, 16(2) (2004), 255–90

Boyd, S., *Child Custody, Law and Women's Work* (Oxford University Press, 2003)

Bracken, L., 'Assessing the Best Interests of the Child in Cases of Cross-Border Surrogacy: Inconsistency in the Strasbourg Approach?', *Journal of Social Welfare and Family Law*, 39(3) (2017), 368–79

Bracken, L., 'Strasbourg's Response to Gay and Lesbian Parenting: Progress, then Plateau?', *International Journal of Children's Rights*, 24 (2016), 358–77

Bradley, A., 'Introduction: The Need for Both International and National Protection of Human Rights – The European Challenge' in S. Flogaitis, T. Zwart and J. Fraser (eds.), *The European Court of Human Rights and Its Discontents – Turning Criticism into Strength* (Edward Elgar, 2013), pp. 1–8

Brandth, B. and Kvande, E., 'Masculinity and Child Care: The Reconstruction of Fathering', *Sociological Review*, 26(2) (1998), 293–313

Brauch, J. A., 'The Margin of Appreciation and the Jurisprudence of the European Court of Human Rights: Threats to the Rule of the Law', *Columbia Journal of European Law*, 11(1) (2004–2005), 113–50

Brems, E., 'Evans v UK – Three Grounds for Ruling Differently' in S. Smet and E. Brems (eds.), *When Human Rights Clash at the European Court of Human Rights – Conflict or Harmony?* (Oxford University Press, 2017), pp. 75–94

Brems, E., 'Islamophobia at the ECtHR: A Test-Case for Positive Subsidiarity'. Unpublished draft paper presented at the ESIL-ECHR *Conference European Convention on Human Rights and Migration* (6 October 2017)

Brems, E., 'Margin of Appreciation Doctrine in the Case-Law of the European Court of Human Rights', *Zeitschrift für ausländisches öffentliches Recht und Völkerrecht*, 56 (1–2) (1996), 230–314

Brems, E., 'Procedural Protection – An Examination of Procedural Safeguards read into substantive Convention rights' in E. Brems and J. Gerards (eds.), *Shaping Rights in the ECHR – The Role of the European Court of Human Rights in Determining the Scope of Human Rights* (Cambridge University Press, 2013), pp. 136–61

Brems, E., 'Protecting the Rights of Women' in G. Lyons and J. Mayall (eds.), *International Human Rights in the 21st Century – Protecting the Rights of Groups* (Rowman & Littlefield, 2003)

Brod, H. (ed.), *The Making of Masculinities. The New Men's Studies* (Allen & Unwin, 1987)

Brod, H. and Kaufman, M., *Theorizing Masculinities* (Sage, 1994)

Bruinsma, F. and Parmentier, S., 'Interview with Mr Luzius Wildhaber, President of the European Court of Human Rights', *Netherlands Human Rights Review*, 21(2) (2003), 185–201

Buchbinder, D., *Masculinities and Identities* (Melbourne University Press, 1994)

Büchler, A. and Keller, H. (eds.), *Family Forms and Parenthood: Theory and Practice of Article 8 ECHR in Europe* (Intersentia, 2016)

Burbergs, M., 'How the Right to Respect for Private and Family Life, Home and Correspondence became the Nursery in which New Rights are Born' in E. Brems and J. Gerards (eds.), *Shaping Rights in the ECHR – The Role of the European Court of Human Rights in Determining the Scope of Human Rights* (Cambridge University Press, 2013), pp. 315–29

Calavita, K., *Invitation to Law and Society – An Introduction to the Study of Real Law* (University of Chicago Press, 2010)

Callahan, D., 'Bioethics and Fatherhood', *Utah Law Review*, (1992), 735–46

Cano Palomares, G., 'Right to Family Life and Access to Medically Assisted Procreation in the Case Law of the European Court of Human Rights' in M. Gonzales Pascual and

A. Torres Perez (eds.), *The Right to Family Life in the European Union* (Hart, 2017), pp. 99–114

Caracciolo di Torella, E., 'Brave New Fathers for a Brave New World? Fathers as Caregivers in an Evolving European Union', *European Law Journal*, 20(1) (2014), 88–106

Caracciolo di Torella, E., 'New Labour, New Dads – The Impact of Family Friendly Legislation on Fathers', *Industrial Law Journal*, 36 (2007), 318–28

Caracciolo di Torella, E. and Foubert, P., 'Surrogacy, Pregnancy and Maternity Rights: A Missed Opportunity for a More Coherent Regime of Parental Rights in the EU', *European Law Review*, 1 (2015), 52–69

Caracciolo di Torella, E. and Masselot, A., *Reconciling Work and Family Life in EU Law and Policy* (Palgrave Macmillan, 2010)

Carozza, P. G., 'Uses and Misuses of Comparative Law in International Human Rights: Some Reflections on the Jurisprudence of the European Court of Human Rights', *Notre Dame Law Review*, 73 (1997–1998), 1217–37

Catlett, B. and McKenry, P., 'Class-Based Masculinities: Divorce, Fatherhood and the Hegemonic Ideal', *Fathering*, 2(2) (2004), 165–90

Charlesworth, H., Chinkin, C. and Wright, S., 'Feminist Approaches to International Law', *American Journal of International Law*, 85 (1991), 613–45

Cherlin, A., 'The Growing Diversity of Two-Parent Families – Challenges for Family Law' in M. Garrison and E. Scott (eds.), *Marriage at the Crossroads – Law, Policy and the Brave New World of Twenty-First-Century Families* (Cambridge University Press, 2012), pp. 287–302

Chinkin, C., 'A Critique of the Public/Private Dimension', *European Journal of International Law*, 10(2) (1999), 387–95

Choudhry, S. and Herring, J., *European Human Rights and Family Law* (Hart, 2010)

Codd, H., 'Regulating Reproduction: Prisoners' Families, Artificial Insemination and Human Rights', *European Human Rights Law Review*, 1 (2006), 39–48

Codd, H., 'The Slippery Slope to Sperm Smuggling: Prisoners, Artificial Insemination and Human Rights', *Medical Law Review*, 15 (2007), 220–35

Coester-Waltjen, D., 'The Impact of the European Convention on Human Rights and the European Court of Human Rights on European Family Law' in J. M. Scherpe (ed.), *European Family Law – The Impact of Institutions and Organisations on European Family Law*, vol. I (Edward Elgar, 2016), pp. 49–94

Collier, R., 'Fatherhood, Gender and the Making of Professional Identity in Large Law Firms: Bringing Men into the Frame', *International Journal of Law in Context*, 15(1) (2019), 1–20

Collier, R., 'From Women's Emancipation to Sex War? Men, Heterosexuality and the Politics of Divorce' in S. Day Sclater and C. Piper (eds.), *Undercurrents of Divorce* (Ashgate, 1999), pp. 123–44

Collier, R., 'In Search of the "Good Father": Law, Family Practices and the Normative Reconstruction of Fatherhood' in A. Sarat and P. Ewick (eds.), *Studies in Law, Politics and Society* (Elsevier Science, 2001), pp. 133–71

Collier, R., 'Law and the Making of Fatherhood in Late Modernity: Reflections on Family Policy in England and Wales 1997–2010' in M. Oechsle, U. Müller and S. Hess (eds.), *Fatherhood in Late Modernity – Cultural Images, Social Practices and Structural Frames* (Verlag Barbara Budrich, 2012), pp. 295–316

Collier, R., 'Masculinities, Law and Personal Life: Towards a New Framework for Understanding Men, Law and Gender', *Harvard Journal of Law and Gender*, 33 (2010), 431–77

Collier, R., *Masculinity, Law and the Family* (Routledge, 1995)

Collier, R., *Men, Law and Gender: Essays on the 'Man' of Law* (Routledge, 2010)

Collier, R., 'Men, Gender and Fathers' Rights "After Equality": New Formations of Rights and Responsibilities in Family Justice' in R. Leckey (ed.), *After Legal Equality: Family, Sex, Kinship* (Routledge, 2014), pp. 59–76

Collier, R., 'The Responsible Father in New Labour's Legal and Social Policy' in J. Bridgeman, H. Keating and L., Craig (eds.) *Regulating Family Responsibilities* (Ashgate, 2011), pp. 47–66

Collier, R. and Sheldon, S. (eds.), *Fathers' Rights Activism and Law Reform in Comparative Perspective* (Hart, 2006)

Collier, R. and Sheldon, S., *Fragmenting Fatherhood: A Socio-Legal Study* (Hart, 2008)

Combs-Orme, T. and Renkert, L., 'Fathers and Their Infants: Caregiving and Affection in the Modern Family', *Journal of Human Behavior in the Social Environment*, 19 (2009), 394–418

Connell, R., *Masculinities* (Polity Press, 1995)

Connell, R., 'Theorizing Gender', *Sociology*, 19(2) (1985), 260–72

Cook, R. and Cusack, S., *Gender Stereotyping – Transnational Legal Perspectives* (University of Pennsylvania Press, 2010)

Costa, J.-P., 'On the Legitimacy of the European Court of Human Rights' Judgments', *European Constitutional Law Review*, 7(2) (2011), 173–82

Craig, L., 'Does Father Care Mean Fathers Share? A Comparison of How Much Mothers and Fathers in Intact Families Spend Time with Their Children', *Gender and Society*, 20 (2006), 259–81

Crouter, A. C., Bumpus, M. F., Head, M. R. and McHale, S. M., 'Implications of Overwork and Overload for the Quality of Men's Family Relationships', *Journal of Marriage and Family*, 63 (2001), 404–16

Crowley, J., 'Taking Custody of Motherhood: Fathers' Rights Activists and the Politics of Parenting', *Women's Studies Quarterly*, 37(3) (2009), 223–40

Curry-Sumner, I., 'ced*E.B. v France*: A Missed Opportunity?', *Child and Family Law Quarterly*, 21(3) (2009), 356–66

Daar, J., 'Accessing Reproductive Technologies: Invisible Barriers, Indelible Harms', *Berkeley Journal of Gender, Law and Justice*, 23(1) (2013), 35–45

Day, R. and Lamb, M. (eds.), *Conceptualizing and Measuring Father Involvement* (Lawrence Erlbaum Associates, 2004)

de Silva de Alwis, R. 'Examining Gender Stereotypes in New Work–Family Reconciliation Policies: The Creation of a New Paradigm for Egalitarian Legislation', *Duke Journal of Gender Law and Policy*, 18 (2011), 305–34

Delmas-Marty, M., *The European Convention for the Protection of Human Rights. International Protection versus National Restrictions* (Kluwer, 1992)

Diduck, A. and Kaganas, F., *Family Law, Gender and the State* (Hart, 1999)

Doucet, A., *Do Men Mother? Fathering, Care and Domestic Responsibility* (Toronto University Press, 2006)

Dowd, N. E., 'Asking the Man Question: Masculinities Analysis and Feminist Theory', *Harvard Journal of Law and Gender*, 33 (2010), 415–30

Dowd, N. E., 'Fathers and the Supreme Court: Founding Fathers and Nurturing Fathers', *Emory Law Journal*, 54 (2005), 1271–334

Dowd, N. E., 'From Genes, Marriage and Money to Nurture: Redefining Fatherhood', *Cardozo Women's Law Journal*, 10 (2003–2004), 132–45

Dowd, N. E., *The Man Question – Male Subordination and Privilege* (New York University Press, 2010)

Dowd, N. E., 'Multiple Parents/Multiple Fathers', *Journal of Law and Family Studies*, 9 (2007), 231–63.

Dowd, N. E., *Redefining Fatherhood* (New York University Press, 2000)

Dowd, N. E., 'Work and Family: Restructuring the Workplace', *Arizona Law Review*, 32 (1990) 431–500

Draghici, C., *Legitimacy of Family Rights in Strasbourg Case Law: Living Instrument or Extinguished Sovereignty?* (Hart, 2017)

Dunn, J., Cheng, H., O'Connor, T. and Bridges, L., 'Children's Perspectives on Their Relationships with Their Non-resident Fathers: Influences, Outcomes and Implications', *Journal of Child Psychology and Psychiatry*, 45(3) (2004), 553–66

Dzehtsiarou, K., *European Consensus and the Legitimacy of the European Court of Human Rights* (Cambridge University Press, 2015)

Ekberg, J., Eriksson, R. and Friebel, G., 'Parental Leave – A Policy Evaluation of the Swedish "Daddy-Month" Reform', *Journal of Public Economics*, 97 (2013), 131–43

Ellison, G., Barker, A. and Kulasuriya, T., *Work and Care: A Study of Modern Parents* (Equality and Human Rights Commission, 2009) online at https://dera.ioe.ac.uk/11030/1/15._work_and_care_modern_parents_15_report.pdf (last access on 15 February 2019)

Esping-Andersen, G., *Incomplete Revolution: Adapting Welfare States to Women's New Roles* (Polity Press, 2009)

Eurofound, *Parental and Paternity Leave – Uptake by Fathers* (Publications Office of the European Union, 2019), online at https://euagenda.eu/upload/publications/untitled-199581-ea.pdf (last access on 15 February 2019)

Eurostat, *Share of Live Birth Outside Marriage*, online at http://ec.europa.eu/eurostat/tgm/table.do?tab=table&init=1&language=en&pcode=tps00018&plugin=1 (last access on 9th February 2019)

Farnós Amorós, E., 'Biology-Based Systems of Parentage and Safety Valves Protecting Social Parenting' in M. González Pascual and A. Torres Pérez (eds.), *The Right to Family Life in the European Union* (Routledge, 2016), pp. 115–30

Featherstone, B., *Contemporary Fathering: Theory, Policy and Practice* (Policy Press, 2009)

Featherstone, B. and Peckover, S., '"Letting Them Get Away with It": Fathers, Domestic Violence and Child Protection', *Critical Social Policy*, 27(2) (2007), 181–203

Featherstone, B. and Trinder, L., 'New Labour, Families and Fathers', *Critical Social Policy*, 21(4) (2001), 534–36

Feldman, D., *Civil Liberties and Human Rights in England and Wales* (Oxford University Press, 2002)

Fenton-Glynn, C., 'International Surrogacy before the European Court of Human Rights', *Journal of Private International Law*, 13(3) (2017), 546–67

Feuillet-Liger, B., 'Preface' in B. Feuillet-Liger, T. Callus and K. Orfali (eds.), *Reproductive Technology and Changing Perceptions of Parenthood Around the World* (Bruylant, 2014), pp. 19–30

Fineman, M., *The Autonomy Myth: A Theory of Dependency* (New Press, 2004)

Fineman, M., 'Beyond Identities: The Limits of an Antidiscrimination Approach to Equality', *Boston University Law Review*, 92(6) (2012), 1713–70

Fineman, M., 'Fatherhood, Feminism and Family Law', *McGeorge Law Review*, 32 (2000–2001), 1031–50

Fineman, M., 'Feminism, Masculinity and Multiple Identities', *Nevada Law Journal*, 13(2) (2013), 619–40

Fineman, M., 'Legal Stories, Change and Incentives – Reinforcing the Law of the Father', *New York Law School Law Review*, 37 (1992), 227–50

Fineman, M., *The Neutered Mother, the Sexual family and Other Twentieth Century Tragedies* (Routledge, 1995)

Fineman, M., 'The Sexual *Family*' in M. Fineman, J. Jackson and A. Romero (eds.), *Feminist and Queer Legal Theory – Intimate Encounters, Uncomfortable Conversations* (Ashgate, 2009), pp. 45–64

Fineman, M. and Thomson, M. (eds.), *Exploring Masculinities – Feminist Legal Theory Reflections* (Ashgate, 2013)

Finley, G. and Schwartz, S., 'Parsons and Bales Revisited: Young Adult Children's Characterisation of the Fathering Role', *Psychology of Men and Masculinity*, 7(1) (2006), 42–55

Føllesdal, A., Peters, B. and Ulfstein, G., 'Conclusions' in A. Føllesdal, B. Peters and G. Ulfstein (eds.), *Constituting Europe – The European Court of Human Rights in a National, European and Global Context* (Cambridge University Press, 2013), pp. 1–24

Føllesdal, A., Peters, B. and Ulfstein, G., 'Introduction' in A. Føllesdal, B. Peters and G. Ulfstein (eds.), *Constituting Europe – The European Court of Human Rights in a National, European and Global Context* (Cambridge University Press, 2013), pp. 389–402

Fortin, J., 'Children's Right to Know Their Origins – Too Far, Too Fast?', *Child and Family Law Quarterly*, 21(3) (2009), 336–55

Franklin, C., 'The Anti-Stereotyping Principle in Constitutional Sex Discrimination Law', *New York University Law Review*, 85 (2010), 83–173

Fraser, J., 'Conclusion: The European Convention on Human Rights as a common European endeavour' in S. Flogaitis, T. Zwart and J. Fraser (eds.), *The European Court of Human Rights and Its Discontents – Turning Criticism into Strength* (Edward Elgar, 2013), pp. 192–210

Fraser, N., *Fortunes of Feminism: From State-Managed Capitalism to Neo-Liberal Crisis* (Verso Books, 2013)

Fredman, S., *Human Rights Transformed: Positive Rights and Positive Duties* (Oxford University Press, 2008)

Fredman, S., 'Reversing Roles: Bringing Men into the Frame', *International Law in Context*, 10(4) (2014), 442–59

Fredman, S., *Women and the Law* (Clarendon Press, 1997)

Freeman, M. *Commentary on the United Nations Convention on the Rights of the Child – Article 3: The Best Interests of the Child* (Martinus Nijhoff, 2007)

Furstenberg, F. and Harris, K., 'When Fathers Matter/Why Fathers Matter: The Impact of Paternal Involvement on the Offspring of Adolescent Mothers' in D. Rhode (ed.), *The Politics of Pregnancy: Adolescent Sexuality and Public Policy* (Yale University Press, 1993), pp. 189–215

Furstenberg, F. and Nord, C., 'Parenting Apart: Patterns of Childrearing after Marital Dissolution', *Journal of Marriage and the Family*, 47 (1985), 893–900

Fuscaldo, G., 'Genetic Ties: Are They morally binding?', *Bioethics*, 20(2) (2006), 64–76

Galanter, M., 'The Radiating Effects of Courts', in K. O. Boyum and L. Mather (eds.), *Empirical Theories about Courts* (Longman, 1983), pp. 117–42

Gallo, D., Paladini, L. and Pustorino, P. (eds.), *Same-Sex Couples, before National, Supranational and International Jurisdictions* (Springer, 2014)

Gans, D., 'Stereotyping and Difference: Planned Parenthood v Casey and the Future of Sex Discrimination Law', *Yale Law Journal*, 104 (1994–1995), 1875–906

Gerards, J., 'Discrimination Grounds' in S. Schiek, L. Waddington and M. Bell (eds.), *Cases, Materials and Text on National, Supranational and International Non-Discrimination Law: Ius Commune Casebooks for the Common Law of Europe* (Hart, 2007), pp. 33–184

Gerards, J., 'The Discrimination Grounds of Article 14 of the European Court of Human Rights', *Human Rights Law Review*, 13(1) (2013), 99–124

Gerards, J., *General Principles of the European Convention on Human Rights* (Cambridge University Press, 2019)

Gerards, J., *Judicial Review in Equal Treatment Cases* (Martinus Nijhoff, 2005)

Gerards, J., 'Margin of Appreciation and Incrementalism in the Case Law of the European Court of Human Rights', *Human Rights Law Review*, 18 (2018), 495–515

Gerards, J. and Senden, H., 'The Structure of Fundamental Rights and the European Court of Human Rights', *International Journal of Constitutional Law*, 7 (2009), 619–53

Gilmore, S., 'Contact/Shared Residence and Child Well-Being: Research Evidence and Its Implications for Legal Decision-Making', *International Journal of Law, Policy and the Family*, 20 (2006), 344–65

Gittins, D., *The Family in Question – Changing Households and Familiar Ideologies* (Macmillan, 1993)

Goldberg, A., *Gay Dads: Transitions to Adoptive Parenthood* (New York University Press, 2012)

Goldberg, A. E., Downing, J. B. and Moyer, A. M, 'Why Parenthood, and Why Now? Gay Men's Motivations for Pursuing Parenthood', *Family Relations*, 61 (1) (2012), 157–174.

Golombok, S., *Modern Families: Parents and Children in New Family Forms* (Cambridge University Press, 2015)

Gonzalez Salzberg, D. A., *Sexuality and Transsexuality under the European Convention on Human Rights: A Queer Reading of Human Rights Law* (Hart, 2019)

Gornick, J. and Meyers, M., *Families That Work: Policies for Reconciling Parenthood and Employment* (Russel Sage Foundation, 2003)

Grabenwarter, C., *European Convention on Human Rights – Commentary* (Hart, 2014)

Gross, O. and Ní Aoláin, F., 'From Discretion to Scrutiny: Revisiting the Application of the Margin of Appreciation Doctrine in the Context of Article 15 of the European Convention on Human Rights', *Human Rights Quarterly*, 23 (3) (2001), 625–49

Gülalp, H., 'Secularism and the European Court of Human Rights', *European Public Law*, 16(3) (2010), 455–71

Gurol, S., 'Challenging Gender Stereotyping before the ECtHR: Case of *Carvalho Pinto v Portugal*', *EJIL: Talk!*, online at https://www.ejiltalk.org/challenging-gender-stereo typing-before-the-ecthr-case-of-carvalho-pinto-v-portugal/ (last access on 11 February 2019)

Haimes, E., 'Recreating the Family? Policy Considerations Relating to the "New" Reproductive Technologies' in M. McNeil, I. Varcoe and S. Yearly (eds.), *The New Reproductive Technologies* (Macmillan, 1990), pp. 154–72

Harkness, S., 'The Household Division of Labour: Changes in Families' Allocation of Paid and Unpaid Work' in J. Scott, S. Dex and J. Wadsworth (eds.), *Women and Employment: Changing Lives and New Challenges* (Edward Elgar, 2008), pp. 234–67

Harris, D., O'Boyle, M., Bates, E. and Buckley, C., *Harris, O'Boyle, and Warbrick: Law of the European Convention on Human Rights*, 3rd edn. (Oxford University Press, 2014)

Harris, D., O'Boyle, M. and Warbrick, C., *Harris, O'Boyle, and Warbrick: Law of the European Convention on Human Rights* (Butterworth, 1995)

Hart, L., 'Individual Adoption by Non-Heterosexuals and the Order of Family Life in the European Court of Human Rights', *Journal of Law and Society*, 36(4) (2009), 536–57

Haverkort-Speekenbrink, S., *European Non-Discrimination Law – A Comparison of EU Law and the ECHR in the Field of Non-Discrimination and Freedom of Religion in Public Employment with an Emphasis on the Islamic Headscarf Issue* (Intersentia, 2012)

Hearn, J., 'Men, Fathers and the State: National and Global Relations' in B. Hobson (ed.), *Making Men into Fathers – Men, Masculinities and Social Politics of Fatherhood* (Cambridge University Press, 2002), pp. 254–72

Helfer, L. R., 'Consensus, Coherence and the European Convention on Human Rights', *Cornell International Law Journal*, 26(1) (1993), 133–65

Hill, J., 'What Does It Mean to Be a 'Parent'? The Claims of Biology as the Basis for Parental Rights', *New York Law Review*, 66 (1991), 353–420

Hobson, B. and Morgan, D., 'Introduction: Making Men into Fathers' in B. Hobson (ed.), *Making Men into Fathers – Men, Masculinities and the Social Politics of Fatherhood* (Cambridge University Press, 2002), pp. 1–22

Hochschild, A. R., *The Second Shift* (Penguin Group, 2003)

Hochschild, A. R. and Machung, A., *The Second Shift: Working Parents and the Revolution at Home* (Viking Penguin, 1989)

Hodson, L., 'A Marriage by Any Other Name? *Schalk and Kopf v Austria*', *Human Rights Law Review*, 11(1) (2011), 170–79

Hodson, L., 'Ties That Bind: Towards a Child-Centred Approach to Lesbian, Gay, Bisexual and Transgender Families under the ECHR', *International Journal of Children's Rights*, 20 (2012), 501–22

Horsey, K., 'Challenging Presumptions: Legal Parenthood and Surrogacy Arrangements', *Child and Family Law Quarterly*, 22(4) (2010), 449–74

Ives, J., Becoming a Father/Refusing Fatherhood: How Paternal Responsibilities and Rights are Generated. PhD thesis, University of Birmingham (July 2007)

Jackson, E., 'Case Commentary – Prisoners, Their Partners and the Right to Family life', *Child and Family Law Quarterly*, 19(2) (2007), 239–46

Jacobs, M., 'Why Just Two? Disaggregating Traditional Parental Rights and Responsibility to Recognize Multiple Parents', *Journal of Law and Family Studies*, 9 (2007), 309–40

James, A., 'Parents: A Children's Perspective' in A. Bainham, S. Day Sclater and M. Richards (eds.), *What Is a Parent? A Socio-Legal Analysis* (Hart, 1999), pp. 181–95

Jänterä-Jareborg, M., 'Parenthood for Same-Sex Couples – Scandinavian Developments' in K. Boele-Woelki and A. Fuchs (eds.), *Legal Recognition of Same-Sex Relationships in Europe – National, Cross-Border and European Perspectives* (Intersentia, 2012), pp. 91–122

Jennings, S., Mellish, L., Casey, P., Tasker, F., Lamb, M. and Golombok, S., 'Why Adoption? Gay, Lesbian and Heterosexual Adoptive Parents' Reasons for Adoptive Parenthood', *Adoption Quarterly*, 17 (3) (2014), 205–26.

Johansson, T. and Andreasson, J., *Fatherhood in Transition – Masculinity, Identity and Everyday Life* (Palgrave Macmillan, 2017)

Johnson, M., 'A Biological Perspective on Parenthood' in A. Bainham, S. Day Sclater and M. Richards (eds.), *What Is a Parent? A Socio-Legal Analysis* (Hart, 1999), pp. 47–72

Johnson, P., '"An Essentially Private Manifestation of Human Personality": Constructions of Homosexuality in the European Court of Human Rights', *Human Rights Law Review*, 10 (2010), 67–97

Johnson, P., 'Adoption, Homosexuality and the European Convention on Human Rights: *Gas and Dubois v France*', *Modern Law Review*, 75(6) (2012), 1136–49

Johnson, P., 'Challenging the Heteronormativity of Marriage: The Role of Judicial Interpretation and Authority', *Social and Legal Studies*, 20 (2011), 349–67

Johnson, P., 'Heteronormativity and the European Court of Human Rights', *Law and Critique*, 23 (2012), 43–66

Johnson, P., *Homosexuality and the European Court of Human Rights* (Routledge, 2013)

Johnson, P., 'Marriage, Heteronormativity, and the European Court of Human Rights: A Reappraisal', *International Journal of Law, Policy and the Family*, 29 (2015), 56–77

Johnson, P., '*X and Others v Austria*', ECHR Blog, 21 February 2013, online at http://echrblog.blogspot.com/2013/02/x-v-austria-judgment.html (last access on 15 February 2019)

Kaganas, F. and Day Sclater, S., 'Contact Disputes: Narrative Constructions of "Good" Parents', *Feminist Legal Studies*, 12(1) (2004), 1–27

Kapotas. P. and Tzvelekos V. P. (eds.), *Building Consensus on European Consensus: Judicial Interpretation of Human Rights in Europe and Beyond* (Cambridge University Press, 2019)

Khaliq, U., 'Transsexuals in the European Court of Human Rights: *X, Y and Z v UK*', *Northern Ireland Legal Quarterly*, 49(2) (1998), 191–201

Kilkelly, U., 'Protecting Children's Rights under the ECHR: The Role of Positive Obligations', *Northern Ireland Legal Quarterly*, 61(3) (2010), 245–61

Kimmel, M., *The Gendered Society* (Oxford University Press, 2004)

Knijn, T. and Selten, P., 'Transformations of Fatherhood: The Netherlands' in B. Hobson (ed.), *Making Men into Fathers – Men, Masculinities and the Social Politics of Fatherhood* (Cambridge University Press, 2002), pp. 168–88

Kratochvíl, J., 'The Inflation of the Margin of Appreciation by the European Court of Human Rights', *Netherlands Quarterly of Human Rights*, 29(3) (2011), 324–57

Krause, H., 'Comparative Family Law: Past Traditions Battle Future Trends – and Viceversa' in M. Reimann and R. Zimmermann (eds.), *The Oxford Handbook of Comparative Law* (Oxford University Press, 2006), pp. 1099–128

LaRossa, R., *The Modernization of Fatherhood: A Social and Political History* (University of Chicago Press, 1997)

Lau, H., 'Rewriting *Schalk and Kopf*: Shifting the Locus of Deference' in E. Brems (ed.), *Diversity and Human Rights: Rewriting Judgments of the ECHR* (Cambridge University Press, 2012), pp. 243–64

Lavrysen, L., *Human Rights in a Positive State – Rethinking the Relationship between Positive and Negative Obligations under the European Convention on Human Rights* (Intersentia, 2016)

Lavrysen, L., 'The Scope of Rights and the Scope of Obligations – Positive Obligations' in Brems and Gerards (eds.), *Shaping Rights in the ECHR: The Role of the European Court of Human Rights in Determining the Scope of Rights* (Cambridge University Press, 2013), pp. 162–82

Letsas, G., 'The ECHR as a Living Instrument: Its Meaning and Legitimacy' in A. Føllesdal, B. Peters and G. Ulfstein (eds.), *Constituting Europe: The European Court of Human Rights in a National, European and Global Context* (Cambridge University Press, 2013), pp. 106–41

Letsas, G., *A Theory of Interpretation of the European Convention on Human Rights* (Oxford University Press, 2007)

Lev, A. I., 'Gay Dads. Choosing Surrogacy', *Gay and Lesbian Psychology Review*, 7(1) (2006), pp. 73–7

Levinet, M., 'Couple et vie familiale' in F. Sudre (ed.), *Le droit au respect de la vie familiale dans la Convention européenne des droits de l'homme* (Nemesis-Bruylant, 2002), pp. 107–60

Levit, N., 'Feminism for Men: Legal Ideology and the Construction of Maleness', *UCLA Law Review*, 43 (1996), 1037–116

Lewin, E., 'Family Values: Gay Men and Adoption in America' in K. Wegar (ed.), *Adoptive Families in a Diverse Society* (Rutgers University Press, 2006), pp. 129–45

Lewis, J., 'The Decline of the Male Breadwinner Model: Implications for Work and Care', *Social Politics*, 8(2) (2001), 152–69

Liddy, J., 'The Concept of Family Life under the ECHR', *European Human Rights Law Review*, 1 (1998), 15–25

Lim, E., 'Of "Landmark" or "Leading" Cases: Salomon's Challenge', *Journal of Law and Society*, 41(4) (2014), 523–50

Lind, C., '*Evans v United Kingdom* – Judgments of Solomon: Power, Gender and Procreation', *Child and Family Law Quarterly*, 18 (2006), 576–92

Lo, W. and Campo-Engelstein, L., 'Expanding the Clinical Definition of Infertility to Include Socially Infertile Individuals and Couples' in L. Campo-Engelstein and P. Burcher (eds.), *Reproductive Ethics II – New Ideas and Innovations* (Springer, 2018), pp. 71–83

Lõhmus, K., *Caring Autonomy: European Human Rights Law and the Challenge of Individualism* (Cambridge University Press, 2015)

Lord Lester of Herne Hill, 'The European Convention in the New Architecture of Europe', *Public Law*, Spring (1996), 5–10

Macdonald, R., 'The Margin of Appreciation' in R. Macdonald, F. Matscher and H. Petzold (eds.), *The European System for the Protection of Human Rights* (1993), pp. 83–124

Mahoney, P., 'The Comparative Method in Judgments of the European Court of Human Rights: Reference Back to National Law' in G. Canivet, M. Andenas and D. Fairgrieve (eds.), *Comparative Law before the Courts* (British Institute of International and Comparative Law, 2004), pp. 135–50

Mahoney, P., 'Judicial Activism and Judicial Self-Restraint in the European Court of Human Rights: Two Sides of the Same Coin', *Human Rights Law Journal*, 11 (1–2) (1990), 57–88

Mahoney, P., 'Marvellous Richness of Diversity or Invidious Cultural Relativism', *Human Rights Law Journal*, 19(1) (1998), 1–6

Margaria, A., '"New Fathers" and the Right to Parental Leave: Is the European Court of Human Rights Satisfied with Just Breadwinning?' in R. Harding, R. Fletcher and C. Beasley (eds.). *ReValuing Care in Theory, Law and Policy: Cycles and Connections* (Routledge, 2017), pp. 131–47

Margaria, A., *Nuove Forme di Filiazione e Genitorialità: Leggi e Giudici di fronte alle Nuove Realtà* (Il Mulino, 2018)

Matscher, F., 'Methods of Interpretation of the Convention' in R. Macdonald and H. Petzold (eds.), *The European System for the Protection of Human Rights* (Martinus Nijhoff, 1993), pp. 63–81

Maurer, T. and Pleck, J., 'Fathers' Caregiving and Breadwinning: A Gender Congruence Analysis', *Psychology of Men and Masculinity*, 7(2) (2006), 101–12

May, A. and Tenzek, K., '"A Gift We Are Unable to Create Ourselves": Uncertainty Reduction in Online Classified Ads Posted by Gay Men Pursuing Surrogacy', *Journal of GLBT Family Studies*, 12(5) (2016), 430–50

May, V. and Smart, C., 'Silence in Court? Hearing Children in Residence and Contact Disputes', *Child and Family Law Quarterly*, 16(3) (2004), 305–15

McCandless, J. and Sheldon, S., 'The Human Fertilisation and Embryology Act (2008) and the Tenacity of the Sexual Family Form', *Modern Law Review*, 73(2) (2010), 175–207

McColgan, A., 'Principle of Equality and Protection from Discrimination in International Human Rights Law', *European Human Rights Law Review*, 2 (2003), 157–76

McGlynn, C., *Families and the European Union – Law, Policy and Pluralism* (Cambridge University Press, 2006)

McGlynn, C., 'Ideologies of Motherhood in European Community Sex Equality Law', *European Law Journal*, 6 (2000), 29–44

McGoldrick, D., 'Religion in the European Public Square and in European Public Life – Crucifixes in the Classroom?', *Human Rights Law Review*, 11(3) (2011), 451–502

Meyer, E., 'Gay Fathers: Disrupting Sex Stereotyping and Challenging the Father-Promotion Crusade', *Columbia Journal of Gender and Law*, 22(2) (2011), 479–529

Mowbray, A., 'Between the Will of the Contracting States and the Needs of Today – Extending the Scope of Convention Rights and Freedoms Beyond what Could Have

Been Foreseen by the Drafters of the ECHR' in E. Brems and J. Gerards (eds.), *Shaping Rights in the ECHR – The Role of the European Court of Human Rights in Determining the Scope of Human Rights* (Cambridge University Press, 2013), pp. 17–37

Mowbray, A., The Creativity of the European Court of Human Rights, *Human Rights Law Review*, 5(1) (2005), 57–79

Mowbray, A., *The Development of Positive Obligations under the European Convention on Human Rights by the European Court of Human Rights* (Hart, 2004)

Müller-Freienfels, W., 'The Unification of Family Law', *American Journal of Comparative Law*, 16(1/2) (1968), 175–218

Mulligan, A., 'Identity Rights and Sensitive Ethical Questions: The European Convention on Human Rights and the Regulation of Surrogacy Arrangements', *Medical Law Review*, 26(3) (2018), 449–75

Nelson, T., *Handbook of Prejudice, Stereotyping and Discrimination* (Psychology Press, 2009)

Nelson, K., 'Reproductive Ethics and the Family', *New Zealand Bioethics Journal*, 1(1) (2000), 4–10

Ní Shúilleabháin, M., 'Surrogacy, System Shopping, and Article 8 of the European Convention on Human Rights', *International Journal of Law, Policy and the Family*, 33(1) (2019), 104–22

Nikolaidis, C., *The Right to Equality in European Human Rights Law – The Quest for Substance in the Jurisprudence of the European Courts* (Routledge, 2015)

Norton, W., Hudson, N. and Culley, L., 'Gay Men Seeking Surrogacy to Achieve Parenthood', *Reproductive BioMedicine Online*, 27 (2013), 271–79

Nozawa, J., 'Drawing the Line: Same-Sex Adoption and the Jurisprudence of the ECtHR on the Application of the "European consensus" Standard under Article 14', *Merkourios – Utrecht Journal of International and European Law*, 29 (77) (2013), 66–75

O'Connell, R., 'Cinderella Comes to the Ball: Article 14 and the Right to Non-Discrimination in the ECHR', *Legal Studies*, 29(2) (2009), 211–29

O'Donovan, K., *Family Law Matters* (Pluto Press, 2003)

O'Donovan, K., *Sexual Divisions in Law* (Weidenfeld & Nicolson, 1985)

O'Mahony, C., 'Irreconcilable Differences? Article 8 ECHR and Irish Law on Non-Traditional Families', *International Journal of Law, Policy and the Family*, 26 (1) (2012), 31–61

Ostner, I., 'A New Role for Fathers? The German Case' in B. Hobson (ed.), *Making Men into Fathers – Men, Masculinities and the Social Politics of Fatherhood* (Cambridge University Press, 2002), pp. 150–67

Pavlich, G., 'Paradigmatic Case' in A. J. Mills, G. Durepos and E. Wiebe (eds.), *Encyclopedia of Case Study Research, vol II* (Sage, 2010), pp. 645–47

Peroni, L. and Timmer, A., 'Gender Stereotyping in Domestic Violence Cases – An Analysis of the European Court of Human Rights' Jurisprudence' in E. Brems and A. Timmer (eds.), *Stereotypes and Human Rights Law* (Intersentia, 2016), pp. 39–66

Perreau, B., *The Politics of Adoption – Gender and the Making of French Citizenship* (MIT Press, 2014)

Plantin, L., Back-Wiklund, M., Kovacheva, S. and Guerreiro, M., 'Comparing Transitions to Fatherhood Across Contexts' in A. Nilsen, J. Brannen and S. Lewis (eds.), *Transitions to Parenthood in Europe – A Comparative Life Course Perspective* (Policy Press, 2012), pp. 67–88

Plantin, L., Mansson, S. and Kearney, J., 'Talking and Doing Fatherhood: On Fatherhood and Masculinity in Sweden and England', *Fathering*, 1(1) (2003), 3–24

Pleck, J., 'American Fathering in Historical Perspective' in M. Kimmel (ed.), *Changing Men: New Directions in Research on Men and Masculinity* (Sage, 1987), pp. 83–97

Pleck, J., 'Fatherhood and Masculinity' in M. Lamb (ed.), *The Role of the Father in Child Development* (Wiley, 2010), pp. 27–57

Polikoff, N., 'Recognising Partners but Not Parents/Recognising Parents but Not Partners: Gay and Lesbian Family Law in Europe and the United States', *New York Law School Journal of Human Rights*, 17 (2000–2001), 711–51

Rainey, B., Wicks, E. and Ovey, C., *Jacobs, White and Ovey: The European Convention on Human Rights*, 6th edn (Oxford University Press, 2014)

Rainey, B., Wicks, E. and Ovey, C., *Jacobs, White and Ovey: The European Convention on Human Rights*, 7th edn (Oxford University Press, 2017)

Rao, R., 'Assisted Reproductive Technology and the Threat to the Traditional Family', *Hastings Law Journal*, 47 (1996), 951–66

Rhoades, H., 'The Rise and Rise of Shared Parenting Laws – A Critical Reflection', *Canadian Journal of Family Law*, 19 (2002), 75–113

Rubio Marín, R., 'A New European Parity–Democracy Sex Equality Model and Why It won't Fly in the United States', *American Journal of Comparative Law*, 60 (2012), 99–126

Ruddick, S., 'The Idea of Fatherhood' in H. L. Nelson (ed.), *Feminism and Families* (Routledge, 1997), pp. 205–20

Ruspini, E., *Diversity in Family Life – Gender, Relationships and Social Change* (Policy Press, 2013)

Ruspini, E. and Crespi, I., *Balancing Work and Family in a Changing Society: The Fathers' Perspective* (Palgrave, 2016)

Ryan, C., 'Europe's Moral Margin: Parental Aspirations and the European Court of Human Rights', *Columbia Journal of Transnational Law*, 56 (2018), 467–523

Sabatello, M., 'Are the Kids All Right? A Child-Centred Approach to Assisted Reproductive Technologies', *Netherlands Quarterly Human Rights*, 31(1) (2013), 74–98

Sadl, U. and Panagis, Y., 'What Is a Leading Case in EU law? An Empirical Analysis', *European Law Review*, 40(1) (2015), 15–34

Scherpe, J. M. (ed.), *European Family Law – Family Law in a European Perspective*, vol. III (Edward Elgar, 2016)

Scherpe, J. M. (ed.), *European Family Law – The Impact of Institutions and Organisations on European Family Law*, vol. I (Edward Elgar, 2016)

Scherpe, J. M. (ed.), *European Family Law – The Present and the Future of European Family Law*, vol. IV (Edward Elgar, 2016)

Scherpe, J. M., 'Medically Assisted Procreation: This Margin Needs to Be Appreciated – ECtHR, Grand Chamber 3. 11.2011 (S.H. and Others v Austria)', *Cambridge Law Journal*, (2012), 276–79

Schokkenbroek, J., 'The Prohibition of Discrimination in Article 14 of the Convention and the Margin of Appreciation', *Human Rights Law Review*, 19(1) (1998), 20–34

Scott, J. and Clery, E., 'Gender Roles: An Incomplete Revolution?' in A. Park, C. Bryson, E. Clery, J. Curtice and M. Phillips (eds.), *British Social Attitudes: The 30th Report*, online at http://www.bsa.natcen.ac.uk/media/38723/bsa30_full_report_final.pdf (last access on 15 February 2019)

Sevenhuijsen, S., 'The Gendered Juridification of Parenthood', *Social and Legal Studies*, 1(1) (1992), 71–83

Shany, Y., 'Towards a General Margin of Appreciation Doctrine in International Law ?', *European Journal of International Law*, 16(5) (2005), 907–40

Sharp, L., 'Blood Ties, Bioethics and the Bright-Line of the Law' in B. Feuillet-Liger, T. Callus and K. Orfali (eds.), *Reproductive Technology and Changing Perceptions of Parenthood Around the World* (Bruylant, 2014), pp. 15–18

Sheldon, S., 'Fragmenting Fatherhood: The Regulation of Reproductive Technologies', *Modern Law Review*, 68 (2005), 523–53

Sheldon, S., 'From "Absent Objects of Blame" to "Fathers Who Want to Take the Responsibility": Reforming Birth Registration Law', *Journal of Social Welfare and Family Law*, 31(4) (2009), 373–89

Shultz, M. M., 'Reproductive Technology and Intent-based Parenthood: An Opportunity for Gender Neutrality', *Wisconsin Law Review*, (1990), 297–398

Simpson, B., Jessup, J. and McCarthy, P., 'Fathers after Divorce' in A. Bainham, B. Lindley, M. Richards and L. Trinder (eds.), *Children and Their Families: Contact, Rights and Welfare* (Hart, 2003), pp. 201–22

Singh, R., 'Is There a Role for the "Margin of Appreciation" in National Law after the Human Rights Act?', *European Human Rights Law Review*, 1 (1999), 15–22

Smart, C., 'Equal Shares: Rights for Fathers of Recognition for Children?', *Critical Social Policy*, 24(4) (2004), 484–503

Smart, C., 'Making Kin: Relationality and Law' in A. Bottomley and S. Wong, *Changing Contours of Domestic Life, Family and Law – Caring and Sharing* (Hart, 2009), pp. 7–23

Smart, C. and Neale, B., *Family Fragments?* (Polity Press, 1999)

Smart, C. and Neale, B., '"It's My Life Too" – Children's Perspectives on Post-Divorce Parenting', *Family Law*, 30 (2000), 163–69

Smet, S., '*X and Others v Austria* (Part II): A Narrow Ruling on a Narrow Issue', *Strasbourg Observers*, 6 March 2013, online at https://strasbourgobservers.com/2013/03/06/x-and-others-v-austria-part-ii-a-narrow-ruling-on-a-narrow-issue/ (last access on 15 February 2019)

Smith, L., 'Clashing Symbols? Reconciling Support for Fathers and Fatherless Families after the Human Fertilisation and Embryology Act 2008', *Child and Family Law Quarterly*, 22 (2010), 46–70

Stalford, H., 'Concepts of Family Law under EU Law – Lessons from the ECHR', *International Journal of Law, Policy and the Family*, 16 (2002), 410–34

Strathern, M., *After Nature: English Kinship in the Late Twentieth Century* (Cambridge University Press, 1992)

Suk, J., 'Are Gender Stereotypes Bad for Women? Rethinking Antidiscrimination Law and Work-Family Reconciliation', *Columbia Law Review*, 110(1) (2010), 1–69

Suk, J., 'From Antidiscrimination to Equality: Stereotypes and the Life Cycle in the United States and Europe', *American Journal of Comparative Law*, 75 (2012), 75–98

Swennen, F. and Croce, M., 'Family (Law) Assemblages: New Modes of Being (Legal)', *Journal of Law and Society*, 44(4) (2017), 532–58

Timmer, A., 'From Inclusion to Transformation: Rewriting *Konstantin Markin v Russia*' in E. Brems (ed.), *Diversity and European Human Rights: Rewriting Judgments of the ECHR* (Cambridge University Press, 2012), pp. 148–69

Timmer, A., 'Toward an Anti-Stereotyping Approach for the European Court of Human Rights', *Human Rights Law Review*, 11(4) (2011), 707–38

Tobin, B., 'The European Court of Human Rights' Inconsistent and Incoherent Approach to Second-Parent Adoption', *European Human Rights Law Review*, 1 (2017), 59–67

Tobin, J. and McNair, R., 'Public International Law and the Regulation of Private Spaces: Does the Convention on the Rights of the Child Impose an Obligation on States to Allow Gay and Lesbian to Adopt?', *International Journal of Law, Policy and the Family*, 23(1) (2009), 110–31

Toulemon, L., 'Fifty Years of Family Change in Europe: Diversifying Partnerships', in D. Mortelmans, K. Matthijs, E. Alofs and B. Segaert (eds.), *Changing Family Dynamics and Demographic Evolution – The Family Kaleidoscope* (Edward Elgar, 2016), pp. 25–49

Townsend, N., *The Package Deal: Marriage, Work, and Fatherhood in Men's Lives* (Temple University Press, 2004)

Van Bueren, G., *International Law on the Rights of the Child* (Kluwer, 1998)

Van den Eynde, L., 'Selecting Landmark Cases', *Strasbourg Observers*, 28 August 2015, online at https://strasbourgobservers.com/2015/08/28/selecting-landmark-cases/ (last access on 11 February 2019)

van der Schyff, G., 'Interpreting the Protection Guaranteed by Two-Stage Rights in the European Convention on Human Rights' in E. Brems and J. Gerards (eds.), *Shaping Rights in the ECHR – The Role of the European Court of Human Rights in Determining the Scope of Human Rights* (Cambridge University Press, 2013), pp. 65–83

Wallbank, J., '"Bodies in the Shadows": Joint Birth Registration, Parental Responsibility and Social Class', *Child and Family Law Quarterly*, 21(3) (2009), 267–82

Wallbank, J., '(En)gendering the Fusion of Rights and Responsibilities in the Law of Contact' in J. Wallbank, S. Choudhry and J. Herring (eds.), *Rights, Gender and Family Law* (Routledge-Cavendish, 2009), pp. 93–118

Weiler, J., *The Constitution of Europe – "Do the New Clothes Have an Emperor?" and Other Essays on European Integration* (Cambridge University Press, 1999)

Weldon-Johns, M., 'EU Work-Family Policies – Challenging Parental Roles or Reinforcing Gendered Stereotypes?', *European Law Journal*, 19(5) (2013), 662–81

Wiegers, W., 'Fatherhood and Misattributed Genetic Paternity in Family Law', *Queen's Law Journal*, 36 (2010–2011), pp. 623–72

Wikeley, N. J., 'Same Sex Couples, Family Life and Child Support', *Law Quarterly Review*, 122 (2006), 542–47

Wildhaber, L., 'The European Court of Human Rights in Action', *Ritsumeikan Law Review*, 21 (2004), 83–92

Wildhaber, L., Hjartarson, A. and Donnelly, S., 'No Consensus on Consensus? The Practice of the European Court of Human Rights', *Human Rights Law Journal*, 33 (7–12) (2013), 248–63

Williams, J., *Unbending Gender: Why Family and Work Conflict and What to Do About It* (Oxford University Press, 2000)

Williams, J. and Segal, N., 'Beyond the Maternal Wall: Relief for Family Caregivers Who Are Discriminated against on the Job', *Harvard Women's Law Journal*, 26 (2003), 77–162

Wintemute, R., 'Strasbourg to the Rescue/Same-Sex Partners and Parents under the European Convention' in R. Wintemute and M. Andenaes, (eds.), *Legal Recognition of Same-Sex Partnerships – A Study of National, European and International Law* (Hart, 2001), pp. 713–29

Wintemute, R., '"Within the Ambit": How Big Is the "Gap" in Article 14 European Convention on Human Rights? Part 1, *European Human Rights Law Review*, 4 (2004), 366–82

Xenos, D., *The Positive Obligations of the State under the European Convention on Human Rights* (Routledge, 2012)

Yodanis, C., 'Divorce Culture and Marital Gender Equality', *Gender and Society*, 19(5) (2005), 644–59

Yourow, H., *The Margin of Appreciation Doctrine in the Dynamics of the European Human Rights Jurisprudence* (Kluwer Law International, 1996)

Zwart, 'More Human Rights Than Court: Why the Legitimacy of the European Court of Human Rights Is in Need of Repair and How It Can Be Done' in S. Flogaitis, T. Zwart and J. Fraser (eds.), *The European Court of Human Rights and Its Discontents – Turning Criticism into Strength* (Edward Elgar, 2013), pp. 71–95

Index

Adoption
 by homosexual(s), 8, 33, 37, 44, 129, 134, 144, 157, 161, 166
 non-consensual, 74, 85–91, 108, 165
 of a surrogacy-born child, 64
 second-parent, 18, 129, 134, 144–151, 161, 163
 single-parent, 18, 33, 44, 129, 134, 144, 157
Adultery, 96
Ahrens v Germany, 27, 28, 37, 91, 104–105
Alexandru Enache v Romania, 114
Anayo v Germany, 27, 76
Article 14 ECHR
 additional rights and, 34, 115, 119, 120, 126, 140, 150
 anti-stereotyping and, 25, 34, 79
 magnifying effects of, 25, 32–34, 115, 121, 126, 137, 140, 154
 substantive equality under, 32
 suspect ground(s) of discrimination and, 39, 116, 124, 134, 142, 145, 162
 very weighty reasons test under, 39, 83, 117, 134, 142, 162, 164
Article 8 ECHR
 applicability of, 25, 52, 53, 67, 90, 137
 close personal ties and, 26, 27, 75, 139, 146
 decision to/not to become a parent, 28, 52, 59, 62
 expansion of, 23, 28, 33–34, 52, 114, 135
 family life under, 26, 28, 29, 44, 55, 67, 75–76, 133, 135
 married heterosexual family and, 27
 positive obligations under, 29–32
 private life under, 26, 28, 94
 procedural requirements, 32, 38, 82–83
 two-stage review, 24–26
Artificial insemination, 6, 17, 49, 51, 54, 59, 60

Assisted reproductive technologies
 advent of, 5, 22, 68, 156
 fragmenting effects of, 6, 17, 48, 49
 heterologous, 6, 49
 homo-parenthood through, 8, 49–50, 129
 prisoners and, 59, 60

B.B. and F.B. v Germany, 31
Balbontin v UK, 79
Berrehab v the Netherlands, 26
Best interests of the child, 31, 80, 81, 84, 87, 106, 137, 141, 144, 148, 156, 159
Biological evidence, 65, 77, 91, 94, 157
Biological link. See Biology
Biology
 as a ground of legal fatherhood, 11, 13, 45, 56, 61, 64, 65, 66–68, 70, 75, 151, 160, 162, 165
 family life under Article 8 and, 67
 indispensability of, 56, 68, 156
 sufficiency of, 61, 68, 75, 82, 88, 101, 107
Birth certificate, 8, 10, 64
Blanket rule, 60, 63
Boeckel and Gessner-Boeckel v Germany, 133
Bonnaud and Lecoq v France, 134
Braun v France, 63
Breadwinning, 8, 14, 16, 35, 46, 98, 100, 109, 115, 116, 143, 157
Breastfeeding, 117
Burden v the United Kingdom, 27, 76

C. and L.M. v UK, 132
Care/ing
 anti-stereotyping and, 35, 77, 80, 81

Index

as a ground of legal fatherhood, 14, 55, 69, 85, 89, 90, 93, 98, 101, 104, 105, 135, 139, 151, 158, 164, 165, 167
as maternal task, 4, 61, 109, 122, 130, 153
family life under Article 8 and, 67, 76–77, 81, 85, 93, 98, 158
public, 30
Carvalho Pinto de Sousa Morais v Portugal, 34
Charron and Merle-Montet v France, 134
Chepelev v Russia, 90
Childcare
-related benefits, 18, 115, 120, 125
shared responsibilities, 8, 110, 112, 117, 121, 123, 125
Christianity, 44
Christine Goodwin v UK, 58
Civil partnership, 128, 131, 134, 145
Cohabitation
family life under Article 8 and, 55, 67, 76, 77, 86, 102
outside marriage, 5, 7, 76, 78, 80, 157
Commitment. *See* Care/ing
Consent
rules on, 59, 63
to adoption, 85, 148
to DNA testing, 97
withdrawal of, 59
Costa and Pavan v Italy, 52
Cross border reproduction, 64

D. and Others v Belgium, 64
Darmon v Poland, 97
Dazin v France, 79
Decision making, 28, 31, 35, 38, 43, 82
Deportation, 89
Dickson v UK, 28, 51, 52, 58–63, 69–70, 157, 160
Diligence, 92, 97, 103, 106, 107, 157, 160
Disability, 148
Discrimination
between married and unmarried fathers, 80, 83
between unmarried heterosexual and homosexual couples, 148
on the grounds of sex, 39, 83, 116, 122
on the grounds of sexual orientation, 33, 39, 132, 133, 144
positive, 124
Divorce/separation
child contact after, 10, 30, 31, 78, 136
child custody after, 7, 12, 30, 31, 78, 80, 84, 86, 87
child support after, 12, 97

fragmenting effects of, 6–8
DNA testing, 5, 7, 11, 45, 64, 73, 91, 93, 96, 97
Doctrinal tools. *See* Doctrines of interpretation
Doctrines of interpretation
consistent application of, 68, 71, 127, 162, 166
ECtHR's construction of fatherhood
productive of, 17, 19, 36, 63, 85, 116, 125, 141, 151, 161
subservient to, 17, 19, 63, 70, 85, 108, 141, 143, 150, 151, 161, 163, 165
inconsistent application of, 43, 77, 91, 135, 149, 154, 161
moral reading of ECHR and, 43, 108, 140, 154
Donor insemination, *See* Artificial insemination
Dynamic interpretation, *See* Living instrument doctrine

E.B. v France, 28, 33, 134, 139–144, 153, 157
Elsholz v Germany, 31, 38, 82
Embryo(s)
frozen, 59
implantation of, 61
Emonet and Others v Switzerland, 147, 153
Employment
women's participation in, 5, 8, 18, 45, 109, 125
Eriksson v Sweden, 30
Eski v Austria, 89, 90
European consensus
as trend among Contracting States, 58, 104
comparative data and, 41, 57, 65, 70, 84, 95, 103, 104, 116, 118, 122, 142, 149, 163, 165
criticism of, 40–41
ECtHR's construction of fatherhood and, 58, 115, 125
evidence of, 41, 57, 163
method of identification and application of, 40–41, 58, 84, 118, 122, 149, 163, 164
moral reading of ECHR and, 44, 84, 150
selective use of, 41, 44, 150, 162
European Convention on Human Rights (ECHR)
moral reading of, 35, 140
European Court of Human Rights (ECtHR)
anti-stereotyping approach of, 34, 79, 82, 95, 106, 114, 116, 118, 121, 122, 123, 126, 137, 138, 143, 161, 164
definition of family life, 26–27, 44
interpretative role of, 21, 166
judicial activism of, 41, 42, 84, 163
judicial creativity of, 20

European Court of Human Rights (cont.)
  judicial self-restraint of, 24, 54, 79
  legitimacy issues, 20, 37, 166
  social change and, 2, 21, 22, 126, 166
Evans v UK, 28, 37, 51, 52, 58–63, 69, 157, 160
Evolutive interpretation, *See* Living instrument doctrine

Face-veil, 43
Family law
  common trends, 9–13
  dominant ideology of the family in, 5, 10
  evolving, 9
  introverted subject, 21–22
  reform, 9
  social change and, 10, 166
Family/ies
  'the sexual family', 4
  bi-parental, 10, 129, 151
  breakdown, 7, 26–27, 31, 45, 73
  dominant ideology of, 4–5, 7, 8, 14, 27
  foster, 31, 87, 165
  fragmentation of, 6
  homosexual, 8, 22, 46, 128
  legal regulation of, 21, 30
  marital, 5
  mono-parental, 103
  social change and, 6, 132, 146, 160
  unmarried, 7, 11, 132, 151
  –work reconciliation, 18, 109, 110, 125, 159, 161
Fatherhood
  'new', 15–16, 62, 69, 82, 85, 86, 90, 101, 115, 121, 125, 155, 161, 163
  as direct/autonomous relationship, 13, 75, 89, 93, 98, 158
  as mediated relationship, 7, 27, 62, 72, 76, 82, 98, 101, 107, 156
  as unitary status, 6, 14, 61, 62, 69, 70, 89, 107, 159, 160
  biological, 6, 11, 12, 13, 14, 97, 162
  care and, 16, 85, 89, 99, 100, 155
  construction of, 2, 17, 19, 25, 46–47
  conventional, 13–14, 48, 54, 55, 61, 63, 69, 76, 82, 89, 90, 107, 110, 116, 125, 126, 127, 131, 139, 141, 143, 152, 155, 163, 167
  ECtHR's moral views on, 63, 71, 108, 119, 135, 139, 143, 154, 161, 163, 166
  employment and, 109

fragmenting, 1, 6, 8, 10, 14–15, 45, 73–74, 75, 110, 126, 158
geneticisation of, 10, 12, 75
heteronormativity and, 14, 49–50, 55, 56, 128, 160
heterosexual, 136, 141, 157
legal regulation of, 9, 13, 15, 35, 49
marital, 14, 82, 86, 90, 97, 101, 106, 108, 157, 160, 165
multi-, 10, 73
post-separation, 31, 74, 152, 156, 159
social change and, 1, 15, 17–18, 46, 123
unmarried, 11, 12, 98
Fretté v France, 28, 37, 41, 134, 139–144, 149, 152, 157

Gas and Dubois v France, 133, 135, 144–151, 158
Gay, 130, 134, 137, 138, 143, 152
Gendered division of labour, 4, 8, 16, 18, 35, 61, 109, 115, 116, 119, 121, 122, 125, 134, 139, 141, 143, 154, 157, 158
Görgülü v Germany, 31, 38, 87, 88, 89, 90

Hämäläinen v Finland, 133
Heteronormativity, 14, 49, 55, 56, 128, 129, 130, 132, 142, 144, 147, 152, 157, 160, 165
Heterosexuality
  as a ground of legal fatherhood/parenthood, 14, 18, 35, 46, 49, 130, 135, 138, 143, 145, 147, 151, 153, 154, 157
  marriage and, 8
Hoffmann v Germany, 39, 82
Hokkanen v Finland, 30, 31
Homo-parenthood, 6, 8, 18, 49–50, 130, 131, 160, 166
Homophobia, 43, 136
Household, 6, 8, 15, 72, 133, 146

Identity
  biological parentage as part of, 38, 66, 68
  father's relationship with his putative child as part of, 94
  gender, 55, 56
  personal, 57
Ignaccolo-Zenide v Romania, 31
Illegitimacy, 39, 78
In vitro fertilisation, 17, 53, 59
Infertility, 128
Inheritance, 57
Intentionality

assisted reproductive technologies and, 6, 48
  family life and, 27
  legal fatherhood and, 1, 51, 59, 62, 69, 89, 135, 160, 165
Interdependence, 159, 160
Islam, 44
Islamophobia, 43
Iyilik v Turkey, 97

J.R.M. v the Netherlands, 54
Johansen v Norway, 38
Johnston and Others v Ireland, 29, 75

K. and T. v Finland, 26, 32, 75
K.A.B. v Spain, 89, 90
Kautzor v Germany, 27, 28, 37, 76, 91, 104–105
Keegan v Ireland, 26, 86, 88, 90
Kerkhoven, Hinke and Hinke v the Netherlands, 135
Kinship, 50, 142
Kroon and Others v the Netherlands, 22, 30, 76, 99, 103

Labassee v France, 66
Lebbink v the Netherlands, 26, 82
Legal certainty, 60, 91, 96, 97
Lesbian, 18, 33, 42, 49, 50, 54, 129, 134, 153
Living instrument doctrine
  Article 8 and, 23, 78
  assisted reproductive technologies and, 53
  criticism of, 41
  European consensus and, 24, 41, 84, 144, 163, 164
  moral reading of ECHR and, 43, 150
  positive obligations and, 23

M.B. v UK, 79
Maillard and Others v France, 63
Male breadwinner model, 4, 8, 45, 110, 112, 143
Mandet v France, 159
Marckx v Belgium, 29, 55, 75, 86, 99, 165
Margin of appreciation
  assisted reproductive technologies and, 53–54, 56–57
  badge of discrimination and, 38, 83, 124
  conventional fatherhood and, 36, 53, 58
  criticism of, 39, 42
  European consensus and, 24, 37, 42, 53–54, 56–57, 62, 70, 117, 122, 126, 141, 161, 163
  homosexuality and, 37, 42

inconsistent application of, 39, 40, 63, 78
intensity of review and, 36, 62, 63, 94, 102
legal diversity and, 23
moral reading of ECHR and, 42, 63
nature of rights at stake and, 38
seriousness of the interference and, 37
transsexuality and, 37
variable effects of, 40, 63, 78
vis-à-vis contact-related claims, 38, 85, 88
vis-à-vis custody-related claims, 38, 84
vis-à-vis ethical and moral issues, 36–37, 53–54, 62, 65, 67, 70, 103
vis-à-vis identity-related claims, 38, 65, 67
width and influencing factors of, 39, 99, 117, 126
Marital presumption, 11, 30, 72, 73, 93, 100, 101, 103
Markin v Russia, 34, 114, 115, 121–125, 126
Marriage
  'special status' of, 76, 146, 149, 150, 153, 158
  as a ground of legal fatherhood, 35, 49, 61, 151
  as father–child connector, 1, 7, 17, 45, 72, 158
  decline of, 1, 5, 7, 11, 17, 73
  for same-sex couples, 131
  heteronormative view of, 135, 151, 154, 158, 162
Masculinities, 16
Mata Estevez v Spain, 132
Maternity
  allowance, 119
  leave, 111, 112, 117
  rights, 111
McMichael v UK, 31, 32
Mennesson v France, 37, 38, 51, 63–71, 156, 160, 162
Military, 121
Minority/ies, 43
Mizzi v Malta, 34, 95
Morality, 22, 42

Nazarenko v Russia, 34
Niedzwiecki v Germany, 114
Nurture, *See* Care/ing
Nylund v Finland, 76, 100–101

Okpisz v Germany, 114
Oliari and Others v Italy, 133
Olsson v Sweden (No. 2), 30
Origins
  right to know one's, 12

Ostace v Romania, 96
Ova donation, 53

Paradiso and Campanelli v Italy, 51, 63–71, 156, 160, 162
Parental leave
  allowance, 112, 117
  legislation, 112, 118, 123
  right to, 114, 117, 121, 124, 157, 159
  take-up, 112, 115, 125
Parental responsibility, 8, 10, 31, 57, 74, 78, 79, 86, 134, 136, 144, 152
Paternity
  acknowledgment of, 76, 81, 165
  disestablishment of, 28, 73, 92, 98, 107, 157, 159
  establishment of, 28, 30, 37, 73, 106, 108, 159, 161, 162
  European consensus and, 37, 91, 95, 103
  judicial declaration of, 93, 95, 96
  leave, 111, 112
  misattributed, 74
  proceedings, 32, 73, 77, 158, 165
  testing, 11, 12, 73, 74, 105
  time limits to bring proceedings, 94, 95
Paulík v Slovakia, 28, 95
Petrovic v Austria, 39, 114, 115, 116–119, 123, 125, 126
Positive obligation(s)
  assisted reproductive technologies and, 53
  conventional fatherhood and, 55
  inconsistent application of, 44–45, 90, 91–92, 99, 162, 165
  moral reading of ECHR and, 44–45, 91, 102, 108, 164
  to ensure child's integration in his family from childbirth, 29–30, 56, 86, 99, 103
  to facilitate reunion of parent with child, 31, 88, 162, 164
  to grant same-sex couples access to marriage, 133, 145
  unconventional family ties and, 56, 66, 91, 164
Pregnancy, 76, 100, 105, 111, 121
Pre-implantation genetic diagnosis, 52

Promptness, 77, 88, 92, 95, 157
Proportionality, 25, 36, 59, 60, 62, 79, 82, 93, 99, 101, 106, 145, 146, 150, 158

R.L. and Others v Denmark, 97
Rasmussen v Denmark, 28, 94, 95
Religion, 37, 44, 103
Różański v Poland, 76, 102

S.H. and Others v Austria, 37, 52, 53
Saenz and Saenz Cortes v France, 63
Sahin v Germany, 31, 33, 38, 76, 80, 82, 83, 116
Salgueiro da Silva Mouta v Portugal, 134, 135–139, 151, 157, 160
Schalk and Kopf v Austria, 132, 145
Schneider v Germany, 27, 34, 81, 84
Secularism, 44
Separation, *See* Divorce/separation
Shavdarov v Bulgaria, 37, 91, 99, 102
Shofman v Russia, 41
Social security, 113, 114, 120
Söderbäck v Sweden, 88, 89, 90
Sommerfeld v Germany, 31, 38, 81
Sperm donation, 49, 50, 53, 54, 134, 144
Stereotype/ing
  best interests of the child and, 81, 84
  compounded, 130, 137
  conventional fatherhood and, 35, 79
  definition of, 34, 118
  dominant ideology of the family and, 5
  gender, 113, 123, 124, 126, 137
  human rights and, 32, 34, 79, 94, 113, 123
  man-breadwinner/woman-homemaker, 35, 114, 115, 118, 122, 124, 126, 137
  sex role, 113, 118, 123, 137, 143
Subsidiarity
  principle of, 20, 21
Surrogacy
  contract of, 64
  European consensus and, 37
  for gays, 129
  immigration restrictions and, 65
  lawfulness of, 37, 64, 68
  national legal checks and, 65
  recognition of family ties created abroad through, 37, 38, 51, 63, 129
  travel authorisation and, 64

Tavli v Turkey, 97
Transsexuality
    fatherhood and, 51, 54–58, 156, 163

Van der Heijden v the Netherlands, 27, 76

Weller v Hungary, 114, 115, 119–121, 126

X and Others v Austria, 133, 135, 144–151, 162, 163
X, Y and Z v UK, 37, 51, 54–58, 65, 69–70, 156, 160, 163, 164, 165

Yousef v the Netherlands, 101–102

Zaunegger v Germany, 34, 80, 83, 85, 163, 164